THE
WEST

Sitting Bull (Tatanka Yotanka) with William F. 'Buffalo Bill' Cody;
steel-tipped arrows, Sioux (inset)

Dodge City street scene, 1879; Log Cabin Library No. 28,
romanticizing the exploits of Jesse James (inset)

THE WEST

**FROM LEWIS AND CLARK TO WOUNDED KNEE:
THE TURBULENT STORY OF THE SETTLING OF FRONTIER AMERICA**

**CONSULTANT EDITORS
WILLIAM C. DAVIS · JOSEPH G. ROSA**

SMITHMARK

A SALAMANDER BOOK

This edition published in 1994 by
SMITHMARK Publishers Inc.,
16 East 32nd Street, New York,
New York NY 10016

9 8 7 6 5 4 3 2 1

SMITHMARK books are available
for bulk purchase for sales
promotion and premium use.
For details write or call the
manager of special sales,
SMITHMARK Publishers Inc.,
16 East 32nd Street, New York,
NY 10016: (212) 532-6600

© Salamander Books Ltd 1994

ISBN 0 8317 9367 8

CIP data is available for this title

All correspondence concerning the
content of this book should be
addressed to Salamander Books Ltd,
129–137 York Way, London
N7 9LG, England

CREDITS

Editor: Richard Collins
Designer: Mark Holt
Filmset: SX Composing Ltd, England
Color reproduction: Scantrans PTE,
Singapore

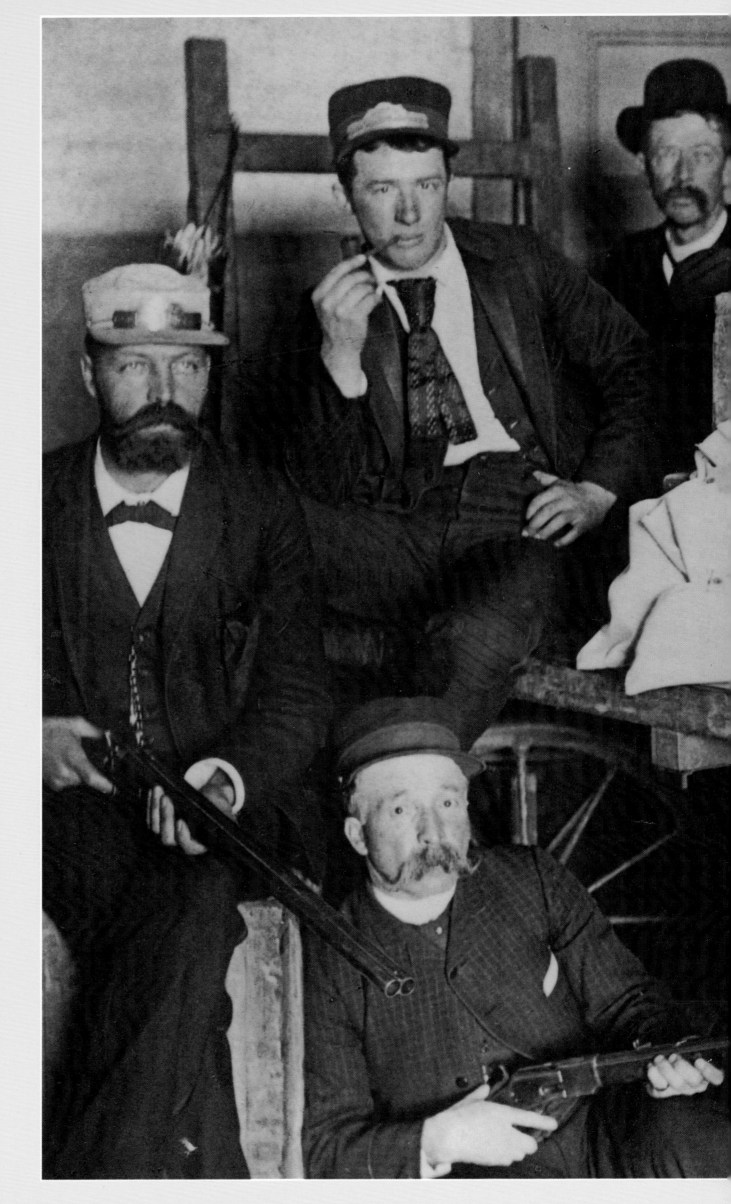

Wells Fargo messengers in Reno,
Nevada, with sacks of silver and
strongboxes, exuding the confidence
their shotguns give them

CONTENTS

Years afterward, when the open-grazing days were over, and the red grass had been ploughed under and under until it had almost disappeared from the prairie; when all the fields were under fence, and the roads no longer ran about like wild things, but followed the surveyed section-lines, Mr Shimerda's grave was still there, with a sagging wire fence around it, and an unpainted wooden cross. As grandfather had predicted, Mrs Shimerda never saw the roads go over his head. The road from the north curved a little to the east just there, and the road from the west swung out a little to the south; so that the grave, with its tall red grass that was never mowed, was like a little island; and at twilight, under a new moon or the clear evening star, the dusty roads used to look like soft grey rivers flowing past it. I never came upon the place without emotion, and in all the country it was the spot most dear to me. I loved the dim superstition, the propitiatory intent, that had put the grave there; and still more I loved the spirit that could not carry out the sentence – the error from the surveying lines, the clemency of the soft earth roads along which the home-coming wagons rattled after sunset. Never a tired driver passed the wooden cross, I am sure, without wishing well to the sleeper.

From *My Ántonia*, by Willa Cather

Child feeding chickens on Montana farm, turn of the century; iron horseshoes (inset)

THE FIRST AMERICANS

Before Columbus came to America, the population of the Native Americans – the first, aboriginal peoples – was reckoned to stand at about 5 million. By 1890, nearly 500 years after his landing, the population stood at 250,000. During the same period, the white population in the United States – called the New World by Europeans – increased from 0 to 75 million. In so doing, it usurped the ancestral lands of Indians who had inhabited the continent for centuries and destroyed the delicate balance of their economy and an age-old way of life.

Before the white man came a complex civilization of peoples inhabited North America, all of them related by distant ancestral ties that, in most cases, lay so long in the forgotten past that one tribe scarcely recognized another as anything other than a potential competitor. Several hundred thousand-strong, they flourished from ocean to ocean, rich with culture, costume and lore. Theirs was no romantic or idyllic life. They struggled against seasons, beasts, and frequently each other. Some hunted and foraged and evolved great warrior societies. Others adopted agriculture and abandoned the nomad's life. They built mounds to their gods and their dead, lived in caves, huts, tipis and even wooden houses, mastered boat-building, domesticated wild horses, and developed cultures as sophisticated as any in Europe.

They came across an ice bridge from Siberia eons before, migrating south through Alaska and Canada over the massive Wisconsin Glacier, following the eastern slopes of the Rockies. Once clear of the glacier, one wing of the migration split away and moved eastward, then divided

Right: A Mikasuki Seminole household in the Big Cypress Swamp, Florida. The Seminole descended from Creek colonists who migrated into Florida in the 18th century. The Seminole lived in the fastness of the Everglades of Florida.

Below: A superb wooden paddle for a small canoe, made and used by the Tlingit of the Northwest Coast. Neighbors of the Haida, they lived a maritime existence among hundreds of islands along the panhandle of Southeastern Alaska.

Below: A Ute camp on the eastern slope of the Wasatch Mountains, Utah. The Utes were Basin people who also lived in the mountain ranges of central and western Colorado.

Above: *Evidence of the First Americans – picture writing and petroglyphs on a rock wall.*

1513
The Spaniard Ponce de Leon lands in Florida. He receives, by all accounts, a hostile reception

1539–43
Hernando de Soto explores deep into the Southeast, with disastrous effects on those he meets

1803
Start of Lewis and Clark's epic journey to explore the Louisiana Purchase territory

1830s
Smallpox all but wipes out the Mandan on the central Plains

Above: Utse-tah-wah-ti-an-kah of the Osage. The Osage lived originally on the southern Plains and were neighbors of the Kiowa, Iowa, Kansa and Missouria, among others. They were speakers of a Siouan language and were part farmers and part hunters.

again, a northern portion slowly moving toward the lush woodlands of the Northeast while the other moved to the Southeast, eventually settling everything between the Mississippi and Florida. Meanwhile the main branch of the exodus continued southward, leaving behind settlements on the Great Plains, while other small groups pushed west of the Rockies to inhabit the Great Basin. By the time the tide reached Texas, yet another group turned westward to settle the Southwest and push on to California, while others crossed the Rio Grande and continued the snail's pace march of civilization through Mexico and Central America, and eventually all the way down South America.

The Algonquians, as the Northeasterners would be called, eventually occupied all of New England and most of the country east of the Mississippi and north of Tennessee. Kickapoo, Sauk and Fox, Winnebago, Potawatomi, Kaskaskia, Peoria, Miami, and more, clustered around the Great Lakes and on the Illinois and Indiana Prairies. Shawnee settled in Kentucky, with the Cherokee below them in Tennessee, the Tuscarora eastward in North Carolina, and Pamunkey, Powhatan, Nanticoke, Delaware, and Susquehanna running up the coastline to New York. Then came the great confederacy tribes of the Iroquois, the Seneca, Cayuga, Onondaga, Oneida, Mohawk, Huron, Mohican, and more, with their highly

Above: A Potawatomi man. This Northeastern tribe were speakers of the Algonquian language and occupied the lands hemmed in by lakes Michigan and Huron. Around 1820 they moved across the Mississippi to reservations in Oklahoma and Kansas.

Left: *The Blackfeet lived on the northern Plains and formed part of the Algonquian linguistic group.*

Below: *Exquisite woven baskets were a trademark of the Pomo of northern California.*

'A Herd of Bison Crossing the Missouri River', by William Jacob Hays, Sr (1830–75)
(Buffalo Bill Historical Center, Cody, Wyoming. Gertrude Vanderbilt Whitney Trust Fund Purchase)

Above: A Nisenan boy from northern California, whose people spoke a root of the Penutian language. His flicker feather headband and the large abalone shell gorget at the neck typify Californian tribes' use of natural and local materials.

Above: A Southern Cheyenne man. Before 1700 these people lived in present-day Minnesota. The tribe was split into two groups – the Northern Cheyenne and Southern Cheyenne – in the 1830s, following the 1851 Fort Laramie Treaty.

developed political and diplomatic system.

South of them settled another equally cultured confederacy of tribes, though less rigidly organized. They would in time come to be called the Five Civilized Tribes. The Seminole spread to the farthest reaches of Florida, while above them in present-day Alabama and Georgia the warlike Creeks ruled a wide domain bordered on the west by the Choctaw in southern Mississippi and the Chickasaw north of them. Their kinsmen the Cherokee lived in north Georgia and Tennessee. A host of sub-tribes, from the Catawba and Tuscaroras of the Carolinas, to the fierce Natchez living on a bluff overlooking the Mississippi, filled out the family tree of these agricultural peoples who built religious burial mounds for their dead, developed – among the Cherokee – a written language, and lived a pastoral life in their rich woodlands and prairies.

Their cousins across the great river lived a much different life. There massive bison herds migrated over the grasslands, and many of the Indians followed them. In Texas the Comanche tamed wild horses and used them to become the greatest horsemen of the Plains, riding swiftly alongside the shaggy bison to kill them, and making everything from clothing to tipis to bowstrings from the tough hides. In latter-day Oklahoma and Kansas the Wichita, Kiowa, Kansa, and especially the Osage reigned, while west of them in Colorado the fierce Cheyenne and Arapaho dominated the western Plains as far as the Rocky foothills. The northern reaches, up to the Canadian border, were the domain of the several families of the Lakotan, or Sioux. Scattered among them were also several other tribes living more or less in peaceful coexistence. The Pawnee, Omaha, and more, inhabited Nebraska, while the Mandan lived in their European style villages on the upper Missouri. West of them the Crow claimed much of Montana, while farther north Blackfeet, Assiniboin, and more, straddled the Canadian line. Among almost all of them there developed a fierce warrior tradition growing out of the hunt and an idealized concept of manhood. Inevitably it led them into occasional conflict with each other, not for land or wealth, but for glory or

Left: A pair of Arapaho moccasins, collected by A.L. Kroeber. The tongues are forked and represent rattlesnakes tongues. The Arapaho inhabited Oklahoma and Wyoming.

Right: A Bannock dwelling in the Basin. They were neighbors of the Northern Shoshoni and Northern Paiute, and joined with the latter in a brief war against the whites in 1878.

Below: A Pawnee earth lodge village. The Pawnee were one of the earliest tribes to arrive on the Plains (about 1300), moving into Nebraska from eastern Texas to live in such villages along the Platte River. Latterly, some Pawnee scouted for the army.

sometimes for nothing more than revenge.

In the Great Basin west of the Rockies lived a host of peoples, many of the tribes small and barely able to subsist in the arid wastes. Paiute, Shoshoni, Ute, and kinsmen eked a meager existence in Utah and Nevada, while Shoshoni and Bannock dominated western Wyoming and southern Idaho and Oregon. The Flathead lived in western Montana, and the noble Nez Perce claimed northern Idaho. A complex of tribes lived in Washington – Skokomish, Puyallup, Wenatchee, Spokan, Walla-Walla, Yakima, Klickitat, Chinook, and more, most of them radically different in dress, custom, and culture, from the Plains peoples. These Indians tied their lives to the ocean, building mighty canoes for hunting and for war, and resembling more closely their earliest ancestors who first crossed the ice bridge. South of them the Klamath and the warlike Modoc held southern Oregon, while California hosted another wide variety of small tribes, most of them pastoral hunter-gatherers, this group being being represented by the likes of the Pomo and Miwok.

Finally, the southwestern tribes of Arizona and New Mexico included some of the most highly developed artisans of all among the Hopi and Navajo. Their neighbors, the several factions of the Apache, were less settled, depending on raiding on Mexicans and other Indians for much of their livelihood, and themselves evolving a rugged warrior cult.

One thing all of the Indian peoples of North America had in common besides their ancestry. They were unprepared for the white man, either for his diseases, which would ravage them, or his concept of property and voracious hunger for land. For all of them as the day of the white explorers and discoverers dawned, there lay ahead a trail of tears.

Above: The interior of a Shoshoni lodge, in 1878. The Shoshoni were a Great Basin people, some of whom moved onto the Plains in the 1840s in order to hunt buffalo, thus bringing themselves into contact with more hostile tribes.

Right: The northeastern Pueblo of Taos, in the Southwest. The village was built in about 1700; the architecture is testimony to the enduring quality of Pueblo architecture.

Below and right: The Navajo of the Southwest have always produced superb silverwork. Shown are a bow guard, a naja, and two conchos to be worn on belts or bridles.

Above: Little Big Man, Oglala Sioux. Sioux is a collective term for seven closely related tribes who are of the Siouan linguistic stock. The Sioux are regarded as the quintessential High Plains people with a proud nomadic tradition.

Above: An Arikara man from the central Plains. Speakers of a Caddoan tongue, and sometimes referred to as 'Northern Pawnee', the Arikara were semi-sedentary people who lived south of their neighbors the Mandan on the Missouri River.

Above: A war captain and chief hunter of the Pueblo of Nambe, New Mexico, in the Southwest. 'Pueblo' means 'village dwellers'; it was a name given by the Spanish which referred to their style of architecture – houses made of stone and adobe.

LEWIS AND CLARK

Never before in history had a nation so suddenly acquired such a massive piece of territory as the Louisiana Purchase. Overnight the United States almost doubled in size. President Jefferson needed quickly to know the extent of the land, its look and layout, and its potential riches. He turned to two young men whose names were to become legends in the West. Together Lewis and Clark made one of the epic journeys of all time, against daunting obstacles. There could be no more glorious way to open the new chapter in American history that would be the West.

The acquisition of the vast Louisiana Territory from France in 1803 more than doubled the size of the United States, and presented at once an opportunity and a challenge. All that land awaited exploitation on the one hand, yet on the other no one knew just exactly what lay out there. There were no maps, no surveys, and only scattered accounts from the few white men who had penetrated portions of the wilderness. President Thomas Jefferson and a young America, anxious to capitalize on their new acquisition, had to know more about what they had bought.

Jefferson turned to his secretary Meriwether Lewis and to the son of Revolutionary War hero George Rogers Clark, William Clark, and commissioned them to lead an expedition of discovery and survey. They were to go to St Louis and the mouth of the Missouri River, then proceed up the long stream to its headwaters, cross the continental divide, and then find their way to the Pacific. Along the way they were to become acquainted with the Indian tribes, collect and study flora samples, note the mineral resources of the region, and prepare maps for those settlers and explorers who would follow. It was a tall order.

Lewis and Clark collected forty-four soldiers and civilians for their expedition and spent the fall and winter of 1803–4 equipping and training them near St Louis. The next spring they set off up the

Right: Despite the incredible hardship of the journey through the new Louisiana Territory, Lewis and Clark suffered remarkably few casualties, and only one death, which was that of Clark's servant Floyd. George Catlin's painting shows Floyd's burial place.

Below: The actual limits of the newly acquired Louisiana Territory were ill-defined, extending some said as far as its owner could push them. In 1803 the undisputed area included the shaded region in the center of the continent, parent of a dozen states.

Above: President Thomas Jefferson sent Lewis and Clark on their way to see what he had bought.

1803
Jefferson buys the Louisiana Territory from France, and sends Lewis and Clark and their small expedition on its way up the Missouri

1805
Lewis and Clark finally reach the Pacific, to winter in the Oregon Territory before starting the return journey in the coming spring

1806
In September Lewis and Clark finally arrive back in St Louis, with 4,000 miles of epic journey behind them

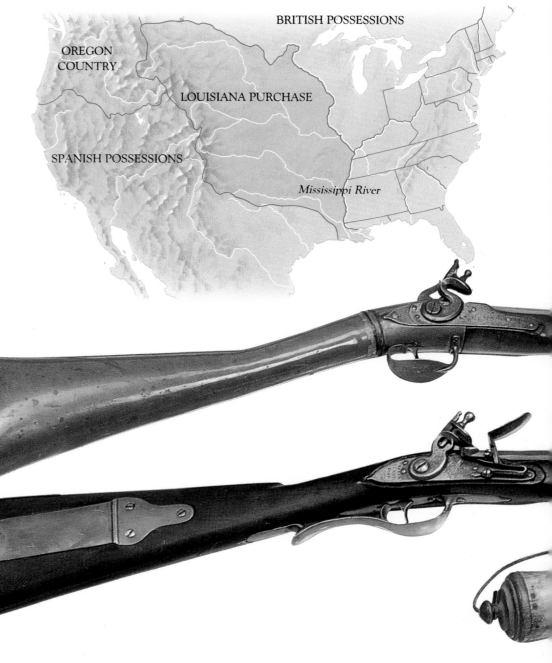

BRITISH POSSESSIONS

OREGON COUNTRY

LOUISIANA PURCHASE

SPANISH POSSESSIONS

Mississippi River

Artifacts courtesy of Buffalo Bill Historical Center, Cody, Wyoming

Above: Meriwether Lewis lived beyond his spectacular adventure in the Louisiana Territory to become governor of the region a few years later. Mentally unhinged by financial debt and accusations of dishonesty, he eventually committed suicide.

Above: William Clark, though less flamboyant than Lewis, was the more stable of the two. His later work in finishing the journals and reports of the expedition furnished an invaluable archive on the first American opening of the far West.

Missouri on three boats and got as far as the Dakotas, where they wintered with the Mandans and Arikaras. The next spring they pressed on in canoes moving west. With them now went a Shoshone woman called Sacajawea – 'Bird Woman' – who helped act as interpreter and diplomat with the tribes they encountered. With her help they reached the Rocky Mountains that summer, crossed the divide in what is now Idaho, and then moved on to the Bitter Root valley and found a succession of streams that eventually led them to the Columbia River. Following its course, they at last saw before them the Pacific in early November.

But their journey was only half done. They built Fort Clatsop and passed a dreadful winter before commencing the return trip in March 1806. Now Lewis and Clark split their company

into three parties in order to cover and map more territory. They covered the Yellowstone and tributaries of the Missouri, then rejoined for the final leg back down the latter to St Louis. When they arrived in September 1806 they had covered 4,000 miles of wilderness, their boats laden with specimens, their journals bulging with information, and with the loss of only a single man who died of disease, and one other who simply abandoned the party. Along the way, though they had a few scares, they fired not a single hostile shot at the Indians they met, and thanks to Sacajawea left behind them friendly relations. Lewis and Clark literally opened the West, and at the same time made themselves immortal for the most successful expedition of discovery any Americans would ever make until men landed on the moon.

Left: A powder horn like those used on the expedition, with a turned wooden plug in the base, and a carved neck. It kept powder dry and – more importantly – close at hand.

Above, top: A Jacob Kuntz air rifle of the kind taken on the expedition. Made in Philadelphia. Air compressed in the hollow metal butt fired the piece with no need of flint and powder.

Above: The elegant Harpers Ferry Model 1803 flintlock rifle, one of the most beautiful American military long-arms of all, and a veteran of the Lewis and Clark expedition.

'Lewis and Clark on the Lower
Columbus', by Charles M. Russell
(1864–1926) (gouache, watercolor
and graphite on paper, 1905. Amon
Carter Museum, Fort Worth)

PIONEERS & EXPLORERS

It took a special breed of men to leave all known trappings of civilization behind them, strike out into the unknown, and set about exploring half a continent. To later generations the achievements of Jedediah Smith, Stephen Long, John C. Fremont, and more, seem almost mythological. Yet they did what history says of them. In spite of the dangers from inhospitable natives, searing deserts, frozen mountain passes, and virtually no information on what lay ahead, these intrepid advance men for empire could not stay their burning curiosity.

Above: *Fremont's Peak in the Wind River Mountains of Wyoming, photographed by W. H. Jackson.*

1803–6
Lewis and Clark traverse the Louisiana Territory from St Louis to the Pacific and back, mapping the way for a tide of exploration to follow

1807
Zebulon Pike explores the Rocky Mountains, leaving his name on a peak he may never have climbed

1826
Jedediah Smith is the first white American to reach San Diego overland

1832
The first immigrant train rolls out of Missouri and across the plains and mountains to Oregon, inaugurating the Oregon Trail

Artifacts courtesy of Buffalo Bill Historical Center, Cody, Wyoming

The epic journey of Lewis and Clark in 1803–6 was only the beginning of the exploration of the new West, and each succeeding explorer built upon the trails left by those who came before, while blazing new ones for those to follow. In fact, even as the two returned to St Louis with the trove of information and samples they collected, Zebulon Pike was already leading a military expedition into the Minnesota country in 1805–6, and then the next year set off on his more epic journey across the plains to Colorado and into the Rocky Mountains and up the Arkansas River.

But then the second war with Britain put a stop to further exploration by the government until after 1820. Meanwhile, ever-opportunistic individuals continued to trickle into the prairies and mountains, not in search of information so much as a chance to profit. John Coulter took his beaver traps into the Rockies in what is now Colorado and Wyoming, followed by a few other hardy men, precursors to the Mountain Men. When others saw what these fellows brought back, the fur companies began their organized expeditions and the annual rendezvous of trappers

Right: *An artist's rendering of the arrest of Zebulon Pike in Santa Fe, an event that capped his 1806–7 exploration of the Rocky Mountains and Arkansas River. The Spanish owners of the New Mexico Territory did not welcome the appearance of an Anglo in their midst, and held him captive for some time before his release and eventual return home.*

Below: *Some of the equipment likely to be found in an early explorer's pack included the English flintlock trade musket, amber, glass and bone beads and pipes, the Hudson's Bay trade blanket, a beaver pelt, and a stout leather trunk. The flintlock would be highly valued.*

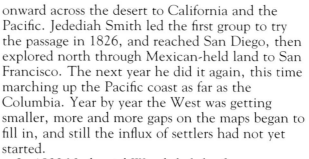

onward across the desert to California and the Pacific. Jedediah Smith led the first group to try the passage in 1826, and reached San Diego, then explored north through Mexican-held land to San Francisco. The next year he did it again, this time marching up the Pacific coast as far as the Columbia. Year by year the West was getting smaller, more and more gaps on the maps began to fill in, and still the influx of settlers had not yet started.

In 1832 Nathaniel Wyeth led the first immigrant train out of Missouri and across the plains on a route Smith had found that led eventually to Oregon. Thus the Oregon Trail was opened. Within a few years all of these several trails began to teem with men and animals and wagons, laden with a few possessions, some seeds and cuttings, and a lifetime of dreams. Meanwhile, along the rivers that were navigable, the advent of steam allowed paddle-wheelers to course up the Missouri, Yellowstone, and other rivers, bringing even more settlers.

It was not a fast journey. The wagon route could take five months or more to reach the Pacific, and along the way lay savage animals, sometimes hostile Indians, swollen rivers, sudden blizzards, and every other peril of the elements. Yet still they came, and when the railroad finally bridged the continent in 1869, even Nature itself could not stay the human tide.

that lasted from 1825 to 1840. Each year the Mountain Men brought more knowledge with them out of the mountains, and spread white knowledge of the wilderness ever westward.

Others looked into the southwest, and in 1821 Robert McKnight opened a route from Missouri to Santa Fe. Behind them came trade, and then settlers on the Santa Fe Trail, and meanwhile at the end of the route more daring men could see before them the Old Spanish Trail that led

Right: Frederic Remington's painting of an Indian trapper, traveling light without a pack pony, the intimidating mountains ahead of him.

THE MOUNTAIN MEN

Out of the misty recesses of a dense canyon, across the waters of a swollen stream, over the parched and steaming plains, the most individualistic of all Americans plied their lonely trade. They were the Mountain Men, dedicated to solitude, trapping, and seeing for themselves what lay beyond the far side of the next hill. They came and went in the winking of time's eye, as the lands they explored were filled up and the beaver they hunted played out. None who met them ever forgot them, their colorful dress, distinctive speech, or impact on the settlement of the West.

Above: John Johnson acquired the nickname 'Liver Eatin'' following his exploits against the Crow Indians.

1822

Trappers ascend the Missouri, hired to hunt fur-bearing animals for two years or more, then bring their pelts to a rendezvous for sale, commencing the era of the Mountain Men

1825

The first 'rendezvous' reaps the rewards of almost three years in the mountains for the first band of trappers

1840

The last rendezvous. The beaver are almost gone, the tide of fashion in the East wants fur no more, and the land is getting too familiar to suit the loners

Artifacts courtesy of Buffalo Bill Historical Center, Cody, Wyoming

I n 1822 one of the most storied and romantic eras in the history of the West began when the first boatload of fur trappers worked its way up the Missouri River toward the faraway mountains. There these men would hunt the beaver and other fur-bearing animals, and then bring their pelts back out of the high fastnesses three years later to a rendezvous where traders would give them money, whiskey and supplies in return for their bounty. Some 120 of these tough men actually made it through those years, and when they appeared in July 1825 in the foothills of the Uinta Mountains they brought more than ninety pack loads of beaver. The days of the Mountain Men had begun.

They were loners almost to a man. Jim Bridger, 'Old Bill' Williams, Jim Beckwourth, and more, went year after year into the Rockies, pushing the known limits of the mountains ever farther west as they trapped out old streams and sought new ones. There was a thriving market in the East for the 'peltries' they brought back, and finding them provided a lifestyle that suited these independent men. They braved savage winters, blistering summers, rough untracked terrain, and often hostile natives, to harvest the streams. In the process, they filled in blank spots on the map of the West from the Canadian border as far south as the New Mexico Territory. They got along with the Indian when they could, often marrying into a tribe in part for company, and as well for survival.

Most of them worked alone, or with only one or two companions, though a few formed what they

Right: Alfred J. Miller's magnificent painting 'Rocky Mountain Trapper' conveys all of the color, spirit, and violence of the lives of these daring men. No wonder so many in the East believed that they had 'gone savage'.

Below: The Mountain Men adopted the Indian style of dress as being most practical and durable for the rugged life on the streams and in the high fastnesses where they set their trap lines. If anything, they were even more colorful than the natives.

called 'brigades', and marched into the mountains, established base camps, then fanned out, each pursuing his own direction. They faced danger and sudden death every day. A broken leg, a lost horse, or an Indian arrow or club, even if not immediately fatal, left a man at the mercy of the elements and the animals. Only the toughest survived. Hugh Glass crawled almost 100 miles after being savaged by a grizzly bear. When Tom Smith broke a leg while out alone, he cut the flesh through with his own knife, snapped off the bone, and thrust the bleeding stump into his camp fire to cauterize the brutal wound. No wonder that these men gave rise to so much of frontier lore and legend, and some of them like 'Old Bill' Williams became such adept story-tellers that they virtually created their own mythology.

Their heyday was pitifully brief. Barely a decade after they started trapping the beaver began to play out, and 1840 saw the last rendezvous, just fifteen years after the first. After that the Mountain Men simply drifted on to other pursuits. Some settled down with their Indian wives. Others became scouts for the army. Several turned to larger game as the demand for bison meat and hides made the huge prairie herds suddenly lucrative. A few became traders. None of them got rich in the beaver trade. They squandered what they got for their pelts almost as soon as the money hit their hands, then set off once more into the high lonesome where they belonged and preferred to be.

Above: Grizzled old Jim Bridger outlived the hazards and hardships of his profession long enough to be alive for a photographer to capture his portrait. Unlike most of his associates, he actually made a good living from the mountains.

Below: Hunters like this man often married Indian women and had families, living in tipis on the Plains as they hunted for furs.

Right: The powder horn made from a hollowed steer horn, was a necessity in the mountains. This one has a turned wood plug.

Above: James Beckwourth became notorious for a skill developed by many of the Mountain Men – lying. His own friends and men who met him in later life never knew which of his exaggerations to believe and which to ignore as pure fabrications.

THE FUR TRADE

With the vast landscape opened to exploitation by the Louisiana Purchase, enterprising Americans began to feel out the riches of the new land. The most visible were its animals, fur-bearing beaver, bison and more, all of them ripe for harvest to feed the comfort and fashion of the peoples in the settled East. Hardy men went into the mountains after them, while other entrepreneurs founded companies to organize the trapping. All of them in their way, from the solitary Mountain Men to the French-Canadian *voyageurs*, played a role in exploration and exploitation at the same time.

At one time or another, all of American was 'the West', and from the time that white men first saw the potential richness of the land and its resources, the furs of its mammals figured high in their calculations. Deer, bear, bison, fox, mountain lion, and more all offered not only warmth for the practical, but at one time or another profit for those who could supply them to the caprices of current fashion. Most of all there was the beaver, the industrious fellow who mastered his environment almost as well as the whites did, yet whose very mastery of the streams made him so easy to harvest and almost eradicate.

As early as 1534 and the explorations of the Frenchman Jacques Cartier, Europeans began to take furs. Quickly the French established monopolies to control and capitalize on the trade, and as their frontier borders advanced, so did their trappers, always some distance in front of settlement. The English carried on the trade, and so did the Dutch when they came, but the great spread came in the early nineteenth century when

Below right: Two voyageurs run their canoe ashore during a fur trapping outing. These colorful French Canadians dominated the northern fur trade, taking part as well in much of the early exploration of the upper continent. Often interbred with the Indians, they traveled widely, and in time covered virtually all of Canada before they disappeared.

Below: A pair of bearskin gloves, lined with fur, were both decorative and incredibly warm in the frigid mountain winters as the trappers sought their 'peltries'. The knife was essential for skinning whatever came along.

Above: *Long after the fur trade all but expired, voyageurs like these still plied Canadian waters.*

1808
John Jacob Astor founds the American Fur Company

1840
The beaver streams play out, ending the era of the Mountain Men as the fur supply dwindles

Artifacts courtesy of Buffalo Bill Historical Center, Cody, Wyoming

Above: *Snowshoes made of rawhide strips woven over ash wood frames allowed trappers to travel relatively easily in deep snow.*

the French sold the great Louisiana Territory to the infant United States. Now there was a resident population whose very character symbolized exploitation of opportunity poised on the edge of a vast continent of riches.

One after another they set out to claim that wealth, and while the Mountain Men who did most of the trapping finished their era with nothing to show for their labors, the fur companies sometimes made staggering wealth. John Jacob Astor, in fact, built one of America's great dynastic fortunes on his American Fur Company's profits. He started in 1808 and within only a few years virtually dominated the trade, even before the Mountain Men started going to the Rockies. He depended on the Indians to bring the furs to him, and in 1811 established his Pacific Fur Company on the western ocean in what became Oregon, in spite of the threat of British interference. That kind of enterprise, though it suffered setbacks, in the end made him one of America's richest men. In 1834 when he left the business and sold his interests, he was a millionaire. A few years later, as the fur trade

itself dwindled and died, so did Astor's old company.

While most of the trade concentrated in the northern climes, from the Great Lakes to the Pacific, the southwest, too, saw a burgeoning business. Men like Christopher 'Kit' Carson and others hunted the streams and foothills of northern New Mexico and southern Colorado. Even Texas yielded furs, and other entrepreneurs made their fortunes here, men like Manuel Lisa and Pierre Chouteau and his son Auguste. They and other businessmen set up regular caravans that crossed the arid southwest from Missouri to New Mexico, bringing supplies and trade goods and returning with pelts. Yet here, too, the 1840s signalled an end to enterprise. Friction with Indians and with Mexico made it increasingly dangerous. The trapping out of the beaver made each year's expeditions and caravans a little less profitable. Then the coming of war with Mexico in 1846 turned Americans' minds to other things, and now men who once explored the unknown streams of the southwest found themselves using their knowledge of the ground to lead tiny armies.

Above: Christopher 'Kit' Carson started life trapping the streams of northern New Mexico, then became a guide for John C. Fremont's explorations, before serving in the Mexican War and even later as a brigadier general in the Civil War.

Above: It all came to this for the Mountain Man. An iron spring-operated trap shuts its jaws on the fur-bearing quarry.

Above: Manuel Lisa, like so many who sought fortune in furs, realized that trapping the animals was only half of the challenge. Getting them to market also offered riches, wealth that Lisa tapped when he organized cross-country caravans.

'The Voyageurs', by Charles Deas (1818–67) (Courtesy Museum of Fine Arts, Boston)

TEXAS INDEPENDENCE

Today's Texan is as fiercely independent as his ancestors during the 1820s and 1830s. Any attempt to change his way of life or interfere with the running of the state is sure to bring an instant reaction. Consequently, it is not difficult to understand how the 'Texians', as they called themselves, reacted when, having been invited by the Mexicans to populate the land, found that they were forbidden any ideas of forming a separate self-ruled state. This led to conflict when the Mexicans tried to impose their own rules, and in the end it was the Texians who won.

For ten years Texas, the largest of the contiguous United States, was an independent nation, with its own government, army, navy, foreign policy, and economy. But no one originally envisioned such a future when the first whites from east of the Mississippi moved west to Texas in the 1820s under what was then a pacific colonization policy by the territory's Mexican rulers. In 1822 they actually encouraged Stephen Austin to bring 200 families with him to settle the fertile land and, as more and more colonists followed, pressure began to rise for this outpost to become a separate state within the Mexican nation. A few more extreme Americans wanted to see the province severed entirely from Mexico, however, either to become an independent nation, or else join the Union as a state.

By 1832 some internal dissent broke out among the American settlers themselves as a faction

Right: The fall of the Alamo, as depicted by Theodore Gentilz. Reporting to Colonel Travis, Crockett said: 'Colonel, here am I. Assign us to some place, and I and my Tennessee boys will defend it.'

Below left: A typical 'Bowie knife' of the period. There were many different types, some resembling meat cleavers or short swords! James Bowie popularized the knife, but it was actually designed by his brother Rezin. Jimi Bowrie is reputed to have used it to good effect at the Alamo.

Bottom: The defenders at the Alamo, from a painting by N. C. Wyeth. The heroic defense of a handful of men, led by the likes of Davy Crockett and Bowie, proved an inspiration to Texans, and the cry: 'Remember the Alamo!' became a rallying call in their fight against Mexican tyranny.

Above: *Sam Houston, the man who defeated Santa Anna and became the Republic of Texas' first president.*

1822
Stephen Austin arrives in Texas

1835
Santa Anna is elected President of Mexico; he stations Mexican troops throughout Texas

1836
(March) the siege of the Alamo ends in massacre of its defenders; (April) the Texians are revenged at the decisive Battle of San Jacinto. Sam Houston is elected President of the Republic of Texas

Above: *This onyx buttoned beaded vest belonged to David Crockett. The vest is of rawhide and was tanned with buffalo brains, in the traditional Indian style. The use of early trade beads probably dates the garment to the early 1830s.*

Left: *These antique gentlemen are survivors of the Texas force that defeated General Santa Anna at the Battle of San Jacinto on 21 April 1836. Even in old age their pride in their achievement still shines through. A gallant band indeed.*

Above: Colonel James Bowie, immortalized both for the knife which keeps his name and his heroic death at the Alamo. His life had been one long adventure. He once fought with the pirate Jean Laffite, hunted alligators and traded in Negro slaves.

Above: Davy Crocket, a legend in his own time. He served as a congressman from Tennessee, and was the subject of many stories and legends, most of them untrue. But he was a larger than life character who was very popular with the public.

pressed ever more for local self-rule. But then the new Mexican dictator Santa Anna made clear his autocratic intentions, including stationing troops throughout Texas to control and intimidate the colonists. Already a few scattered outbreaks of violent resistance occurred, but then in October 1835 actual revolution began at Gonzales, followed by two insignificant but humiliating Mexican surrenders at Goliad and San Antonio. Santa Anna reacted by raising his army and marching into Texas in February 1836, intent on a brutal quelling of the rebellion.

The first impediment in his path was a Texan garrison in an abandoned mission at San Antonio called the Alamo. With several thousand troops, Santa Anna laid siege to the 180 defenders, a mixed group of Americans and Mexican supporters, and after thirteen days stormed the fortress and slew them to the last man. But the defenders bought time for Sam Houston to build a small army and also form a government and constitution at Washington-on-the-Brazos on 2 March. In spite of another severe blow when nearly 400 Texans captured at Goliad were summarily executed, Houston finally met Santa

Anna in battle at San Jacinto on 21 April and delivered a decisive defeat, capturing Santa Anna himself and sending his army back to Mexico.

While Santa Anna never recovered from his humiliation, and only grudgingly agreed to Texan independence to secure his own release, the new Republic of Texas was an accomplished fact. For the next ten years it grew with Houston as its first president, and its government modeled on that of the United States. At first Houston and others looked forward to permanent independence, since Texas was larger than many European nations, enjoyed fertile domestic resources, and had good sea ports available on the Gulf of Mexico.

But by 1841 the expanding cost of independence, the constant menace of Mexico to the south and hostile Indians on all its borders, made Houston and others think again. The Republic was broke and over $8 million in debt. Both Houston and his successor Anson Jones recognized that annexation by the United States was the only logical solution and, after considerable skillful manipulation on all sides, Texas joined the Union on 29 December 1845, ending its ten-year flirtation with independence.

EARLY SETTLERS

Long before laws made homesteading possible, and very often even before America owned the land in question, settlers moved into new territory. They were the kind who lived perpetually on the fringe of civilization, some of them moving every year as even the sound of a neighbor's axe signalled that the region was becoming too crowded. They were the ultimate opportunists, and migration got into their blood. Some started in Georgia and did not stop until by the end of their lives they reached California. Life was always going to better over the horizon.

Above: A settler family, heading west, smiles, anxiety and determination on their faces.

1821
The Santa Fe Trail swings into operation, linking the United States with the southwest and providing a highway for an early trickle of settlement

1842
The Oregon Trail starts to see the first waves of immigration leaving Independence, Missouri, bound for the Pacific Northwest

Artifacts courtesy of Buffalo Bill Historical Center, Cody, Wyoming

First to last, the West was a place to settle. From the aborigines who initially crossed the Bering Strait's ice bridge, to the latest European or Asian immigrant, all of them – farmers, miners, merchants, exploiters – whatever their reason for coming, shared one common purpose. They were coming here to live.

Setting aside the wanderers like the Mountain Men, the first real settlers were the families who came in their overland wagons, or riding their lathered horses, or even on their own two feet. And they were perhaps the boldest of all, for their aim focused not on the edge of the known civilized frontier but the distant boundaries of the continent itself. Starting in the 1840s, they loaded their plows and their spinning wheels, their children and their chickens, tied a milk cow to the back of their wagon, put a few fruit tree cuttings on its floor, and set out for Oregon and

Right: Rugged though their frontier lives and conditions might be, settlers took the aspiration for education with them, as evidenced in the school children gathered outside this log and stone school house on the prairie in the early days.

Below: It might look like a family ready to head west, but in fact they are already there, and happily posing with the team that pulled them, probably the wagon they rode, and very possibly one of the children born along the way.

California. Those who had trades brought their tools with them, counting on plying their craft with their fellow settlers.

The first to make the trek were native born whites, leaving behind them lands and farms that in many cases would come into the hands of immigrants from Europe. Some of them, in fact, were almost professional movers. Men like Gideon Lincecum, who had moved twelve times already, starting in South Carolina, and never staying put more than two years before he pressed on westward, finally lighting in Texas in the 1840s. The pioneering spirit, the opportunistic urge, and the rootless curiosity of the frontiersman, motivated a host of them. They moved first when they were young, then again when growing families outstripped the productivity of their existing soil. Some moved again in middle age, having left their old places to their grown children, or else seeking newer and larger lands to house several related families.

Then, too, there came the 'Pikers', poor whites who had nothing to lose by leaving their old homes, and who in spite of poverty and illiteracy

Above: At first in small bands, and then in the tens of thousands, the settlers who moved west took with them what they could from their old life as they sought a new one. Most of all they took the animals that would be essential in carving a new life.

Below: Tools of the farmer's trade on the prairies. His scythe cut the high grass. The mattock dug up roots. The axe split wood and the shingle splitter shaped it after the bow saw cut the logs.

Above: An early immigrant train might have looked much like this, though oxen more likely would have pulled the wagons.

somehow hoped things might be better to the west. Along with them moved a small legion of single young men, setting out to make a place for themselves before the burdens of family came to bear on them. Generally all of these pioneers moved on their own at first, then informally banded together in immigrant trains for safety. But some eastern communities moved almost en masse, forming virtual colonies of New Yorkers in Kansas and elsewhere. Anxious to find new homes, still they took with them intact the society and culture they had known in their old villages and towns.

Whatever motivated them, these first settlers were, qualitatively, probably the best. They brought the most daring and determination to their enterprise. They came not to make quick exploitation, but to settle and build, first homes, then communities. And they brought with them experience of a lifetime of pioneering in many cases. Most of all, they brought the willingness to risk everything on this chance in the wilderness, since for most of them there was no going back and nothing to go back to. To them, the West meant commitment.

RIVERBOATS

Before the arrival of the railroad, the steamboat was the most comfortable and generally relaxing means of travel anywhere in the West. If one were prepared to accept and ignore the seamier side (gamblers, prostitutes and others) and could afford to do so, one traveled first class, and was treated to good food, music, wines and other comforts. But less well off passengers were not neglected: the banjo and piano abounded and later came the steam calliope, an organ-like instrument that was much admired – even though the operator risked being scalded from burst pipes!

The distant sound of a whistle, the thrashing of paddle wheels and the appearance around the bend in the river of a large, flat-bottomed boat with high smoke stacks and either a stern or side paddle wheels usually sent smaller craft scurrying. For the steamboat had right of way, and held its own on the Mississippi, Missouri and other rivers for more than fifty years.

The era of the steamboats was a fascinating part of the growth of America. They played a role in both its economic and social advance, and provided a romanticism and color that will never come again. Long, low-lying 'floating palaces' that embodied every luxury then known, they were also the haunt of the gambler and others anxious to relieve fare-paying passengers of their wealth. The gambling fraternity may well have caused problems, but the captains knew that, if they were monitored and controlled, their cut of the action could amount to $4,000–$5,000 a year. Yet despite such hazards, the steamboat attracted elite members of society, some of the finest chefs and noted musicians, many from Europe. Many captains owned their vessels, and a captain of a steamboat in the years prior to and immediately after the Civil War was treated almost like royalty.

On a par (almost) with the captain was that other romantic figure of fact and fiction – the pilot. These men had spent years on the river and (so they claimed) knew every sandbar, snag and hazard there was. In fact one of the most famous of them all, was Samuel L. Clemens, better known as Mark Twain (his adopted name came from the leadsman's cry 'mark twain' as his weighted chain registered two fathoms when thrown into the river to check the depth). He declared that only someone who had hit every snag, run aground on every sandbank or made every possible error could call himself an experienced pilot!

Right: A view of the Natchez showing her low-lying hull and the huge paddle wheel housings. Her long smoke stacks also bear her name, and their height graphically illustrates the efforts made to keep sparks from combustible cargoes.

Below: The levee at St Louis, one of the busiest ports at the 'gateway to the West'. It took great skill to manoeuver in such crowded waters, and collisions were a common occurrence. Note the bales of cotton piled up on shore.

Above: The steamboat Natchez; *note the cotton bales stowed on deck. They could be a fire hazard!*

1844
The steamer *J. M. White* sets a record of 3 days, 23 hours and 9 minutes for the journey between New Orleans and St Louis

1870
The *Robert E. Lee* and the *Natchez*, mastered by John W. Cannon and T. P. Leathers respectively, rerun the race. The *Robert E. Lee* wins in just over eighteen hours

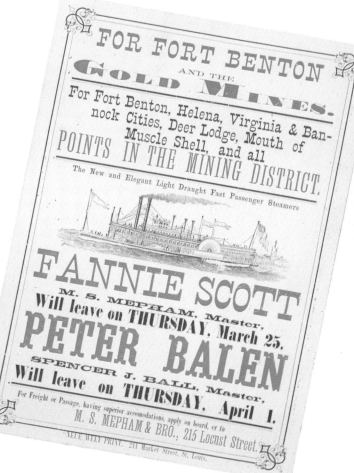

FOR FORT BENTON
AND THE
GOLD MINES.

For Fort Benton, Helena, Virginia & Bannock Cities, Deer Lodge, Mouth of Muscle Shell, and all
POINTS IN THE MINING DISTRICT.

The New and Elegant Light Draught Fast Passenger Steamers

FANNIE SCOTT
M. S. MEPHAM, Master,
Will leave on THURSDAY, March 25,

PETER BALEN
SPENCER J. BALL, Master,
Will leave on THURSDAY, April 1.

For Freight or Passage, having superior accomodations, apply on board, or to
M. S. MEPHAM & BRO., 215 Locust Street.

Left: A typical broadside either handed out or pasted up on hoardings, or some other handy spot, advertising a departure date and destinations.

Above: Samuel Clemens, the inimitable 'Mark Twain', in his later years. He more than anybody else brought before the public the era of steamboat travel, and his romantic yarns have captivated a worldwide audience. His home even resembled a steamboat!

Mechanically, and compared with modern vessels, steamboats were primitive, but for their time they were remarkably efficient. The tall smoke stacks created powerful drafts and, if the boat was a wood-burner, they helped keep the huge sparks clear of the vessel. In fact, if the wood-burning steamboat carried cotton, as many as eight men were kept fully employed watching with water buckets handy as the sparks streamed down like a firework display.

But there was also the danger of a boiler explosion. Charles Dickens made a trip on a steamboat in 1842, and was informed that 'the steamboats generally blow up forward', which was true; so in order to avoid contact with the boilers, the best accommodation was in the stern. Fuel used was more often coal than wood, but when racing, either against time or another vessel, kegs of resin, turpentine or even pork fat were heaved into the fireboxes.

Rivalry among the riverboat captains was well known, but perhaps the most famous was that between Captain John W. Cannon of the *Robert E. Lee* and Thomas P. Leathers, Master of the *Natchez*. Neither man liked the other, and fiercely contested any suggestion that either boat was faster; but the public wondered which vessel was capable of beating the record set up in 1844 by the steamer *J. M. White* of three days, twenty-three hours and nine minutes between New Orleans and St Louis. The two vessels were both scheduled to leave New Orleans for St Louis on 30 June 1870. Both captains denied that a race was in the offing. But race they did, and the *Robert E. Lee* won in a time of eighteen hours and fourteen minutes, a record that still stands.

Above: Captain Thomas P. Leathers, master of the *Natchez*. He was embittered by the South's defeat in the Civil War and refused to fly the United States flag. Instead he flew the Confederate flag until 1885 when he relented. He died in 1896.

Above: Captain John W. Cannon, master of the *Robert E. Lee*, whose victory over the *Natchez* electrified the South and gladdened the heart of the *Lee*'s illustrious namesake, the South's greatest general, who died some months later. Captain Cannon died in 1882.

Above: *This vessel is purported to be the J.M. White circa 1878–86, but we do not believe it is the same one that set up a speed record in 1844.*

Right: *A rare item of 'steamboat memorabilia', a complimentary pass issued by the Keokuk Packet Co., to H. E. Bridge, President of the Union Pacific R.R.*

IMMIGRANTS

America the 'melting pot' really did not start to bubble until the nineteenth century when immigrants from all around Europe began to pour into the open fertile spaces of the northwest, and after the Civil War to the plains and prairies. They came in millions, driven by necessity and dreams. A polyglot culture of a sort that never would have emerged in the rigid confines of European national borders, here erupted rapidly as people kept their native customs and folkways, but rapidly assimilated into a whole larger than the sum of its parts.

Above: A typical young immigrant family in front of their sod house on a now-forgotten prairie.

1848
In the wake of a series of revolutions and upheavals in eastern Europe, tens of thousands of Germans, Hungarians, Italians, and Irish, begin emigrating to America. Many will settle in the West

1849
While Europeans start to crowd the East, Japanese and Chinese make their way to California to work in the gold rush

Every American is an immigrant. The horse is native to the continent. So is the potato. Man is not. From the first ancestors of the Indians to the latest arrival, every American has come from somewhere else. If the fabled 'melting pot' has not worked quite to the extent that social planners and myth makers proclaim, still the fact is indisputable that no other spot on the globe has seen such an intermingling of races, colors, and nationalities.

Following the arrival of the first – and inaccurately named – Native Americans, millennia passed before more newcomers arrived. Setting aside the disproved claims of arrival from outer space, ancient Israel, and similar nonsense, the first verifiable immigrants to follow were the Norsemen who carved precarious settlements out of the northeastern coast in the centuries immediately preceding Columbus. The Spaniards came after him, of course, but mainland immigration really began with the English in the days of Roanoke and Jamestown and Plymouth Plantation. It would be much the same centuries later when the population spread jumped the Mississippi and raced across the West.

Yet the opening of that vast new territory beckoned to others from literally around the world. The English-speaking peoples – Scots, Welsh, Irish, and Englishmen – rushed to the new land almost neck-and-neck with a flood of Germanic peoples fleeing the upheavals in Europe of the 1840s. Swiss came over, too, and Poles and Hungarians. They went to Texas and Missouri at first, though gold in California lured them to the Pacific coast as well. After the Civil War Scandinavians came in hordes to settle the high plains territory. In California by the 1870s almost a third of the population were non-native born, and the Irish alone in San Francisco made up a sixth of the city dwellers.

A decade later, as the land absorbed the influx of European settlers, a new wave appeared from other points of the compass. Tens of thousands of Chinese – and later Japanese – settled the far west, coming as railroad workers or laborers to the cities, but soon spreading throughout the region. Across the Atlantic came a flood of Italians, many of them not stopping in their migration until they reached northern California. At the same time, the world's perpetual travelers, European Jews,

Far right: With the opening of new territory, companies advertized to lure willing immigrants to become settlers.

Below: In Colorado the Schuch family established a community of Germans that thrived on their hard work like many other Europeans of the time.

began to settle in small pockets here and there.

The cultural richness that resulted was a marvel of human variety. A synagogue could go up on the same street as a Buddhist shrine. A babble of tongues filled the market place, and place names from a hundred nations began to dot the new communities. Folk song, foods and crops, national dress, and more, made a kaleidoscope to the West, with every facet of humanity and its ways in evidence. Naturally enough, the immigrants tended at first to keep to themselves, to form small ethnic communities for comfort, and in some cases safety. But eventually most assimilated into the general population, while at the same time contributing some of their distinctive speech, foldways, and interests to the mix that produced the modern West.

Above: *The Hagebaks of Norway settled in this sod house near Madison, Minnesota in 1872. Mrs Hagebak sits in the foreground.*

Left: *A truly magnificent 'soddy', this one near Broken Bow, Nebraska, was built by Belgian Isadore Haumont in 1884–5.*

Right: *In the gold and railroad camps of the far West, many Chinese immigrants established small communities around the inevitable laundries that sprang up there.*

THE MORMONS

For so many who went west, a dream preceded the move, and for none more so than the Latter-day Saints. Whether or not their leader Brigham Young actually said 'this is the place' when he saw the Salt Lake valley, the fact is that the Mormons _made_ it the place. A civilization sprang up from the rocky desert, a monument to the determination of a religious sect's members, and a shining example of what Americans of all creeds could do in the wilderness. It came at the price of hardship, persecution, and in spite of their own resistance to expanding Federal authority.

For some people, the impetus to settle in the West came not so much from economic opportunity as the chance to get away. Some fled debts. Others escaped the law. And a few like the Latter-day Saints became immigrants in order to leave behind persecution and intolerance.

They originated in the imagination of Joseph Smith, who organized the Church of Jesus Christ of Latter-day Saints at his home in western New York in 1830, following several visions and revelations. As he told it, Christ, following the Resurrection, visited the ancient peoples of America and founded his church among them. Angels now revealed to Smith the history of that church as told in a text called the _Book of Mormon_. From the first, Smith met opposition and intolerance to his new denomination, and he soon moved with his growing band of followers to Ohio, then Missouri, and on back to Illinois. Everywhere called heretics and damned for their polygyny and other practices, the Mormons still survived even the murder of Smith. Finally

Right: Brigham Young, now an old man, sits in the chair at center, surrounded by church elders and younger followers.

Below: An early artist's romanticized view of the Great Salt Lake. It was hot, often stank, discouraged flora, but no one else wanted to live there.

Bottom: A view in Salt Lake City taken after the Civil War. It rapidly became a center of Western civilization and immigrant travel.

Above: Founder of the Church of Jesus Christ of Latter-day Saints and its first prophet, Joseph Smith.

1830
Joseph Smith organizes the Mormon Church in New York, quickly attracting the enmity and suspicion of neighbors

1846
The Mormons, under Brigham Young, move west in search of space to grow and escape the persecution of opponents

1847
Young and his followers first arrive at Salt Lake, determining that this should be where they created their Zion on earth

Above: Brigham Young combined the elements of visionary and practical organizer, to become the dynamic leader that the Mormons needed to survive persecution in the East, and the hard trek to and life to come in the West.

Brigham Young assumed the leadership in 1844, and two years later he led them west. They went first to Iowa, but then pressed on, Young holding before his followers the dream of a promised land beyond the great mountains where persecution would not find them, and where they could turn the desert into a garden.

He spoke of Utah, and in the summer of 1847 his first advance parties set foot in the Salt Lake valley. A few months later the rest arrived. 'This is the place', Young supposedly told them. It was a barren reach, bordered by the mountains on the east, and by the massive Salt Lake to the west. But thanks to Young's inspiring leadership, within a few years the Saints did make the desert blossom. Salt Lake City became a prosperous and self-sufficient small city, and the headquarters of their faith. It helped that the United States became embroiled in a war with Mexico when the settlement commenced, and even after peace came, Utah was simply too far away to attract either attention or continued intolerance.

Isolation gave the Mormons the freedom of worship they craved, though they could not stay out of larger events indefinitely. By the late 1850s, as Young persistently tried to ignore Federal laws that, he maintained, had no authority in his domain, Washington decided that the Mormons were virtually in rebellion and sent a military expedition to control them. While the Saints harassed the soldiers and delayed their operations, in the end resistance was futile. Without actual bloodshed, Young finally gave in, the troops occupied Salt Lake City, and peace prevailed. The Civil War came and went, and so did the subsequent Indian wars, with little involvement by the Mormons. But eventually they sought statehood, and once they renounced polygyny, Utah became a star on the flag in 1896.

And as for Salt Lake City, its magnificent temple became the centerpiece of its people's religion, and the city itself grew into a state capital and a thriving Western center of commerce and culture, as it remains today.

Above: Proponents of polygyny – the practice of one man having multiple wives – the Mormons held rigidly to the principle until they gave it up for statehood. Brigham Young had many spouses, including this woman many years his junior.

THE MEXICAN WAR

The Mexican War was the first offensive war undertaken by the young United States which was relatively unconfused by world issues. Its causes, in essence, were the refusal of Mexico to accept the 1845 annexation of Texas with its boundaries and the expansionist tendencies of the U.S. as it moved inexorably westward. When Texas was admitted into the Union, the U.S. wanted to ensure its boundary claim – which it now adopted – stood. It also wanted Mexican California. A struggle was inevitable. War came in May 1846.

When Mexico gained her independence from Spain and became a republic during the early 1820s, she also gained the territory now known as Texas. Originally, she welcomed American colonists into the territory, but by the early 1830s, when it was realized that they were becoming a dominant force, she took action which led to the fall of the Alamo, the defeat of the Mexicans under the leadership of General Santa Anna at the hands of Sam Houston and the declaration of the Republic of Texas in 1836. But the Mexicans still harbored a desire to

Below: The colored sections of the map show the areas disputed by the United States and Mexico in the first half of the 19th century. Texas had declared itself a republic in 1836 and was admitted to the Union in 1845. The extensive blue area indicates the territory the United States ultimately intended to acquire from Mexico.

Above: U.S. President James Polk, whose declaration of war was soundly backed by Congress.

1846
(May) War between Mexico and the United States formally declared. The Americans are victorious at Palo Alto and Resaca de la Palma

1847
(February) The army of Brigadier General Zachary Taylor is victorious at Buena Vista. In September Mexico City is taken

1849
The ratification of the Treaty of Guadalupe Hidalgo ends the war

Above: The Battle of Resaca de la Palma, fought in May 1846. American cavalry makes a desperate charge through Mexican lines, climaxing the opening of the Mexican war.

Right: On 7 August General Winfield Scott, commanding the U.S. army in Mexico, marched out of the city of Pueblo en route for Mexico City, which surrendered on 14 September.

retrieve what had once been theirs, while the Texans, recalling the execution of survivors of the Alamo at the hands of Santa Anna's men, grew to hate Mexicans – a reaction that existed for several generations.

While Texas enjoyed her new status, she nevertheless had problems with Mexico and the occasional incident involving clashes with troops or battles between their respective navies. In 1845, with mutual agreement, the United States annexed Texas. The United States and Mexico were already at loggerheads over disputed claims and the latter's refusal to accept the annexation of Texas and the Rio Grande as an international boundary between both countries. Although the United States was prepared and equipped for war, Mexico was not, for she was in the middle of internal strife; but the annexation of Texas proved too much, and in April 1846 the two nations went to war.

History recalls that the Mexicans, although greatly outnumbered and poorly equipped, nevertheless put up a good fight. President Polk ordered General Zachary Taylor to move troops to the border and Congress, in mid-May, officially declared war and authorized the recruitment of 50,000 volunteers for twelve months' service. The regular army (numbering about 7,200) was increased to nearly 16,000, and included several new regiments, among them the United States Mounted Rifles, whose officers included the former Texas Ranger Samuel Walker. He persuaded the government to negotiate with Sam Colt for revolvers which were supplied in 1847 to his own regiment and the Texas Rangers.

The Americans soon realized that the Mexicans were determined to fight every inch of the way and, in the pitched battles that followed, successfully defeated sometimes numerically superior Mexican troops (at the Battle of Buena Vista on 22 February 1847 Taylor met and defeated their old enemy Santa Anna). By early 1848 the Americans were occupying Mexico City. On 24 August an armistice was declared, and on 14 September the American flag was raised in the Grand Plaza.

Following negotiations in the village of Guadalupe Hidalgo, some miles from Mexico City, on 2 February 1848, the Mexicans were forced to sign the 'Guadalupe Hidalgo Treaty' that ceded to the United States a vast territory that included present-day California, Texas and New Mexico. Within weeks of the signing, word reached the world that gold had been found at Sutter's Mill, California. In July 1848, American forces finally withdrew from Mexican soil.

Above: Mexican General and virtual dictator Santa Anna already had a score to settle with the Anglos thanks to his humiliating defeat and capture by the Texans in 1836 after the Battle of San Jacinto. His 1846–8 war did nothing for his reputation.

Above: James 'Jim' Bowie was already a part of frontier legend thanks to his brawling ways, his notorious drinking, and the famous long knife that he helped design. His death at the Alamo made him one of the most enduring heroes of Texas.

Above: Samuel Walker led a detachment of United States dragoons whom he got equipped with the Colt Dragoon Revolver, which soon became known as the Walker Colt. It was the biggest military handgun in American history.

Below: A rare Walker Colt, the massive 44 caliber six-shooter that gave dragoons awesome firepower.

GOLD RUSHES

Gold . . . for eons men hungered for it, fought and died for possession of it. In the middle of the last century they crossed a continent at the merest whisper of gold. Some have even lusted after it as another might yearn for a beautiful woman. The gold strikes in California, the Klondyke and other parts of the West created wealth for some, but for others it meant misery or death. But demand for the precious metal far outweighed concern for the dangers involved. For come what may, gold was the ultimate goal . . . greed did the rest and did for many who sought it.

When the United States and Mexico signed the Treaty of Guadalupe Hidalgo early in 1848 which ended the war between the two countries, unknown to both sides gold had been discovered at Sutter's Mill, California, only weeks beforehand. But it was some months before news of it spread across the nation and eventually the whole world. Thousands descended upon California, arriving by sea and overland, and by 1849 the population was such that the territory petitioned the government for statehood which was granted in 1850. The social implications of gold and silver rushes simply echoed the inherent greed and selfishness of people lured toward what they honestly believed would lead to a life of riches and splendor. Naturally, few realized such grand ambitions, for the majority of them were faced with the reality of staking claims, fighting to keep them, and the hard day-to-day drudgery of working all hours in the hope of finding 'dust' or a 'nugget or two'.

California, Montana and later the Klondyke had their share of gold and silver rushes that attracted all manner of people. Many were honest, hard-working individuals who had left home and family in the hope of striking it rich and returning

Right: The main gold and silver locations, where thousands flocked at the thought of quick riches from strikes or some other means of grabbing instant wealth. But the locations of the strikes, often in mountainous areas, soon separated the men from the boys.

Below: Typical gold camp equipment: an iron-bound wooden staved barrel; metal and glass lantern (oil fueled); and various pry bars, picks and the inevitable wash bowl or shallow pan.

Bottom: This photograph, of a long tom flue near Auburn, California, in 1852 is interesting because of the lady carrying what may be a lunch basket. Women were a rare commodity in the early days.

Above: A typical "forty-niner with his 'wash bowl on his knee' sifting 'dust'.

1848
Treaty of Guadalupe Hidalgo ends war with Mexico; California is wrested from Mexican control. In January gold is discovered at Sutter's Mill

1849
Gold fever reaches the East: the rush is on

1859
Discovery of gold in Colorado Territory

Artifacts (pp. 38, 39, 41) courtesy of Buffalo Bill Historical Center, Cody, Wyoming

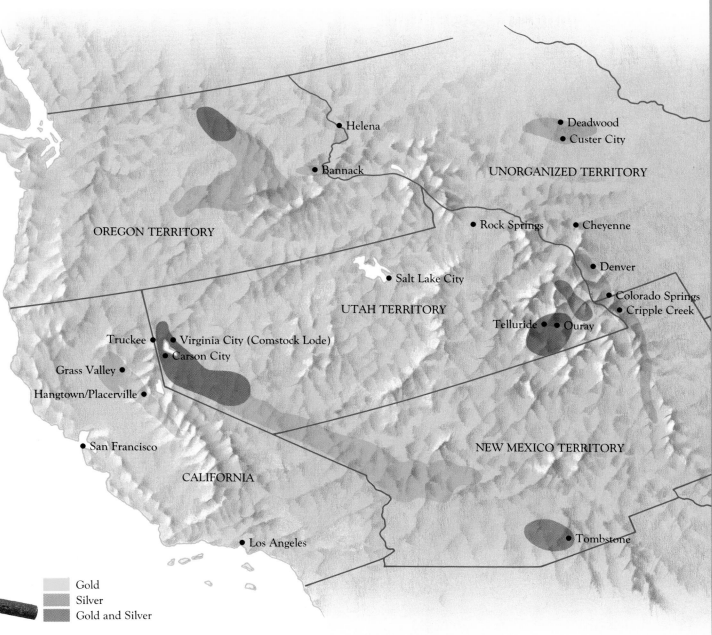

Gold
Silver
Gold and Silver

Above: John Bidwell, who made a massive gold strike on 4 July 1848. He later became a wealthy and very influential landowner. His success was typical of those 'on the ground' when gold was discovered. By the end of the year, however, the place became 'overcrowded'.

Above: John Sutter, whose lumber mill on the American River at Coloma sparked off perhaps the greatest gold strike in history, when yellowish 'specs' discovered in the mill race turned out to be gold. James Marshall confirmed the find and reported to Sutter.

Left: A rare sight at the 'diggings' were blacks, many of them escaped or freed slaves who had fled to California. A free or non-slave territory and later state, California was considered to be a safe haven.

Below: Gold was valued by weight, either in 'dust' or 'nugget' form. These brass, iron and wooden scales were an essential part of every assayer's office.

GOLD RUSHES

to a hero's welcome. Others, however, had simply deserted their families or employers and fled to the 'diggings', for such was the lure of gold and silver that it acted as a drug to some.

Individuals anxious to protect either their claims or hard-fought 'dust' were always armed, and the gunmakers back East made fortunes on the shipment of weapons. Quite ridiculous prices were paid for Colt's revolvers (as much as three hundred dollars at one point), and even cheap and shoddy weapons sold for a couple of dollars back East suddenly went for four or five times their value. By 1851, however, Colt had successfully flooded the market and prices tumbled.

Montana's gold rush had been overshadowed by the California experience, but it was nonetheless as important. As early as 1851 gold deposits had been found, but it was 1862 before a big strike was made. This was at Bannack. A year later Alder Gulch boomed with the discovery of gold, and in other parts of the West gold and silver strikes presaged population explosions that served eventually to speed up settlement and civilisation.

The effect upon communities and individuals involved in gold and silver rushes was marked. Some people invested their sudden wealth in property, or set up businesses, while others were only too anxious to gather what they could and

Above: A typical Chinese 'coolie' who flocked to the diggings. Thousands of them had been in California since the 1840s, refugees from oppression and starvation in their native land. They proved to be good workers and rivalled the Irish 'navvies'.

Right: The Chinese – with their extraordinary drive and determination – made an enormous contribution to the growth of the nation. This scene shows two miners working a stream with shovel, pan and a 'cradle'.

Below: What it was all about: a large nugget. 'Gold out there, and everywhere/ And everybody is a millionaire' went one of the ditties.

leave before the temptations of gambling or whoring led to the loss of luck or even their lives. More sober individuals, having 'made their pile', could now book passage on ships and head for New York or other eastern cities. Even so they ran the risk of hurricanes. Perhaps the most famous gold ship tragedy was that of the *Central America* which sank in a storm in 1858 with the loss of many lives. More than a century later, much of the gold coinage she was carrying, and other artifacts belonging to passengers, was salvaged. The risks were always great but, over land or sea, the lure of gold or silver was such that few bothered to consider them.

Above: This wild-eyed prospector, an 'oldtime miner of the Black Hills', carries (out of the picture) an 1873 Model Winchester. If California could be hazardous, the Black Hills of Dakota on the northern Plains were another story altogether.

Above: Another view of Auburn, at the head of Auburn Ravine. The flue or sluice was an essential feature of some facets of goldmining.

Above right: An iron-bound hooped wooden stave whiskey barrel typical of the kind found in most mining communities. The boots are wooden soled with leather uppers, suitable for use in damp areas. The 'pepperbox' pistol is a .31 cal. Blunt & Syms.

Left: Bannack, from a plate made in the 1860s. This appears to be some kind of a parade – the leading carriage carries a long pole from which flutters the 'Stars and Bars'. Behind them other vehicles reflect a festive air.

Right: As early as 1853, an enterprising miner worked out that, by using high pressure hoses, gold could be 'washed out' of gold-bearing deposits.

41

VIGILANTES

Today, the word 'vigilante' frightens the liberally minded, but for those who prefer justice rather than debate, it suggests positive action, which is why that facet of the history of the Old West continues to receive much attention. But vigilantes have always been controversial. Those formed to provide 'people power' were well intentioned, but for others, it was the way to achieve political and economic control of communities. Vigilantes acted wherever the law was lacking, and notably in the gold and silver towns of the early territories.

Above: *Jose Forner, executed by the vigilantes at San Francisco in December 1852.*

1862
First big gold discovery made at Bannack. All sorts of elements, including the lawless, are attracted

1863
(December) Execution of George Ives, a roadagent, by vigilantes at Nevada City

1864
(March) Vigilantes hang the notorious Jack Slade, for persistent crimes, at Virginia City

Artifacts courtesy of Gene Autry Western Heritage Museum, Los Angeles, California

On 23 September 1865, the Vigilance Committee, Virginia City, Montana Territory, declared that 'the practice of drawing deadly weapons, except as a last resort for the defense of life, being dangerous to society and in numerous instances leading to affrays and bloodshed, notice is hereby given that the same is prohibited and offenders against this regulation will be summarily dealt with . . . '

That statement sums up the attitude of most of the vigilante groups that sprang up in the mid-nineteenth century in frontier America. In 1851, in response to public alarm and an increasing use of violence by its population, the city of San Francisco found itself 'policed' by vigilantes who had adopted the age old belief that in the absence of law and order 'people power' took over. California, at that time in the grip of the gold rush, and faced with a population swelled by thousands of wouldbe goldseekers, among them criminals from as far away as England and Australia, was grateful if reluctant to tolerate vigilantes. And in the early days they did fulfill a useful role. At first, offenders were hauled before a committee and made to account for their actions.

Right: *James Daniels learned the hard way that when the vigilantes of Montana imposed a 'suspended sentence', it meant what it said. Frontier justice was both harsh and expedient. Some argued that vigilantes acted in a similar manner to the 'Committee of Public Safety' during the French Revolution of 1789–95. Whatever its ethics vigilanteism was at least effective.*

Below: *Virginia City, Montana, from a photograph in the mid-1860s. Already the tents and shacks are being replaced by more permanent structures. In the center can be seen what appears to be the city's main street; false-fronted buildings and hitching racks predominate.*

Below: *A San Francisco 'vigilante sword' and scabbard. Both sword and scabbard are gold-washed. Below are an ivory club and a silver pocket watch.*

Above: Another prominent member of the Montana vigilantes was Charles Behrer, who made his name as the man who broke up the notorious Henry Plummer gang; Plummer's role as a sheriff disguised his activities for a long time.

Sometimes, a flogging or some other punishment was ordered. Only later did it become necessary to hang persistent offenders or those who murdered or robbed their fellow prospectors. Those hard cases who perished from 'lead poisoning' or 'rope burns' were comparatively few; for the most part, fear of the consequences was enough to persuade many criminals into a less dangerous existence.

Vigilante humor, like that which amused most Westerners, was considered macabre to say the least. When a religiously inclined individual was hanged, he was 'jerked to Jesus', and to the vigilantes a 'suspended sentence' included a rope. And, of course, there are the innumerable tall stories. One time, a man knocked at the door of a shack and asked for the widow Jones. 'I'm not a widow,' she said. 'Do you want to bet on that?' A jury in Carson City was deliberating over its verdict when there came a knock on the door. 'Will you be long? Only we need somewhere to lay him out.'

As late as 1869, Hays City, Kansas, found itself in need of law and order. The elected sheriff had disappeared, and, following a riot between civilians and black troops from nearby Fort Hays, the post commander had threatened martial law; but the state governor interceded. However, he made no move to install a temporary sheriff. The local vigilante committee then took it upon themselves to advise undesirables to leave town. This led to a lot of bad feeling, but most of the unruly element obeyed the order for fear of the consequences. By August, however, the governor had made no provision for an acting sheriff, despite a petition from many citizens; so it was that the county commissioners, aided by the vigilance committee, elected Wild Bill Hickok as acting sheriff pending the November elections. Despite that, the vigilance committee continued to keep a wary eye upon local toughs, but left it to Hickok to enforce the law.

Vigilanteism was, and still is, frowned upon by officialdom which points out that the authorities and not the individual are responsible for enforcing the law. But as those places mentioned knew to their cost, where there was no law at all it was the individual's or the community's duty to enforce what law they could. Vigilantes are now much a part of Western tradition and, good or bad, they served their purpose.

Above: Captain James Williams, a prominent member of the Montana vigilantes. Anxious to avoid publicity, he asked Thomas Dimsdale (author of *The Vigilantes of Montana*) not to mention him by name in his narrative.

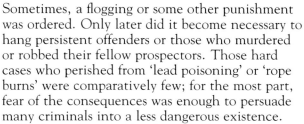

Right: Stephen ('Big Steve') Long was hanged at Laramie City, Wyoming, in the late 1860s. The photographer also exposed another plate showing satisfied onlookers.

Above: John X. Beidler, who acted as chief hangman for the Montana Vigilantes. He took his job seriously and endeavored to 'elevate' his clients to greater glory with as little discomfort as possible. He later served as a U.S. Marshal in Dakota Territory.

WELLS FARGO

Wells, Fargo & Co. are world famous. Ever since its formation in 1852, the company has been in the public eye. From its earliest days in the express and stagecoach business, when it was confronted by numerous rivals, the company sought to beat them at their own game. It finally succeeded in taking over most of them and incorporating their routes into their own. Later, when the banking side of the business became its prime concern, Wells Fargo expanded and has branches in other parts of the world. But it is its 'stagecoach' image that attracts us most.

Henry Wells and William G. Fargo both had banking and express experience by the time they formed the most famous stagecoach empire of them all on 18 March 1852. Wells had learned the stagecoach and mail business back East, where he took over Pomeroy & Co.'s express route from Albany to Buffalo – much of the time driving a coach or helping out with other chores. Later, the firm became known as Wells & Company's Western Express, and operated from the Eastern seaboard to as far west as St Louis, Mo. Fargo was originally one of his employees who proved to be so able that Wells took him on as a partner. The pair later acquired John Butterfield, whose own stageline was well known, together with several smaller outfits. This company was the real beginning of a famous ally – the American Express Company.

By the late 1850s, Wells Fargo were one of the fastest growing stagecoach companies in the West. Freight it left to its rivals such as Russell, Majors & Waddell, who were rivaled in turn by such outfits as Jones & Cartwright. Ironically, both Russell, Majors & Waddell and Jones & Cartwright foundered (in 1862 and 1861 respectively). As we have noted elsewhere, William Russell's ambitious Pony Express excited the world and the company pinned its hopes on it; but it proved to be a financial failure. Wells Fargo, who had themselves used 'pony riders' and 'express messengers' during the 1850s, then took over the Pony Express. On 8 May 1862, the *Daily Alta California* announced that 'Wells, Fargo & Co. have received a transfer of the Pony Express and everything referring thereto from W. H. Russell,

Right: This tough-looking individual is a typical 'Conductor' or 'shotgun' guard (although the barrels on this version are longer than usual). Note the gold 'bars' and the strongbox.

Below: The banking side of the business proved to be the most profitable, and shown are several items of interest. The check is numbered '1' and dated 19 July 1852. The 'flyer' has a list of every place in the United States and Canada that accepted their checks. Below are examples of gold nuggets and an octagonal 50 dollar gold piece dated 1852.

Above: *The original Wells Fargo office, San Francisco, in 1852. Its name conjures up images of the West.*

1852
The most famous stagecoach firm of them all begins its life in March, founded by Henry Wells and William Fargo

1862
Rival freighters in the shape of Russell, Majors & Waddell cannot maintain their impetus and the company fails

1870–84
Over fourteen years, Wells Fargo record a total of 313 stage robberies, 34 attempted holdups and a loss of $405,000, averaging 25 incidents yearly, with annual losses of $30,000

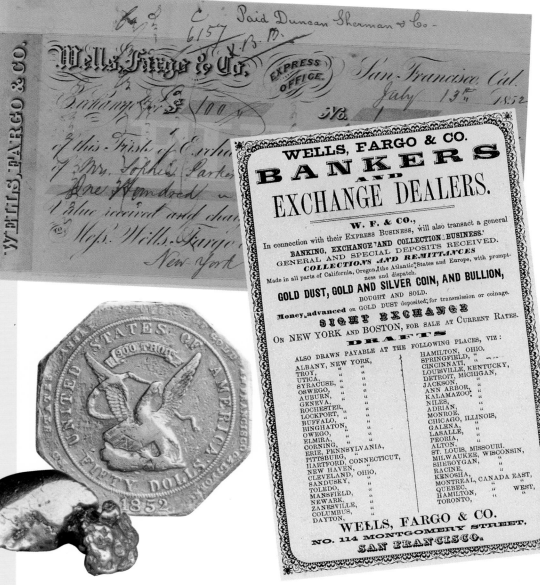

and the first thing they do is to advertise a material reduction in the charge for conveying letters . . .' Wells Fargo's 'pony express' ran until the railroads made it unnecessary. But during deep snow drifts and other hazards, the 'pony' was still a viable alternative.

With the end of the Civil War in 1865, the nation prepared for a westward expansion. The railroads were a priority and, during the construction of both the Union Pacific and the Central Pacific, Wells Fargo decided to expand their own business interests. In fact, a 'grand consolidation' of all the major stagecoach and express companies west of the Missouri River was contemplated. Ben Holladay, whose own mail and express routes had been great rivals, was persuaded to sell out his interests. He was followed by the Overland Mail Company; the Pioneer Stage Company, and a number of express companies. They were all merged under the control of Wells, Fargo & Co., who promptly sought business with the railroads. Eventually, they provided the transport and communications between the Union and Central Pacifics until the two lines were joined in 1869, together with services to other parts of the West.

The company's reputation was built upon its integrity, reliability and organization, for the transportation of gold dust and bullion was a major hazard at a time when goldseekers were often outnumbered by speculators who cared little how they got their 'dust' or from whom. Therefore, the company's employees were well armed and enough of them were available to protect their precious loads.

Wells Fargo changed with the times. In place of the colorful stagecoaches they resorted to armored trucks, and railroad cars to transport valuables. The company is still in business today, but it concentrates more upon its banking interests.

Above: Henry Wells wrote in 1852 that California was 'a great Country and a greater People', and noted that his company had just despatched by steamer the largest shipment of gold ever sent from San Francisco. Soon the company would expand.

Above: William G. Fargo, whose loyalty and business sense so impressed Wells that he promoted him from an employee to a full partner, a decision he was never to regret. Between them they forged an empire on wheels, and a national institution.

Below: The magnificent Abbott-Downing 'Concord' stagecoach that plied the West for more than fifty years. With its vermillion coachwork and its yellow chassis, it was an attractive vehicle. Note the door panel picture.

WELLS, FARGO & COMPANY.

S. MAIL

THE PONY EXPRESS

The Pony Express service set up in 1860 by Russell, Majors & Waddell may not have been the first of its kind, but it was the most famous. Hard-riding 'gallopers' or 'express' messengers had been in use for centuries – indeed, news of the victory at the Battle of Waterloo in 1815 was rushed to London partly by such riders – but Russell, Majors & Waddell were the first to establish relay stations and plan a route and times. What followed – in its all too brief life – was an epic in endurance, for animal and man, many of the latter lost in obscurity.

The Pony Express was the brainchild of Russell, Majors & Waddell, whose Central Overland California and Pike's Peak Express Company was already well-established by the time the Pony Express was inaugurated in 1860. Rivals for lucrative government mail contracts prompted the partners to think in terms of a horseback mail service to speed up deliveries. Russell's personal enthusiasm was not shared by his two partners, but they agreed to the gamble and the hope that if it was successful Congress would reimburse them for their costs and later award them with a franchise for the shorter central route across the continent – the one their riders would follow.

A series of relay stations was set up from St Joseph, Missouri, to Sacramento, California, about fifteen miles apart and stocked with remounts. In February 1860, the company advertised for two hundred gray mares 'from four to seven years old, not to exceed fifteen hands high, well broke to the saddle and Warranted Sound, with black hoofs, and suitable for running the "Overland Pony Express"'; a month later the press advertised for 'Young skinny wiry fellows not over eighteen' who should be expert riders willing to face death daily – 'orphans preferred'. All this was for the princely sum of $25 per week, which was still better than most laborers could earn.

The first mail run was on 3 April 1860, and the cost per letter was $5 per ounce. Wrapped in oiled silk to protect it from the weather, the mail was then placed in locked pockets on a leather *mochila* that fitted over the rider's saddle and was easily removed. So adept were the riders that they soon

Below: The Pony Express relay station at Echo Canyon, Utah. The building is typical of those built every fifteen miles across the 2,000-mile route. Horses were kept fed and watered and saddled in readiness for the quick changeover as riders arrived on exhausted mounts.

Above: Four Pony Express riders, photographed at St Joseph, Missouri.

1860
The Pony Express, the brainchild of Russell, Majors & Waddell, inaugurated. In April the same year the first mail run takes place. Western luminaries such as Buffalo Bill Cody and Wild Bill Hickok are said to have been pony riders

1861
The Western Union Telegraph Company reaches Salt Lake City, linking existing line to San Francisco; the Pony Express ends its short life

Artifacts (p. 46) courtesy of Buffalo Bill Historical Center, Cody, Wyoming

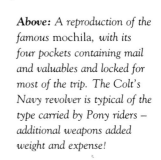

Above: A reproduction of the famous mochila, with its four pockets containing mail and valuables and locked for most of the trip. The Colt's Navy revolver is typical of the type carried by Pony riders – additional weapons added weight and expense!

developed their own style of mounting and dismounting. As a rider was seen to approach a relay station, his new mount was led out, already saddled and bridled and held by an hostler. Once the rider came in, he swung out of the saddle, grabbed his *mochila*, and, on the run, slung it across the saddle of his fresh mount which was then released by the hostler. The rider then urged the pony forward and leapt into the saddle. All in less than thirty seconds!

The hazards were many: hostile Indians, roadagents, and the perils of desert and mountains in bad weather, and a need to keep on the move, ensured that the riders never wasted any time. Originally, they were armed with one or a pair of

Colt's Navy revolvers and sometimes a Colt's revolving carbine; but the company begrudged the weight, and this was reduced to one revolver and perhaps a spare loaded cylinder carried in a belt pouch.

Such was the fame of the 'pony riders' that travelers eagerly looked for them. Mark Twain's comment in *Roughing It* is typical. The cry: 'Here he comes!' as a distant speck was noticed by the stage driver, and instantly heads were thrust out of windows and eyes strained for a sight of him. Seconds later in a cloud of dust, the rider thundered by, accompanied by a whoop and a hurrah from the coach, his brief wave in return, then he was gone, 'so sudden is it all, and so like a flash of unreal fancy, that but for the flake of white foam left quivering and perishing on a mail sack after the vision had flashed by and disappeared, we might have doubted whether we had seen any actual horse and man at all, maybe'.

In later years Buffalo Bill Cody claimed to have ridden 'the pony' but his service was confined to acting as a boy messenger between the company's Leavenworth offices and the fort some three miles away, several years before the Pony Express was organised. But he nonetheless publicized its epic story world-wide.

Russell, Majors & Waddell's enterprise led to a financial failure, and they did not get the coveted franchise, and in October 1861, when the Western Union Telegraph Company reached Salt Lake City to link up with the existing line to San Francisco, the original Pony Express came to an end. But several 'pony express' ventures continued to operate in some of the more sparsely populated regions (the most famous that run by Wells, Fargo and company).

The Pony Express may have been a financial failure, but in terms of human endeavor, courage and inspiration, it was a resounding success.

Above: Richard Egan was one of the Pony Express riders who, in appearance at least, lived up to the company's requirements; they advertised for young, skinny, wiry fellows, not over eighteen years and preferably orphans. Egan fit the bill.

Above: Buffalo Bill Cody claimed in 1879 that he had ridden for the Pony Express, but in truth his only connection was as a small boy working for Russell, Majors & Waddell at Leavenworth for some months in 1857. But his was a good yarn.

Left: 'Lincoln Elected', an imaginative painting by Maynard Dixon of a Pony Express rider dressed immaculately and carrying his pistol – wrongly – in a saddle holster. Pistols were worn on the belt.

Below: A Wells Fargo cover for the Pony Express. In 1861 it cost about $5 per half ounce for a letter; telegrams despatched from Eastern routes via available telegraph lines to San Francisco cost $6.90 for a 10-word message.

STAGECOACH AND ROUTES

The era of the stagecoach has inspired artists, writers and, latterly, filmmakers, to portray a mode of travel that to those who experienced it was a chore, something to be endured and to be completed as soon as possible. How, then, does one equate that with the present-day reaction to the vehicle? The answer, of course, is nostalgia and a romantic affection for an era of excitement and expansion, during which the stagecoach played an important role. Most people know of the Concord coach, of which the famous Deadwood Stage is a good example.

The stagecoach is perhaps the most instantly recognizable vehicle associated with the Old West, even more than the covered wagon or the wood-burning steam locomotive. Its appearance in any Western film adds excitement to the visual effects. Indeed, some might say that the stagecoach is symbolic of an era.

Based upon the heavier and more cumbersome European-style mail coaches, the Western coach was adapted to its environment. There were a number of manufacturers, but the best known was Abbot-Downing of Concord, New Hampshire, whose 'Concord' coaches were used all over the West, and exported worldwide (the famous Cobb Company used them on its Australian routes). Buffalo Bill introduced them to Europe when he included the 'Deadwood stage' in his Wild West Exhibition.

The Concord coach was strongly built, and was slung on leather thoroughbraces attached to the chassis. When in motion, the coach rocked on its 'braces, and at speed or over rough country travel sickness was common. Nine passengers could ride inside, and the same number (including the driver and conductor or messenger – remembered today as the 'shotgun guard') crammed on top. Depicted as a six-horse-drawn vehicle, most Western coaches, once the going got rough, were pulled by mules. In *Roughing It*, Mark Twain noted that their six 'fine horses' were replaced by six half-wild Mexican mules that had to be restrained while the

Right: This maximum load effect was photographed at the Branco stage station about 5 miles below Silver City, Idaho, and depicts a typical six-horse Concord coach. Note the driver's foot pressed firmly on the brake. The photograph also gives some indication of how cramped traveling could be.

Right: This 'staged' photograph was made at Bodie, California, in its later years. The place was renowned both for its gold and silver mines and its legendary 'Bad Man from Bodie' image.

Below: This map illustrates the main stagecoach routes that covered most of the West. The hazards of both the country and the elements played a great part in establishing the various routes. Rivers and mountain passes always posed serious problems for the stage.

Above: The stagecoach from Harlem, Montana, which was pulled by two pairs of horses.

1854
Formation of the California Stage Company consolidates most of California stage lines

1857
Overland Mail Company is formed; Wells Fargo become involved in development of a major stage line

1858
The same company begins first regular transcontinental mail and passenger service; also called the Butterfield Line after its president

Artifact, stagecoach and stage stop courtesy of Buffalo Bill Historical Center, Cody, Wyoming

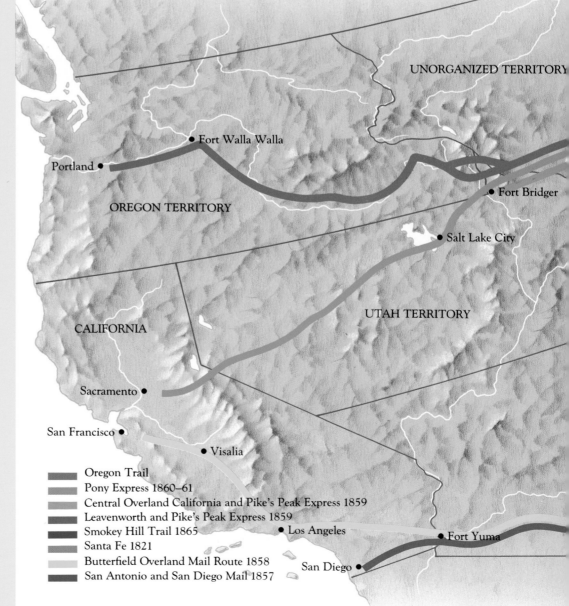

Oregon Trail
Pony Express 1860–61
Central Overland California and Pike's Peak Express 1859
Leavenworth and Pike's Peak Express 1859
Smokey Hill Trail 1865
Santa Fe 1821
Butterfield Overland Mail Route 1858
San Antonio and San Diego Mail 1857

driver prepared himself, and then set off at a wild gallop unabated for 'ten or twelve miles'.

Few stagecoach passengers would appreciate the nostalgia felt by today's generation: for most of them it was a nightmare experience. Crossing the country took several weeks, with frequent changes of horses or mules; infrequent stops for food or 'natural breaks' and overnight stops were few. Most folk slept in the coach, and only on rare occasions when the country made night travel dangerous did the coach park for a few hours. Attacks by Indians or roadagents and the occasional broken wheel or delay caused by flood or a migrating buffalo herd were acceptable hazards, so it was with some relief that the passengers reached their destination.

Above: William H. ('Shotgun') Taylor was one of the company's best known drivers and division agents during the late 1860s. He is dressed in the familiar 'furs' associated with those who drove coaches through the High Sierra snows and other hazardous routes.

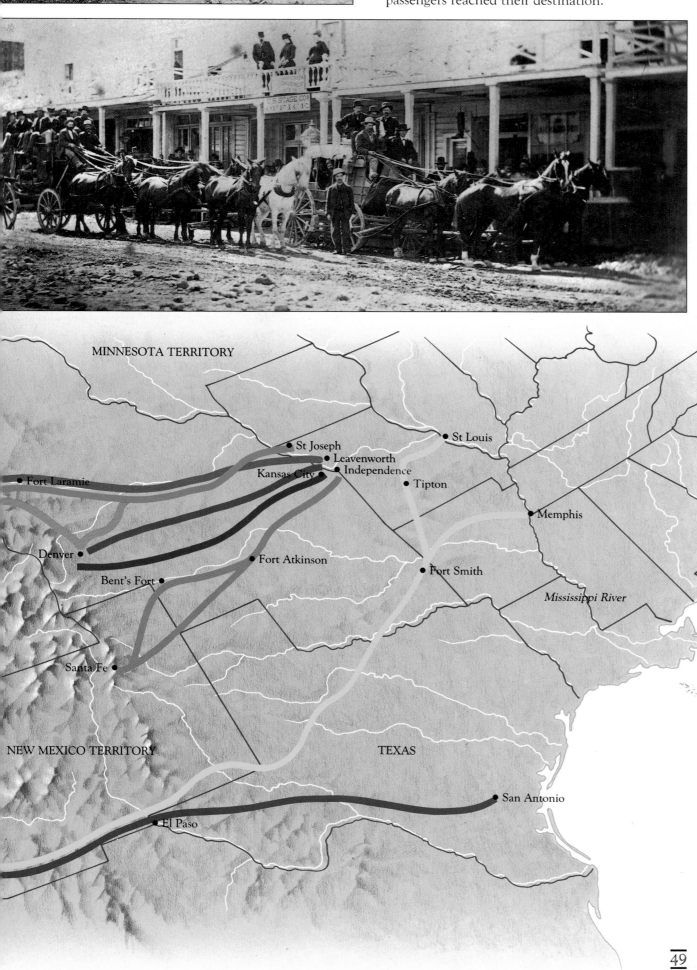

MINNESOTA TERRITORY

St Joseph
St Louis
Leavenworth
Kansas City
Independence
Fort Laramie
Tipton
Memphis
Denver
Fort Atkinson
Bent's Fort
Fort Smith
Mississippi River
Santa Fe

NEW MEXICO TERRITORY
TEXAS

San Antonio
El Paso

Above: The legendary stagecoach driver Hank Monk. He is reputed to have given New York *Tribune* editor Horace Greeley – he of 'Go West, young man' fame – a memorable ride down the Sierra into the goldfields in Placerville, California, in 1859.

Above: The dapper 'Uncle Jim' Miller, another notable stagecoach driver. Only hinted at is the finery in which he is arrayed – a well cut suit with vest, broad brimmed hat, and a silver topped whip. He also has a dalmatian on a leash, regrettably out of the picture.

49

STAGECOACH AND ROUTES

The *Omaha Herald* of 3 October 1877 published some interesting comments on coach travel. If the team were to bolt, one should 'sit still and take your chances. If you jump, nine out of ten times you will get hurt.' Liquor consumed in cold weather meant that one would 'freeze twice as quickly'. And comments about the food at stations was frowned upon – they usually did their best. Smoking inside the coach was discouraged, and one should 'spit on the leeward side'. Discussing religion or politics was out as was 'shooting', which tended to frighten the horses. And finally: 'Don't lag at the wash basin. Don't grease your hair, because travel is dusty. Don't imagine for a moment that you are going on a picnic. Expect annoyance, discomfort, and some hardship.'

If one were to pick out one of the truly memorable features of stagecoach travel it would have to be the drivers. They were a remarkable breed of men, prepared to risk their lives in hostile Indian country, all kinds of weather and the ever-present danger of mishap on the road. Their skill in the handling of a four- or six-team of half-broke horses or mules was legendary. In manner and dress they would be described as ordinary – muffled up and engulfed in huge capes or overcoats surmounted by a cap or broad-brimmed sombrero. In the summer they also wore dark green goggles to protect themselves from the sun.

In 1864, one young driver, Robert Emery, was in Atchison, Kansas, when word reached him that

Above: Pearl Hart, who as a young girl is credited by some with 'America's Last Stagecoach Robbery' near Globe, Arizona. Accompanied by an ex-miner named Joe Boot, the young boarding-school student got away with nearly $500.

Above: This typical, basic nineteenth-century stage station set out at the Buffalo Bill Historical Center reflects its time and the way it was used and equipped.

Above: This gaudily painted Concord coach, minus its leather boot coverings or curtains, is an excellent example of the basic coach that plied the plains for more *than fifty years. Note the chassis design with its spring steel supports for the leather 'thoroughbraces' that cushioned the worst of the bone-crushing jolts.*

his brother Charles and family, who kept the stage station at Liberty Farm, had been killed by the Indians and the station burned. Many of the older drivers refused to take their stagecoaches any further. But Bob Emery decided for the sake of his family he should go. He left Atchison with seven men and two lady passengers on 9 August. Ambushed by about fifty Indians, he managed to turn the coach and outrun them. The coach was covered in arrows. He was hailed as a hero and later presented with a ring inscribed to his bravery. Sadly, the young driver died a year later from a fever.

The era of the stagecoach lasted until the turn of the present century, but its days were numbered once the railroads criss-crossed the country. Nevertheless, it played a major role in bringing civilization to the West.

Above: Black Bart (Charles E. Bolton), who robbed Wells Fargo coaches and left behind poems signed 'Black Bart PO-8', was finally caught through a laundry mark. He never fired a shot during his robbing career, and after he left prison he disappeared.

Below: Ben Holladay had many interests. Apart from his stage line, he ran the 'Holladay Inn' at Westport, Mo., where he also had owned a brewery.

Right: A Wells Fargo strongbox on which lies a double-barreled side hammer breech-loading 12-gauge shotgun, and a Sharps 1859 model carbine, among others.

Above: Guess who? Highway robber William 'Bill' Brazelton robbed a number of stagecoaches in Arizona Territory during the late 1870s, before a posse ended his career. Supported by his left thigh is a Remington rolling-block carbine.

THE TEXAS RANGERS

Since their humble beginnings in the early 1820s, the Texas Rangers have earned themselves a place in history and a continuing adulation from their fellow Texans. It is a mystique that outsiders often fail to appreciate and who see them as a throwback to another time and another place. But today's Texas Rangers (there are only about sixty-two of them these days) are a dedicated organization of men highly trained in the latest techniques to help them fight crime. Yet when the situation demands it, they still mount up and ride off into the brush country in pursuit of villains.

Above: Heavily-armed Texas Rangers in front-garb pose for the cameraman.

1823
Rangers organized by immigrants in what was to become Texas to fight warlike Comanches. Conflicts continue throughout early parts of the century

1847
.44 caliber Colt-Walker model revolver issued to Rangers. The affect on their foes is devastating

1861
Outbreak of Civil War sees temporary disbandment of Rangers. They are reinstated once the Union army quits Texas

1874–90
The Rangers continue to bring law and order to the Texas frontier

Artifact courtesy of Gene Autry Western Heritage Museum, Los Angeles, California

The Texas Rangers share the mystique of the North-West Mounted Police and the United States Marshals in that their exploits have become so fictionalized that in their dealings with outlaws they are attributed with the power of 'judge, jury and executioner'. In reality, of course, the Rangers are today an official police force, but when they were organized in 1823 by immigrants into what later became Texas, they were little else but local militia formed to protect settlers from warlike Comanche Indians. By 1826, the colonists had appreciated their worth, and it was decided to keep about twenty or thirty Rangers in permanent service, increasing their numbers as and when required.

The defeat of Santa Anna following the fall of the Alamo and the declaration of Texas as a Republic led to the establishment of a corps of Rangers to be stationed in some of the more remote areas to protect outlying settlements against Indian attack. By the outbreak of the war with Mexico in 1846, the Rangers were considered to be a force to be reckoned with. When the Texas government purchased a number of Colt's revolving rifles and pistols in the late 1830s (the latter intended for the Navy), it was the Rangers who proved their worth when, in 1844, they defeated a large band of Comanches. In 1847, Colt's new revolver, the massive .44 caliber Colt-Walker model (named after Captain Samuel Walker, a former Ranger who had been responsible for Colt's government contract) was issued to troops and the Texas Rangers, the Texans proved their own and the pistol's worth in combat.

When the Civil War broke out the Rangers were disbanded. Following the war, the occupying Union army took over policing the state of Texas on a martial law basis. In 1870, F. J. Davis was elected governor and, to safeguard himself and his administration, he organized a 'State Police'. Most of the troopers were blacks under the command of white officers. Soon all manner of crimes were laid

Below: A group of Rangers at Camp Rioletas. The man in the center holding a cup is reputed to be Bass Outlaw. To his left and seated on the camp stool is Major Frank Jones, who led the hunt for Sam Bass in the 1878 and killed him at Round Rock.

against the force by those claiming that the blacks were having their revenge for previous treatment during slavery. Opinion was sharply divided between those who supported the police and those who hated them. It was not resolved until the Union army left Texas at the end of so-called 'Reconstruction', at which point the Rangers were then reinstated. From 1874 until the 1890s, they helped bring law and order to the Texas frontier. Much of this latter work was undertaken by the 'Frontier Batallion' while normal policing and more general duties were fulfilled by a 'Special Force of Rangers'.

By the turn of the century, in their fight against crime, the Texas Rangers had achieved a reputation second to none, and they kept their place, prestige and independence until 1935 when they became a part of the 'Department of Public Safety', of which they still form a part. To some they are an anachronism, a throwback to the frontier days when rough justice demanded sometimes rough measures to implement it, a time when it was said that 'one Ranger could take care of one riot'. And despite efforts in recent years to disband the Rangers, they are still very much alive (and kicking), a reminder to most Texans of a time when such men fought for freedom sometimes in the face of overwhelming odds.

Above: John Armstrong, the man who captured John Wesley Hardin, was regarded as one of the great Rangers – he never hesitated to 'administer extreme unction' to those who refused to be handled without fuss, and his exploits are legion within the force.

Above: Bass Outlaw, whose unfortunate surname did not deter him from his law-enforcement career, was promoted to sergeant in the Rangers. But drink was his downfall and he was forced to resign. He died in an El Paso gunfight in 1894.

Above: *Colt's 'Texas Paterson' 5-shot revolver with a rammer added later. These were favored by the Rangers.*

Left: *Rangers in camp at Camp Leona. The organization did not have official uniforms during its frontier days. This photograph is interesting because it depicts Bass Outlaw (to the right of the seated negro cook).*

Texas Rangers, Frontier Battalion, Company D, taken in 1885
(Courtesy Robert G. McCubbin)

RAILROAD SURVEYS

It took intrepid men to explore the vastness of the West. It took men of another kind of vision and courage to attempt to span that new world with iron rails. Impassable mountains could not daunt them. Unbridgable chasms could not stop them. Unfriendly natives, drought, blizzard, and all the perils the elements could muster, did not deter them. Backed by the promise of untold riches, spurred by Eastern politics and Western ambition, they looked until they found paths through the wilderness. If an Indian or a mountain goat could cross the land, so could the iron horse.

Almost from the moment that an iron monster belching smoke and steam first pulled itself along iron rails, the idea of bridging the two oceans by a transcontinental railroad fired the imaginations of American entrepreneurs. Long before the work even commenced, men with an eye to a profit began buying property in Illinois, Missouri, Wisconsin, Nebraska, and other places, all in anticipation of lavish profits if the final route of such a line should choose to cross their land.

But any such profit hinged first on the decision of where to locate the line. Before the Civil War Southerners wanted it below Mason and Dixon's line. Naturally, Northerners wanted it built in higher latitudes. All depended on surveys that would determine the easiest, cheapest, and most practical route. During the 1850s the government financed several separate survey teams, all of them heavily influenced by politics. At the instigation of Secretary of War Jefferson Davis of Mississippi, southern routes were explored, one – the Pope–

Below: In the 1850s a host of proposed routes for the first transcontinental rail line were proposed. Virtually all were tied up with the sectional politics of the time. Southerners favored a southern route from Arkansas or Texas; Northerners proposed a link starting in Chicago or St Paul. In the end, the War Department commissioned several surveys. The Civil War eliminated the southern surveys, and practicality eliminated the northern lines in favor of the road that ran straight across the middle – the Theodore Judah–Grenville Dodge surveyed route.

Above: *A Union Pacific survey crew in Kansas in 1867. They are under cavalry protection.*

1850–60
Railroad surveys are run west from the Mississippi to the Pacific Northwest, Northern California, Sacramento, Los Angeles and San Diego

1869
The Union Pacific and Central Pacific complete the first transcontinental railroad, linking Omaha, Nebraska, on the Missouri River, with Sacramento, California

Parke survey – starting on the Red River on the northeastern border of Texas, then running across the state to El Paso and on westward along the Mexican border to San Diego. Another – the Whipple survey – was mapped commencing at Fort Smith on the Arkansas River and shooting across the plains of the Indian Territory, over northern Texas, and across the New Mexico territory through Albuquerque, to Los Angeles.

Meanwhile, far to the north the Stevens survey projected a line starting at St Paul, Minnesota, and shooting westward over unorganized lands to the Oregon Territory, and thence to Portland, with several variant routes laid out as it approached the Columbia River. Meanwhile across the middle of the country, the Gunnison–Beckwith survey started at St Louis, Missouri, passed through Independence, then sallied out across Kansas and into future Colorado and Utah to Salt Lake City. From there it would cross future Nevada and on to Fort Reading on the Sacramento River in California.

In the end railroads would chug along all of these routes one day, but it was the Theodore Judah–Grenville Dodge survey that won the first prize. It would commence at Omaha, Nebraska, on the Missouri River, follow the Platte River west to Fort Phil Kearney, cross the Rockies some distance north of Denver, and then pass on north to the Great Salt Lake to pierce the Sierra Nevada Mountains near Virginia City, finally terminating at Sacramento. By 1860 this was the chosen path, and only the coming of the Civil War delayed its implementation. Yet hardly were North and South reunited than work commenced, and in 1869 Americans finished the great Union and Central Pacific lines. Suddenly the vast West seemed to grow perceptibly smaller as a journey that once consumed months could now be reduced to a few days.

Men had done more than conquer mountains and bridge impassable rivers and gorges. They had completed one of the greatest political, economic, and social achievements in human history. It was the final door unlocked in opening the West to the surge of settlement which would very soon follow.

Below: A railroad surveyor's compass used for measuring distances and directions as precisely as possible.

Above: Theodore Judah was a brilliant, if eccentric and irascible, engineer. Judah was chiefly responsible for finding ways around the seemingly impassable obstacles along the Union Pacific line through the Rocky and Sierra Mountains.

Below: A railroad surveyors' camp in California. The original Union Pacific camps would probably have looked much the same as the one shown here.

Above: A gang of tracklayers at work in 1867 not far from Hays, Kansas. A scene which would be repeated all across the continent for generations.

Below and left: A surveyor's chain and a surveying transit, the latter used by the B & O's chief engineer at one stage in his career.

COMSTOCK STRIKE

The whole history of the West was tied up in the dreams men had of opportunity and riches. It was fitting that in time the most fabulous wealth in all of America should be found there, hidden in the streams and hills of the ore-bearing regions of Nevada and California. The Comstock Lode, most glittering of all, spent two decades in the headlines of the world for the wealth coming out of its labyrinthine tunnels. Perhaps half a billion dollars worth of ore eventually enriched its owners before the bonanza played out. There was never anything like it, before or since.

Above: A crew of miners from one of Virginia City's mother lode mines.

1859

Prospector Henry Comstock accidentally finds silver near Virginia City, starting the bonanza that took its name from him

1873

The greatest strike of all is found, the so-called 'big bonanza' that made the California Consolidated Mine one of the richest in American history

1879

After twenty years of frenzied activity, the Comstock Lode begins to play out, leaving abandoned mines and ghost towns in its wake

For twenty years, from 1859 to 1879, a once barren place near Virginia City, Nevada, reigned as one of the most famous, and undeniably the richest, places in the world. An itinerant prospector and trapper named Henry Comstock one day in 1859 stumbled on to the gleam of silver on a claim he had filed, and from it would spring the richest silver lake in American history.

Comstock sold his claim for what seemed a fortune to him at the time, some $11,000, hardly suspecting that in the ensuing two decades more than $300 million – some said as much as $500 million – would erupt from the ground. Indeed, it would become Nevada's single greatest economic asset. In fact it was more than a single mine. The Comstock Lode of ore ran for some distance beneath the soil, and spawned a number of mines, some of them the deepest yet drilled in America. A host of the most modern machines for drilling, blasting, and hauling ore, were brought to Virginia City to harvest the silver and gold that seemed to come endlessly from the ground. In 1873 the greatest strike of all, called the 'Big Bonanza', made the owners of the California Consolidated Mine vast fortunes.

Handling all of that ore called for engineering marvels almost equal to the sparkling wonder of the metals themselves. The miners repeatedly encountered underground lakes of geothermal

water that had to be cleared before they could continue, leading Adolph Sutro to design and implement a tunnel five miles long to drain the pits into the Carson River. At the same time, several methods of ore extraction were practiced in the mines, the lavish wealth justifying the expenditure and experimentation.

The wealth spread near and far. Virginia City grew almost overnight from nothing to a city of 40,000, one of the largest and per capita the wealthiest cities in the West. Financiers built an artificial lake to hold water in the summer months, then piped it thirty miles to the townspeople, all at a profit. Meanwhile Sutro and the major investors in the mines amassed huge fortunes that they exhibited by building lavish mansions in San Francisco, where they preferred to live. Indeed, not since the Gold Rush of 1848 did that city experience such an influx of wealth, including the building of amply funded new

Right: An artist's rather crude depiction of the discovery of the Comstock Lode in 1859. The man seated at the left is Comstock himself, looking remarkably composed for someone who has just taken center stage in a maelstrom.

Right: A cross-sectional view of the expanding underground labyrinth of the Comstock strike. Gallery upon gallery penetrates ever-deeper into the earth as the miners follow the glimmering seam of precious ore. The Consolidated Virginia mine was even larger.

Above: The earliest known photograph of Virginia City was taken in 1862 during a parade of firemen and their proud new equipment. Many of them spent their days in the darkness of the mines.

Right: At the Ophir Mine in 1875 ore plummeted out of hoppers into rail cars for shipment. The ore left Virginia City in staggering quantities for more than two richly rewarding decades before the seams played out and the mines and miners quickly ceased what had now become an unprofitable operation.

Above: Artemus Ward was known in the mining camps as one of the 'Three Saints', though it hardly described their boisterous living. His real name was Charles Farrar Browne, and he and Twain liked to walk Virginia City rooftops when drunk

Above: Dan de Quille went to California and Nevada in 1857 to prospect for silver and gold. Unsuccessful at this, he became a journalist and later the city editor of the *Territorial Enterprise*. He wrote *The Big Bonanza*, a history of the Comstock Lode.

banks, and even the opening of its own stock exchange.

After twenty years the seam of ore began to play out. Miners had to go deeper and deeper to bring out less and less. In the end the California mine ran more than 600 feet long, while the Consolidated Virginia stretched another 710, and all around them a rabbit's warren of lesser tunnels sought to eke out every last ounce from a seam of silver that in places extended hundreds of feet in width. When the ore ran out, so did the miners and the capitalists, and Virginia City quickly retreated into a near ghost town. But, thanks to the Comstock Lode, a major surge of wealth played a vital role in the rapid growth of the post-Civil War West.

Above: Samuel Clemens, alias Mark Twain, brought the rowdiness and violence and humor of the gold camps back to his readers in the East, and in the process established for himself a reputation as one of America's foremost humorists and literary heroes.

U.S. MILITARY UNTIL 1871

The United States army, following the Revolutionary War and that of 1812, was a comparatively small organization, and was stretched to its limits. The situation changed with the war with Mexico in 1846, but it was not until the Civil War in 1861 that there were sufficient troops to cover the whole country. After the war, however, the peacetime force was again reduced in size. This was unfortunate because troops were soon needed on the frontier to guard railroad workers and settlers against hostile Indians. Posts were built, most of them under strength.

From the very first appearance of United States soldiers in blue, the mission of the army in the West was several-fold. It must maintain peace and order on the frontier, at the same time protecting whites from native peoples, and the Indians from white exploitation and mistreatment. It must spearhead exploration and surveying routes into the wilderness, then afford surety that travelers on those routes could move safely. It must also defend against other threats, both foreign and domestic. And the challenge was to do all this with an understrength, under-funded cadre of only a few thousand soldiers spread all across the frontier in a host of isolated outposts.

The army commenced its Western involvement with the men it sent on the early surveys, men like Captain Zebulon Pike and Major Stephen Long. Then came the War of 1812 with the British and the army suddenly had other things on its mind. Hardly a soldier was to be seen west of the Mississippi during those years, but when the war ended and settlement began to push across the river in earnest, the military was in the vanguard. Then came another war, this time with Mexico in

Below: Fort Marcy, at Santa Fe, New Mexico, was the headquarters of the Federal Department. Few Western forts or 'posts' were stockaded. Most of them were open-plan and relied upon a stone blockhouse for defense should hostile Indians get past the outer pickets.

Bottom: An artilleryman's 'shell jacket' with red facings to indicate the branch of the service (the cavalry uniforms were almost identical except that they had yellow facings). The forage cap, or 'kepi', was adorned with brass insignia to denote the branch and number of the regiment. The style of uniform shown here was in use until the early 1870s.

Above: *John Charles Fremont, soldier and Western explorer, by Mathew Brady.*

1775
Formation of the 'Continental Army' later commanded by George Washington. This later became the United States army

1820s–1840s
The army consisted of about 10,000 officers and men. Its numbers were increased during the Seminole Wars and later during the Mexican War

1866
The army reaches its highest peacetime strength: 57,000

1870
The army is reduced to less than 30,000, and remains so until the 1890s

Artifacts courtesy of Buffalo Bill Historical Center, Cody, Wyoming

Above: General Zachary Taylor, who led the American forces in the war with Mexico. He was a veteran of the Seminole Wars and was known as 'Old Rough and Ready' to his troops. In 1849 he became the twelfth president, and died in office in July 1850.

Above: The cavalryman's version of the shell jacket with yellow facings. First introduced in the 1850s, if not properly tailored, they could be uncomfortable to wear. Accompanying the jacket is a Colt's New Model Army revolver introduced in 1860, and favored by the cavalry.

Left: The Civil War was fought primarily in the East, but out West there were a number of battles that contributed toward the eventual outcome. Illustrated is Glorieta Pass, New Mexico, where on 12 March 1862 a Confederate force 'whipped the Yankees'.

Above: Fremont's military and civil activities have long been controversial, but he was a man of action who displayed a keen interest in what lay over the horizon. As a result he became one of the first men to make a complete circuit of the West.

1846-8, and the military suddenly became very familiar with the West. John C. Fremont, Stephen Watts Kearney, and others led expeditions to California in 1846 that made the first halting attempt to wrest that province from Mexico. General Zachary Taylor assembled an army on the Rio Grande to protect Texas and then thrust south into Mexico itself. An expedition penetrated the New Mexico Territory to Santa Fe, took it for the United States, then pressed on to California. When the war concluded, the military had added a virtual domain to the American map.

After 1848 the army began its first defenses against sporadic Indian outbreaks, especially on the Plains. By the 1850s, however, it had to deal with white violence as sectional difficulties turned Kansas and Missouri into battlegrounds leading up to the Civil War. When that war came, the West was finally a full partner in the affairs of the East. Both Union and Confederacy courted Indian

support, and then the armies of each had to try to counter the depredations of the natives supporting the other. The Confederacy launched a small campaign to try to take New Mexico, but it failed in the little battle at Glorieta Pass, and with it the South's dream of penetrating on to the Pacific. Other than small expeditions to deal with occasional Indian raids, the armies of both sides thereafter contended chiefly with battles against each other in Missouri, Arkansas, and Texas.

Union victory in 1865 saw the United States army the largest ever assembled on the continent, but it quickly demobilized. However, a renewed press westward after the war led inevitably to more and more frontier clashes with the Indians, and that in turn impelled Washington to send more and more soldiers to its western outposts. By 1870 the potential for white and red confrontation all across the frontier, from New Mexico to Canada was so great that the era of the Indian wars was almost inevitable.

Above: Henry Hastings Sibley, soldier and politician. He was successful in several campaigns against Indians (notably in 1862 when he defeated Little Crow at Wood Lake, which effectively ended the Sioux uprising in Minnesota). He also invented a military tent.

BLEEDING KANSAS

Kansas Territory was regarded by many as the 'gateway to the West', and for centuries the land had witnessed events that influenced the history of the nation. In 1541 an expedition of some forty men led by Francisco Vasquez de Coronado marched into the country from the Southwest and spent time in the area occupied by the Wichita Indians. Later came the French and the English. And then in 1854 people from all over the world came to settle in 'Bleeding Kansas'. James Lane and John Brown would become notorious during the grim events of the ensuing years.

Above: An illustration of a typical Missouri 'Border Ruffian', in broad-brimmed hat.

1854
Signing of the Kansas–Nebraska Act opens up Kansas Territory for settlement

1859
John Brown is hanged at Harpers Ferry, Virginia

1861
Kansas becomes a state of the Union

Artifact courtesy of Buffalo Bill Historical Center, Cody, Wyoming

On 30 May 1854, President Franklin Pierce signed the Kansas–Nebraska Act opening up the territory to settlement, and, in the process, set a match to a powder keg of intolerance, hypocrisy and downright wickedness. For Kansas was to be the scene of much of the violence that would manifest itself in the border states of Missouri, Arkansas and parts of eastern Kansas during the Civil War.

The Act set out the boundaries of Kansas to the east of the Missouri state line as far west as present-day Colorado (at that time a part of the original Kansas Territory). It was a vast expanse of land, 200 miles long by 700 miles wide, encompassing prairie, stream and mountains that were home to nomadic tribes of Indians, roaming herds of buffalo and other animals.

According to the original Act, the people of the newly created territory would have a say in their own destiny and high on the list was the question of slavery. That 'peculiar institution' which pervaded much of the southern states' thinking both socially and economically had long been a bitter issue. As early as 1820, the 'Missouri Compromise' had ensured that newly created states would enter the Union on the basis that there would be an equal number of 'free' and 'slave' states. The 'Missouri Compromise' simply meant that the state would have no restrictions on slavery, but would be unable to exclude free Negroes and mulattoes. Since California had been admitted to the Union in 1850 as a free state, the Missourians assumed that the new Kansas Territory would eventually enter the Union as a 'slave' state. Many of the newly arrived immigrants thought otherwise, and as the Act gave them the right to vote on their future, pro-slavery Missourians were fearful that, if Kansas became 'free', she would be a haven for runaway slaves.

It was not long before pro-slavery Missourians began to filter into the territory and soon earned themselves the hated name 'border ruffians'. In return, the Kansans were dubbed 'Jayhawkers' by the Missourians after a mythical bird that was noted for its thievery. However, the possibility of violence did not deter wouldbe settlers who poured into the territory seeking land and a new life. With them came opportunists whose object was to speculate rather than participate. As a result, both sides soon resorted to violence to achieve their aims. There were numerous pitched battles between both factions and men like 'General' James Lane, leader of the so-called 'Free State Army' and John Brown – whose soul is still marching on – became household names. Lane claimed that his military activities were for the

Right: The 'Free State Battery' photographed at Topeka (or Lawrence, depending upon which reference one accepts) posing with their one and much prized cannon.

Below: The Sharps Model 1852 .52 caliber slanting breech carbine that became a feature of the Kansas–Missouri Border Wars. Well-meaning religious organizations shipped in arms, and the Reverend Henry Ward Beecher sent in several hundred in cases marked 'Bibles'.

Below: This group of Freestaters was photographed at Lawrence in 1858 following their rescue of Dr John Doy. The original is a tintype printed in reverse.

good of the state, whereas Brown shielded behind a religious fervor and proclaimed desire to protect and free slaves, and in this latter respect he did enable many to escape, some as far as Canada. But when he embarked upon a series of murderous attacks against sometimes unarmed Missourians, both sides grew to hate him. His attack on Harpers Ferry led to his arrest and subsequent trial and hanging in 1859.

Among the so-called 'free-staters' were such religious leaders as the Reverend Henry Ward

Beecher, whose contribution was to send boxes of 'Bibles' which turned out to be Sharps rifles and carbines, that are today remembered as 'Beecher's Bibles'

By the late 1850s, however, most Missourians were forced to accept the fact that Kansas would remain a slave-free state. But on both sides, the men of violence would soon have another killing ground in which they could exercise their particular talents – as guerrillas on either side during the Civil War.

Above: John Brown is regarded either as a homicidal maniac or a religious zealot whose aim was to 'free the niggers' at any cost, and he was not much concerned how he did it. Some of his atrocities against unarmed men sickened both sides.

Above: Dr John Doy who was captured by pro-slavery Missourians and placed on trial at Weston, Missouri, and jailed for slave-stealing. The Kansas Legislature voted to donate $1,000 toward his defense; but other fee-soilers later freed him from jail.

CIVIL WAR IN THE EAST

From the moment of the firing on Fort Sumter and the secession of Virginia, the eyes of most Americans turned to the Old Dominion and the area between two rival capitals, Washington and Richmond. Separated by a mere 100 miles, it would be the scene of four years of the most bloody fighting as one Union army after another sought to take the Confederate capital and put its principal army, Robert E. Lee's Army of Northern Virginia, out of the war. Along the way, Americans North and South revealed the heights to which heroism and sacrifice could aspire.

Even that great watershed tragedy in American history, the Civil War, was itself inextricably intertwined with the West, for the West meant land, fortune, opportunity and power. Throughout the first half of the nineteenth century North and South increasingly battled over the balance of power in the national government. Compromise after compromise patched over their differences, all of them in the end coming down to slavery, and slavery, in turn, being the defining instrument of power. So long as there was an even number of free states and slave states, then North and South would have parity in their representation in the United States Senate. Let the anti-slave North achieve a majority there however, and that added to the inevitable majority in the House of the more populous free states would mean that laws or even constitutional amendments containing or abolishing slavery could be pushed through. The only way for Southerners to protect slavery where it already existed was to spread it to the new western territories, create more slave states, and thereby stay even with the free states in the Senate.

And thus the West, and its potential for new states that would be decisive in the power struggle in Washington, helped to bring Americans in the East to war with one another. For four years they fought, in two theaters of conflict that were themselves at the time referred to as the 'East' and the 'West'. What East meant, in fact, was chiefly Virginia, while the 'West' in Civil War terms encompassed all of that ground between the

Right: The banks of Bull Run, along and over which Blue and Gray met in the first major battle of the Civil War in the East. Pluck and good fortune made it a Rebel victory.

Below: A typical U.S. model cavalry saber and steel scabbard, as issued to hundreds of cavalry regiments in the Union army.

Bottom: A bridge across Antietam Creek near Sharpsburg, scene of the bloodiest day of the entire Civil War in September 1862, and the first defeat for Robert E. Lee.

Above: President Abraham Lincoln led through defeat after defeat, to eventual triumph.

1861
On July 21 Confederates win the first major battle of the war at Bull Run, near Manassas

1862
At Antietam, in September, Union forces give Lee his first defeat in a marginal victory that Lincoln uses as a pretext for issuing the Emancipation Proclamation

1864
Lincoln appoints U. S. Grant general-in-chief of all Union armies, trusting him to coordinate the efforts of all Yankees everywhere

Above: One man dominated the Civil War in the East for three years. General Robert E. Lee handed the Union a string of defeats and eclipsed successive Yankee commanders before U. S. Grant finally brought him to Appomattox.

Appalachians and the Mississippi, and from the Ohio River south to the Gulf of Mexico.

From the first, most eyes focused on Virginia after the first shots of the war were fired at Fort Sumter in Charleston harbor, South Carolina. For two years, in battle after battle, the Confederacy bested the Union. At First Bull Run in July 1861, then in a series of battles through the spring, summer, and fall of 1862, the Army of Northern Virginia, led by Robert E. Lee, defeated a succession of Yankee commanders. Not until the Battle of Antietam in September 1862 did the Union's Army of the Potomac claim its first

victory. But then that December at Fredericksburg, and again in May 1863 at Chancellorsville, Lee handed new Union commanders devastating and humiliating defeats.

Finally Lee's turn came in July 1863 when he invaded the North and was stopped cold at Gettysburg in the costliest battle of the war. Though he fought on for two more years, his army was never entirely the same again. At the same time, the war took a different turn thanks to men from the 'West'. Out there the war went well for the Union from the first. This western war turned largely on the rivers, especially the Mississippi,

Above: Ambrose Burnside commanded the Army of the Potomac in the Battle of Fredericksburg, where his performance would be remembered only for humiliating defeat. His name lasted long, reversed – to describe 'side burns'.

Left: The Trostle house on the field at Gettysburg. In July 1863 the hottest fighting of that climactic battle swirled around it.

Below: A simple Confederate canteen, covered with cloth that could be soaked to keep it cool.

Above: James Ewell Brown 'Jeb' Stuart was Lee's boldest and most dramatic cavalryman. Time after time he rode around enemy armies, gathering booty and intelligence. His loss at Yellow Tavern was a great blow to Robert E. Lee.

Above: U. S. Grant's strength and determination show in his face. A man who had failed at everything he tried before the war, he proved to be a brilliant general-in-chief when he found the one thing at which he was truly good, making war on a grand scale.

Above: Brilliant, erratic, at times unstable, William T. Sherman became Grant's right hand, a man of limited battlefield skills, but gifted at large-scale strategy. Ironically, he loved the Southern land, and yet made war upon it literally 'hell'.

Above: 'Damn the torpedoes – flank speed.' So said Admiral David G. Farragut in the Battle of Mobile Bay, as legend would have it. Undoubtedly the Union's greatest naval commander, he helped seize the western rivers from the Confederacy.

and the Tennessee and Cumberland, all of them highways into the heartland of the Confederacy. Early in 1862 the Yankees took defenses at forts Henry and Donelson that opened the last two for use in invasion. A narrow Federal victory at Shiloh in April 1862 paved the way for Ulysses S. Grant to become a hero of national proportion, and when he captured Vicksburg on the Mississippi on 4 July 1863 – the day after Lee's Gettysburg defeat – he cemented the Union's hold on the great river and cut the Confederacy in two.

The rise of Grant and the successes in the West brought a number of new men to the fore. Grant himself would become general-in-chief of all Union armies early in 1864, entrusted to direct the entire war effort. To command behind him in the West he left his most trusted lieutenant William T. Sherman. David G. Farragut, who played a vital role in taking the Mississippi, became the Union's first admiral. It helped that to combat them there had been no Lee, but rather a succession of second-rate Confederate commanders, and especially Braxton Bragg – who made better war on his own generals than on the

Above: A dead Rebel was dragged into these rocks to show the Devil's Den position opposite Gettysburg's Little Round Top.

Left: Here the Union XI Corps stood in the Wilderness before being routed during the Battle of Chancellorsville in May 1863.

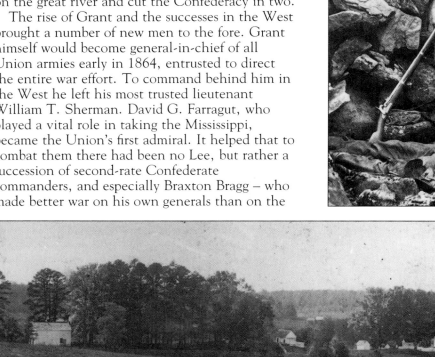

enemy – and Joseph E. Johnston, too proud of his reputation to risk it by giving battle.

With the dawn of 1864 the war, now dominated on the Northern side by these westerners, entered a grim new phase. Grant planned a campaign of pressing the South on all sides without let-up. In Virginia he moved with the Army of the Potomac, hammering Lee day after day through a succession of battles – the Wilderness, Spotsylvania, North and South Anna, Cold Harbor – until he drove him back to the defenses of the Confederate capital at Richmond, and there laid siege to him. Meanwhile in the West, Sherman based himself at Chattanooga, Tennessee, and drove south into Georgia, pushing the timid Johnston before him until he captured the important rail and manufacturing center at Atlanta in the summer. That done, Sherman pushed on east to Savannah on the Atlantic.

By the end of 1864, the North had the South almost at bay. Lee had been taken out of the war effectively, bottled up in Richmond and Petersburg where time ran steadily against him. In Georgia, Sherman stood poised to march north through South and North Carolina, and elsewhere east of the Mississippi the Confederacy could field only vestigial forces whose efforts to resist the Yankee tide were increasingly futile. As a result, when the end came, it came swiftly. Late in March 1865 Grant started the final pressure on Lee that forced him to make a flight to save the lives of both his army and himself, with Grant pursuing him until he surrounded him finally at Appomattox, and there on 9 April the proud Confederate surrendered. Sherman, meanwhile, marched through North and South Carolina almost without resistance, brushed aside Johnston's feeble efforts to stop him, and later in April finally forced Johnston, too, to accept terms. Though a few scattered gray-clad commands held out a few days or weeks longer, the war east of the Mississippi was now virtually over. Fittingly, however, out in the far West, that expanse beyond the Mississippi that played such a vital role in fomenting the conflict, the war itself would continue to drag on for many more weeks before it would finally end.

Right: Late in 1863 Major General U. S. Grant, standing at left, cigar in mouth, gazes at some of his men on the rocky summit of Lookout Mountain following his victory there in November.

Above: The backbone of the Union and Confederate infantryman. A typical .58 caliber muzzle-loading rifle, with triangular bayonet and scabbard.

Left: The cost of the war was brutal to the South in particular, showing most of all in the devastated ruins of Richmond, Virginia, after a fire started during its evacuation in 1865.

Right: The final Union victory celebration took place in May 1865 with the Grand Review of the armies in Washington. President Andrew Johnson and various dignitaries sit behind the bunting at front.

Above: No more hapless or bumbling man led a Confederate army than General Braxton Bragg, despised alike by his generals and his soldiers. All that kept him in command was his lasting friendship with Jefferson Davis.

Above: General James Longstreet, whom Lee called 'my old war-horse', was solid, steady, dependable, yet slow and often unimaginative. He would be the center of a controversy that still rages over the loss of the Battle of Gettysburg.

Above: The mournful-eyed General John B. Hood lost a leg in one battle and the use of an arm in another. Yet his fighting determination never wavered. He rose to army command in 1864, only to meet disaster and humiliation at Franklin and Nashville.

UNION & CONFEDERACY

Some predicted as early as 1808 that North and South would go to war over slavery. In 1861 the prediction came true. Suddenly America was the focus of world attention as two and one-half million Americans rushed to arms to defend whichever definition of Americanism most appealed to them. In more than a thousand fights they struggled and died, defining themselves and the nation they would leave behind after 1865. The Confederacy, in some ways, typified America every bit as well as the Union, which is why at war's end they returned so quickly to peace.

Above: Jefferson Davis, stern, dedicated president of the Confederacy.

1860
South Carolina secedes in December, to be followed by ten more states as the wave of disunion rolls over the South

1861
On 12 April the war begins when batteries fire on Federals in Fort Sumter, forcing its surrender the next day

1863
After two years of defeats, twin Union victories at Gettysburg and Vicksburg in July leave the Confederacy split, crippled, and on the road to defeat

1865
On 9 April Robert E. Lee surrenders to U. S. Grant, ending the war in Virginia. Within weeks the rest of the Confederacy's armies will yield

The men in the ranks, Blue and Gray, entertained very distinct views of their nations and their causes, feelings that sustained them as they risked and shed their blood on America's battlefields.

Contrary to widespread misconception, the Southern fighting man – 'Johnny Reb' his foes would call him, a sobriquet that he would himself adopt with pride – had little or no interest in the issues of slavery and power that brought about the war. Only a fraction of Confederate soldiers either owned a slave or had any stake in the institution itself. Almost to a man, these young Southerners went to war out of the enthusiasm of youth, and because their homeland was to be invaded. Viewing their home states with the kind of loyalty that other peoples applied to their nations,

Right: If the Civil War was brother against brother, so also was it brother with brother. These four siblings all enlisted in the same Union regiment as sharpshooters.

Below top: A typical battleflag of a Confederate infantry regiment, this one showing service in the Army of Northern Virginia.

Bottom: Three Georgia Confederates, all from the same regiment, yet showing a wide variety of headgear.

Confederates went to war to protect home and hearth. It was their roads that invading Yankees would tramp, their fields they might lay waste, their simple dwellings that could feel the torch of the invader. Indeed, not even the notion of Confederate independence and nationhood motivated them nearly as much as the simple instinct for self-defense.

Ironically, there lay one of the great weaknesses of the Confederacy. Most of its people, both in and out of uniform, never really developed an attachment to the idea of a Southern nation. First and last, their eyes rested chiefly on their own locality, their state, even their country. Try as President Jefferson Davis did, he never succeeded in instilling a notion in his people that the way to protect their local interests was by subordinating those interests to the good of the Confederacy as a whole. That the Confederate government lasted as long as it did, as a result, was due more than anything else to the sacrifice of the Confederate fighting man who, once in the army, stayed with it in spite of hardship – to the Georgians who gave their lives in Virginia, to the Texans who sent their sons to Mississippi, to the men from every state who followed their generals into other regions at the risk of leaving behind home and family to the ravages of the invader.

By contrast, 'Billy Yank' as he and his enemy called the Union fighting man, also had little interest in the slave issue. Scarcely one in a thousand of the Yankees who wore the blue went to war in the cause of black freedom. Instead, overwhelmingly they enlisted to avenge the insult to the Stars and Stripes caused by Confederate 'rebellion', and to ensure that the Union remained whole and paramount. If emancipation or abolition came along with it, that was fine, but it was incidental to the perpetuation of the United States.

When Billy Yank finally achieved his victory in 1865 it was due more than anything else to his showing the same kind of courage and determination as his foe, for the Yankees stayed with the war in spite of years of humiliating defeats, bad generals, widespread anti-war sentiment at home, and appalling losses. North and South, it was the courage of the men in uniform who made the war last as long as it did, and as well determined its outcome.

Left: A typical, if somewhat bemused, looking Federal infantryman, in full field dress.

Below: The guidon of the 3rd Pennsylvania Cavalry, Company C, proudly displays the actions in which it engaged from April 1862 until the end of the war in Virginia. Typically it misspells Spotsylvania.

Above: Johnny Clem quickly became known and romanticized as the 'Drummer Boy of Shiloh' thanks to his service in that April 1862 battle. He served the Union throughout the war, and eventually became a general in the U.S. army.

Above: A fierce-visaged Confederate soldier holds his double-barreled shotgun, and poses with bowie knife in his belt, the picture of Southern determination. Three-quarters of a million like him fought the South's battles in innumerable encounters.

Above: Henry Kelly of the Confederate 1st Virginia seems almost dwarfed by his uniform, but the Colt revolving carbine in his hands makes him a formidable source of fire power nonetheless. He used it in the first battle of the war.

CIVIL WAR IN THE WEST

When North and South went to war, neither realized that East and West would soon become a part of their vocabularies. Two very different wars emerged on either side of the Mississippi. To the West men emerged who would raise the level of warfare to a brutality rarely before seen on the continent. There, too, vast spaces saw cavalry covering hundreds of miles in campaigns. In a land once their own, the Indians became a factor, wooed by both sides, and the names of places like Lawrence, Pea Ridge and Wilson's Creek were added to the lexicon of bravery and infamy.

Above: *A very youthful William C. Quantrill, failure-turned Confederate terrorist.*

1861
In August the Confederates deliver a stunning blow to the Union with their victory at Wilson's Creek, Missouri

1863
Quantrill and his raiders sack Lawrence, Kansas, wreaking havoc on civilians and their property

1864
Confederate General Sterling Price leads the last major invasion of the North as he drives unsuccessfully for the Missouri River in the fall

West of the Mississippi, North and South fought a radically different war with each other from the one they waged to the East. It covered a vast territory, involved whites, blacks, and Indians, sometimes was fought over issues that went back to old rivalries and grudges held long before the war came, and all too often degenerated into the most brutish sort of savagery. It was a war within a war, and one that lasted for some time, long after the official fighting ceased.

When secession came, Texas, Arkansas and Louisiana left the Union to join the Confederacy, while Missouri's Southern sympathizers tried mightily – but futilely – to take it out, too. Everyone in those Western states and the territories beyond had been intensely interested in the struggles of the 1850s over 'Bleeding Kansas', and the border war that sought to decide whether Kansas would enter the Union slave or free. Thus, when Civil War broke out in 1861, battle lines were already drawn.

It did not take long for new battles to erupt. In August 1861 Confederates invaded Missouri, and at Wilson's Creek inflicted a defeat that opened much of the state to them. They proved unable to hold it, however, and the next spring, at Pea Ridge, Arkansas, Federals managed to push their foes out of much of Arkansas as well. For the next two years Missouri and Arkansas remained predominantly in Union hands, but suffered increasingly from the bloody raids of savage guerrillas like William Quantrill and William

Right: *George Stidham with his family in 1869. He was a leader of mixed-blood Creek aristocracy and supported the Confederacy.*

Below top: *The regimental flag of the 4th Missouri Infantry, CSA, its 13 stars including Missouri and Kentucky.*

Bottom: *A street in Lawrence, Kansas, down which Quantrill's raiders rode spreading death and destruction.*

'Bloody Bill' Anderson, ostensibly Confederate partisans who, in face, proved an embarrassment to their own side thanks to their propensity for rapine and plunder. When Quantrill sacked Lawrence, Kansas, in August 1863 he murdered over 150 civilians, becoming almost an outcast within his own forces.

In 1864 the Confederacy attempted to regain Arkansas and Missouri, first in a spring campaign that pushed the Yankees back to Little Rock, and then that fall when General Sterling Price led an army all the way to the Missouri River before defeat at Westport ended his hopes in what was the last major Confederate offensive of the war. Meanwhile, the previous spring a Union campaign also came to naught when General Nathaniel Banks led an expedition up the Red River to the Louisiana interior, hoping to take a foothold in Texas, damage Confederate cotton crops, and pin down possible Confederate reinforcements from crossing east of the Mississippi. He conducted an inept campaign that almost saw him trapped, and which in the end accomplished little.

By the end of the war, fighting had become increasingly brutal on the plains and prairies. Cherokee and other Indian tribes were wooed by both sides, and often fought in blue and gray, adding their own kind of warfare to the savagery of the conflict. Indeed, Stand Watie, a Cherokee, became a Confederate brigadier general, and was the commander of the last organized body of Rebels to surrender at the end of June, more than ten weeks after Lee's capitulation. Even then, the wildness and hatreds engendered by the war out here lasted on, becoming a foundation of the Wild West to follow as men like Frank and Jesse James and others refused to put down their guns and continued their lawless plundering ways.

Above: A crude wartime portrait of Quantrill, the uniform of a Confederate colonel – a rank he never held – painted on. His calm, boyish face belied the psychopath within, who used the excuse of a war to wreak vengeance for personal disappointments.

Above: When the Federals finally tracked Quantrill down in Kentucky in May 1865, Clark Hockensmith attempted to save his commander, but was shot in the act, even as Quantrill also took a mortal wound. Quantrill would die 6 June 1865.

Above: Sporting a captured 'US' belt plate (not shown in this picture) probably taken from a victim, John Jarrett – who called himself 'captain' – lived through his bushwhacker service in the war to join old cronies Frank and Jesse James on the outlaw trail.

CIVIL WAR GUERRILLAS

William C. Quantrill . . . William ('Bloody Bill') Anderson . . . even today their names send shockwaves through the minds of those who study or whose families recall their Civil War exploits. Anderson in particular was vicious. General John B. Sanborn described him as 'the most cruel and merciless of the guerrilla leaders', while Quantrill was regarded as a 'disgrace' by most of the Confederacy's professional officers. Their viciousness inspired others, and the disregard for human life during hostilities would lead to retribution after the war.

The Civil War for most people centered around the Eastern states with a few battles in the mid-West and toward the North-West. The slaughter on both sides was horrendous and quite rightly receives much attention from historians. But there was another war, equally or perhaps more vicious, that was fought in the mountains of Missouri and Arkansas and parts of eastern Kansas. It was a war between factions loyal to the Confederacy or the Union, and both sides displayed a contempt for life that lingered long after the war was officially ended.

When the Union army assumed control of much of Missouri early in the war, in particular St Louis and the railroads, and made the population of that state aware of the fact, many of the young men, torn between an allegiance to their state, and that of their pro-Southern beliefs, soon slipped away to join the Confederate army. For those that remained, conscription into a Union regiment was abhorrent, so they joined guerrilla bands and sought to wreak havoc among the 'blue bellies'.

Right: George Maddox, dressed in typical guerrilla style with plumed hat, top boots and sporting an assortment of Colt revolvers and holding a pair of .44 Remington New Model Army pistols.

Below: Although the Colt Navy was the favored weapon of guerrillas on both sides, Colt's .44 caliber New Model Army pistol of 1860 was also prized. This is an early version.

Bottom: Ike 'One Arm' Berry (left) and Sue Mundy (Marcellus J. Clarke), two Kentucky guerrillas who plundered the town of Hickman, Ky, with Quantrill early in 1865.

Above: William ('Bloody Bill') Anderson photographed soon after he was killed. Note the bullet holes.

1861
Kansas 'Red Legs' are formed to try to combat Quantrill's raiders

1865
Hickman, Kentucky, is plundered by Quantrill – one of many bloody actions. On 6 June Quantrill is killed

By far the most notorious of the Confederacies' guerrilla leaders was William Clarke Quantrill, a former school teacher. His merry band of cut-throats also included such notables as William ('Bloody Bill') Anderson, who some said was even more vicious than Quantrill. He accompanied Quantrill on his attack on Lawrence, Kansas, in August 1863, when 150 men and boys, many of them unarmed, were slain. Later, Anderson was to set up on his own and live up to his 'bloody' name.

A major problem for anyone living in any of the guerrilla-ridden states was one of trust. Few people could trust anyone, sometimes not even family members. And it was common for individuals to be 'visited' at night and to be found hanged or shot the next morning. Both sides tended to dress in each other's military uniforms and cause further havoc, which only added to the people's miseries.

A typical guerrilla on either the Northern or Southern side was dressed in nondescript clothing, slouch hat, sometimes with a feather stuck in it, thigh high boots, fancy shirt (with ruffles and often called a 'guerrilla shirt'), and around his waist a belt that housed sometimes eight revolvers stuck into it or in holsters strung around it. A similar number of pistols were often carried in saddle bags or accompanied by spare loaded cylinders. In action, the guerrillas proved themselves equal to many of the military units pitted against them. They were excellent horsemen and could ride into action with their horse's reins between their teeth, kneeing the animal into movement, so that they could fire two pistols at once.

By the close of the war, Quantrill and Anderson were dead, but many of their followers, notably the James brothers, lingered on and became outlaws. And in later years, many of those who had served as guerrillas and survived, celebrated the event in annual reunions. But now they forgot the atrocities and remembered only the 'cause' for which they claimed to fight in the first place.

Below: The ruins of Lawrence, Kansas, in August 1863, following Quantrill's infamous raid. More than 150 (mostly unarmed) men and boys were killed.

Above: Jesse Woodson James as a young guerrilla, from a tintype made c. 1864. He was wounded during the war, and following the conflict was refused a pardon (as was granted to most of the former 'rebel guerrillas'); one reason given for his turn to crime.

Above: Colonel Charles R. Jennison, whose 7th Kansas Cavalry were known as 'Jennison's Jayhawkers'. Buffalo Bill Cody was a member of this outfit, but he was not among those who were recruited into the infamous 'Red Legs'.

Above: Richard ('Dick') Liddell, photographed during the war years. He later consorted with the James gang and was believed to be involved in the plot to kill him. His involvement enraged Jesse's mother – she publicly denounced him as a 'trailor'.

BUFFALO HUNTERS

George W. Brown, an early Kansas buffalo hunter, later recalled his own part in the slaughter of the animals: 'I used a big fifty caliber Sharps rifle. It shot a hundred and twenty grains of powder, and the bullets were an inch and a quarter long. When one of these big leads would hit a buffalo, whether it hit the right place or not, it would make him sick. It wouldn't be long before I put another into him.' That comment was typical of many of those who hunted the Lord of the Plains. Their actions were responsible for the demise of both buffalo and Plains Indians.

Above: *Dead buffalo lie scattered over the prairie, grim evidence of hunters at work.*

1872
A new Sharps cartridge is issued – the .50-90, or 'Big Fifty'. It can drop a buffalo in its tracks

1872–4
1.5 million buffalo hides are carried from the Plains by the Kansas railroad alone

1884
The great herds of buffalo have all but gone from the Plains. The slaughter is complete

Artifacts courtesy of Buffalo Bill Historical Center, Cody, Wyoming

It has been claimed that during the early years of the nineteenth century an estimated sixty million bison inhabited the Great Plains, parts of Texas, the northern plains toward Canada and, to a limited extent, the eastern states. Early explorers had mistaken the animal for the kind of buffalo found in parts of Indian and Africa, hence the name 'buffalo' by which it is best known.

The buffalo was essential to the survival of the American Plains Indian. He fed from its meat, made tipis and rugs from its hide, and its sinews, intestines and bones served other domestic needs.

But to the whites the animal posed a threat to their attempts to tame a wilderness, so its extermination was inevitable.

There were two main herds: the northern and southern. The southern herd occupied parts of Kansas, Nebraska and Texas, southern Wyoming and Indian Territory (now called Oklahoma); the northern herd ranged across Montana, Dakota and northern Wyoming up into Canada. In appearance the animal was ox-like with a humped back that tapered down to its rump. Although afflicted with a poor sense of smell and hearing, once it became aware of an enemy it could move at remarkable speed, sometimes outrunning a horse.

Buffalo hunting as a profession only became lucrative following the Civil War when mass migration and the arrival of the railroads put pressure on the authorities to destroy the herds. The Indians, naturally, resented the loss of their staple diet and the need to rely upon agency beef, whereas the hunters, who could make good money

Below: *A typical buffalo hunter, buckskin-clad, and armed with a Sharps 1874 model rifle. Many were chambered for the .45–90 cartridge, but some were produced in .50–170–700 (that is .50 in. caliber, 170 grains of black powder and a lead bullet weighing 700 grains), and dubbed the 'Big Fifty'.*

Right: *A typical hunters' dugout on the prairie. Men could live quite comfortably in these 'sod houses' for months at a time. Here they could also fortify themselves from possible attack by hostile Indians.*

Far right: *Once the hunter had killed the buffalo, he was followed up by his 'skinner' who retrieved the carcass, removed the 'hide' and pegged it out to dry for a few days before rolling it up for transportation.*

Right: A seven-shot Spencer in .50 caliber and fitted with a set trigger. These proved popular with the hunters, for the Spencer (in its carbine and rifle form) was among the most desired weapons on the plains. Indeed, until shortly before Custer's Last Stand his troops had been armed with them. The government then decided to issue the single-shot .45–70 Springfield Model 1873 carbine. Below the buffalo skull is a skinning knife and a brass-studded leather belt.

Above: William Frederick Cody, alias 'Buffalo Bill', who made his name as a hunter for the Union Pacific Railway Company (Eastern Division) in 1867–8 helping to feed the track-layers. He was adept at riding into a herd and shooting the animals on the run.

Above: William ('Billy') Dixon, whose reputation as a buffalo hunter was enhanced in 1874 at the Battle of Adobe Walls when he shot an Indian at more than 1,000 yards with his buffalo rifle. Dixon had served as Chief of Scouts for General Miles.

out of hides (and later bones for fertilizer) pressed on with the slaughter. Good hides could fetch $2–$3 each or more (depending upon demand), and a hunter usually reckoned on making at least $2,000–$3,000 a year.

Although the United States government made no open comment on the slaughter, it was generally understood that the only way to control the Indians was to destroy the buffalo. Arms manufacturers were not slow in producing weapons suitable for the task. Christian Sharps' rifles were among the most popular, with calibers ranging from .45-70-500 (.45 in. caliber backed by 70 grains of powder firing a 500 grain lead bullet) to the mighty .50 caliber Sharps known as the 'Big Fifty'. Others, including Remington, also produced similar weapons. By the late 1870s, when the buffalo was almost extinct, the government stepped in to protect the survivors.

During the heyday of the buffalo hunter, many famous frontiersmen were engaged in the hunt, among them Wild Bill Hickok, Wyatt Earp, Bat Masterson, Bill Tilghman and others including Billy Dixon – said to be the most successful hunter of them all. But probably the most famous buffalo hunter was William F. Cody, who earned the name 'Buffalo Bill' when employed by the Union Pacific Railway Company, Eastern Division (renamed Kansas Pacific Railway Company in 1869).

In shooting the buffalo, most hunters would creep up on a herd or group of buffalo, set up their rifles and steadily pick off the animals as they grazed. It was usual to remain more than two hundred yards from the herd, otherwise the boom of the heavy caliber guns might cause the animals to stampede or move away. Normally, only when the other buffaloes smelt blood did they panic and stampede. Some hunters, Cody among them, would actually ride into the herd shooting the creatures as they raced along side them. This was not only very dangerous but was also spectacular. Today the buffalo is protected, a living monument to the era that saw him as the Lord of the Plains.

HOMESTEADERS

Nothing so typified the basic ideal that made one an American as the hope – indeed, the demand – for free land. There was a continent sitting there ready for the taking, and the American wanted his piece of it. At every new push west, the free land aspirants moved at the forefront of the advance. Finally Congress gave them what they wanted, but it came at a price. Incredible hard work, endless hours of labor against elements and native inhabitants, all faced the homesteader. If he won, he owned a farm. If he lost, there were thousands waiting to come after him.

Above: Her hard life telling on her face, a homesteader's wife collects bison dung to burn for fuel.

1862
After years of debate, Congress passes the Homestead Law granting a quarter of a square mile to every family willing to settle

1877
Black citizens, many of them recently freed slaves, organize immigrant groups to move west and claim homesteads

1889
More than 50,000 take part in the Oklahoma land rush when the Cherokee Strip is opened for homesteading

Artifacts courtesy of Buffalo Bill Historical Center, Cody, Wyoming

Americans began to agitate for free land in newly acquired territories as early as the late 1700s without success, but always the cry went on, and especially after the population spread west to the Mississippi. Yet it was not until the Homestead Law of 1862 that finally Congress authorized opening the public lands to 'any person who is the head of a family, or who has arrived at the age of twenty-one years, and is a citizen of the United States, or who shall have filled his declaration of intention to become such'. By paying a small handling fee for making his application, he could receive a quarter-section of land – one fourth of a square mile – at no cost so long as he put it under his plow and lived on it for at least five years.

During the years of the Civil War at least 15,000 such homesteads were granted, and uncountable thousands more followed the return of peace. In just the Hays City, Kansas, land office for the year 1878–9, 327,008 acres of homestead land were entered. For those who could not stay put the whole five years, amendments to the legislation allowed them to buy their land for next to nothing – twenty-five cents an acre – after only six months of occupancy.

And it was not easy to stay on those claims. Once he got his house built and his crops planted, the homesteader simply had to wait for rain, seasons, and luck and hard work to bring him a return. Meanwhile he fought the elements and the vermin. Fleas, lice, centipedes, flies, and worse, were his constant companions, even in bed, not to mention the bedbugs. Snakes crawled into their homes. Livestock wandered away, might be stolen by Indians, or killed by drought, bad water, or lightning strikes. Men and women who spent seemingly endless days in isolation sometimes went mad. When they did go to the nearest town, they found prices of everything too high. Eggs went for seven cents a dozen, and a pair of socks cost a quarter. Even when prices like those fell, the prices paid for the homesteader's grain also fell, and usually more, so that he seemingly never got ahead.

Below top: The Smith family, with children, oxen, and goat, at their sod house on the Plains. Father Jacob Smith stands at far right. He and his wife Alice, far left, needed all those children to work the homestead.

Bottom: A Sabbath, a celebration, or perhaps a funeral, bring a score and more of neighbors together outside a typical sod house. Always at the mercy of nature, days were long, work incessant, and there were precious few hours for people to socialize.

It did not help that the large livestock ranchers resented the homesteaders' breaking up of large tracts of once-open prairie whose grass fed vast herds of cattle. Friction between the cattlemen and the homesteaders always lay beneath the surface, and on more than one occasion in Kansas, Wyoming, and elsewhere, broke out in open violence.

In the end, the arrival of mechanized farming swallowed many if not most of the homesteaders' claims. They could not compete with their hand and animal labor. Instead they sold out to larger agricultural combines, then moved on west looking for better land, or else remained to take day jobs as farm workers. Many could not bear to leave all the sacrifice they had planted with their crops. Dead children and perished dreams filled the earth around the sod houses. 'Oh the memories,' exclaimed a homesteader's wife years later when she returned to look at the old claim. Another wrote movingly: 'I saw a vast expanse of prairie country in sunset, but it looked so very lonesome, and so I cried, in a moment of longing for my family so far away.' Such words said it all.

Above: In Loup Valley, Nebraska, a pioneer family stand beside their 'prairie schooner', the small covered wagon they used to travel in, sleep in, and carry their worldly goods on the westward trek to find themselves a homestead in 1886.

Below: The simple kitchen implements of the frontier – an iron cooking pot, stoneware jug, and carved wooden bowls and tools.

Top: In 1877 organizers encouraged homeless blacks to emigrate to the Kansas plains, promising to get them there for only five dollars.

Above: A typical general store on the Plains sold everything from cigars to cider, as well as being a post office and social center.

SODBUSTERS

There was nothing romantic about the farmer, yet he was the bedrock on which America and the westward movement were built. Cattlemen and others dubbed him the 'sodbuster', yet the nation lived on what he grew, and expansion depended upon his willingness to invest the blood of himself and his family in the dream of making a home for themselves on the fringes of civilization. They lived in houses made of dirt, shared their homes with livestock, and at death returned to the obscurity from which they came. But without them there would have been no American West.

Above: *Everybody posed for the camera at a sodbuster's cabin, even the animals.*

1865
Following the Civil War, the westward tide of farmers sweeps across the plains and prairies

1874
Barbed wire is invented, making fencing against cattle practical, and enraging stock raisers as the range rapidly starts to close

1892
The Johnson County War in Wyoming signals the last desperate attempt of organized cattle raisers to stop the spread of farmers and their barbed wire

Artifacts courtesy of Buffalo Bill Historical Center, Cody, Wyoming

Cattlemen and speculators looked disdainfully on the farmers whose plows cut the earth and reshaped it with season after season of planting. 'Sodbusters' they called the men and women who settled on the Kansas prairies, yet in time the epithet became a sobriquet adopted with pride even by the farmers themselves. They came to the West to stay, to set down roots, to build rather than just exploit.

In part, their name came from their initially very intimate relationship to the prairie sod itself. Settling on a flat, dry landscape with scarcely a tree to be seen except the cottonwoods along the occasional stream, the settlers found no sources of building material. So they turned to the earth itself. They cut the grass-bound sod into 'bricks' sometimes one foot wide and two feet long, and perhaps six inches thick. The grass and its roots held the earth together as it dried in the sun, baking hard. Then they simply piled the sod on itself like masonry, in the end making a house with walls of incredible strength and durability. A roof of wooden boards, sometimes covered with more sod, completed the house, and it could last for decades. If or when the farmer became more prosperous, or as his family grew, he could add to the house, and eventually most people abandoned them altogether to be used as barns and animal pens while the family moved to a new frame home as lumber became available.

They furnished their homes with whatever they brought with them from the East or the old country, but most lived very simply. A central iron stove heated the one- or two-room 'soddy', the source of fire coming not from wood, which was too scarce, but from buffalo dung or 'chips' gathered on the prairie. It was smoky, dirty, and smelled awful, but it burned well enough for cooking and heating.

Right: *Among the thousands of families who sought the cheap land and the hard life of the Plains were many blacks, like this family in front of their well-appointed soddy. The windmill pumped water up from a well in their back yard.*

Below: *The 'bricks and mortar' of Plains living lay in the sod, here being cut into sections a foot wide and about two feet long. Several wagon loads of cut sod would be enough to make someone a smelly, damp, but secure home.*

Below: *Some settlers lived in combination homes, half soddy and half dugout. The sash window was a real luxury.*

A considerable number of the original sodbusters were immigrants, some even from eastern Europe and Russia. They brought only their sweat and determination, and their small bags of seed for corn and wheat. But the prairies were fertile and easily broken to the plow once the sod was turned and the rich earth beneath exposed. If a farmer could outlast the cholera and the Indians, the droughts, the tornadoes that roared across the land in the summer, the torrential rains that sometimes drove in the roof or caused leaks so bad that people slept in their raincoats, then he might just produce a bountiful land-holding. In the early days especially, the greatest enemy of man and woman alike was the emptiness, the isolation, and loneliness. A sodbuster lived on his plot of ground for months at a time without going to town – if there was a town. Society, such as it was, revolved around the church or school. There was little time for visiting, and neighbors could be miles away. In such an atmosphere, even the paltriest society became prized, and only the mentally and emotionally fit survived.

Above: Seated in front of their 'soddy', a young and growing prairie family wear their very finest, even though clean clothes – let alone fine ones – seem an anachronism to people living in a house made of mud, and grass roots, and perhaps shared with a cow.

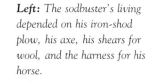

Left: The sodbuster's living depended on his iron-shod plow, his axe, his shears for wool, and the harness for his horse.

Above: There is a certain look of success in this soddy, with its smart sash windows, and its owner proudly displaying his plow, his wagon and teams, and his substantial wife.

RAILROADS

As early as the 1840s plans were afoot to link the eastern states with the Pacific coast by means of a transcontinental railroad. But it was not until the close of the Civil War that the plan was realized. When the news spread across the nation that the 'golden spike' had been driven in and the Central and Union Pacific routes were one, it was a momentous event. Bret Hart described the moment when both locomotives edged toward each other and 'touched pilots' as 'half a world behind each back'. And in innumerable places locomotive whistles 'schreeched' for joy.

Above: *Union Pacific director T. C. Durrant's private car. He sits with other railroad dignitaries.*

1825
The first 'railway' opened in England

1830
The first American-built locomotive

1866
The Union and Central Pacifics begin building to link East and West

1869
The meeting of the rails at Promontory Point, Utah, on 10 May

The railroad, more than any other means of transport, brought civilization to the West, for with it came organized law and order, government and other trappings of civilization that went toward order and wellbeing. But in its early years, the railroad met much opposition, particularly from the Indians who believed that the 'iron horse' would only bring more whites to take over their land. And, of course, their fears were fully justified.

But in the East, where speculation was rife about the benefits to be gained by an intercontinental railroad link, dollars and cents counted for more than Indian fears of survival. And there were economic reasons, too. Communities cut off by thousands of miles of prairie or mountain ranges could, with the advent of a railroad, create trade, and with trade would come people, and with them civilization.

The railroads that spread across the Eastern states during the mid-1830s until the outbreak of the Civil War presaged the demand that would come for a Western extension once the war was over. By 1866 the Central Pacific was building east, utilizing mainly Chinese labor, while from the east heading west came the Union Pacific, with its predominently Irish work force. Four years

Right: This scene depicts a construction camp on the Central Pacific in April 1869, only days away from the joining of the rails. It all seems to be organized chaos and confusion!

Bottom: Probably one of the most famous photographs in the West: moments after the Union and Central Pacifics' locomotives had 'touched pilots' and East and West were joined. One of a large number of plates made by Andrew J. Russell.

Below left: The legendary 'golden spike' that cemented the two railroads. It was replaced later by an iron one.

Below right: This announcement of the opening of the railroad West was printed in full color.

Above: General Grenville M. Dodge, the Union Pacific's chief engineer. He and Thomas C. Durant, vice-president and chief promotor, fell out when Durant, anxious as ever for quick profits, changed many of Dodge's surveyed routes.

later on 10 May 1869, at Promontory Point, Utah, the two lines met and with the driving in of a 'golden spike' the nation was joined.

Meanwhile, the Union Pacific Railway Company, Eastern Division (in 1869 renamed the Kansas Pacific Railway), was building across Kansas en route for Denver. The work force, whether Irish, Chinese or other races, earned its money the hard way, and the Irish 'navvies'

(navigators) who build the Union Pacific set up a record for building so many miles of track in a day that was not bested. They all lived hard, drank hard, fought hard and often died hard. The perils of normal railroading were made worse by the climate, too much whiskey and Indian attack. But they won through and built a network of lines that is still a monument to their extraordinary endeavor.

Above: The legendary Charles Crocker of the Central Pacific. He was the man who suggested that the Central Pacific use Chinese labor. It proved to be a good move, for the 'little yellow men' became giants of sweat and toil and were much respected.

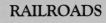

'The Driving of the Last Spike,' by Thomas Hill (1829–1908)
(Courtesy California State Railroad Museum, Sacramento)

RAILROADS

Above: Collis P. Huntington, a vice-president of the Central Pacific. As early as 1860 he became interested in the possibility of a railroad linking East and West. And he also knew that there would be vast profits to be made from railroading ventures.

Above: Oakes Ames who, with his brother Oliver, was involved in the Central Pacific, was a Congressman of some influence. He and his brother owned a shovel-making business, and the pair worked hard to win favors and influence the right people.

Early locomotives, although picturesque and still much admired, were not very powerful, and like most wood-burning steam locomotives depended a great deal on the availability of fuel. The bulk of these engines were 4-4-0 which in railroad parlance means four leading 'bogie' or 'truck' wheels (to negotiate curves) and four driving wheels. Designs varied but the locomotives were normally equipped with twin domes on top of the long boiler casing, the rear one over the fire-box containing the whistle, and safety valves. Ahead of the leading dome, or sandbox, was the engine's bell which was rung each time a train entered or left a station.

The huge diamond or balloon smoke stack was a practical as well as a decorative fixture. Fitted with a spark arrester, it cut down much of the danger from still-burning fragments.

The government allowed the various companies to cut timber on their lands, but many illegal 'wood choppers' who cut trees for railroad ties were arrested and either fined or jailed. Later, when coal replaced wood, the locomotives became more efficient and improved rolling stock not only

Above: Emigration via rail soon became big business both for the railroads and real estate speculators. This photograph depicts a railroad-promoted town lot sale in Kansas in the 1880s. Decking out locomotives with flags was popular at the time.

Below: 'Poetry in motion' was how some railroad fanatics are inclined to describe the much loved 'American 4-4-0' locomotive that was the workhorse of the early railroads. This version is one of the early types. Note the huge spark arrester.

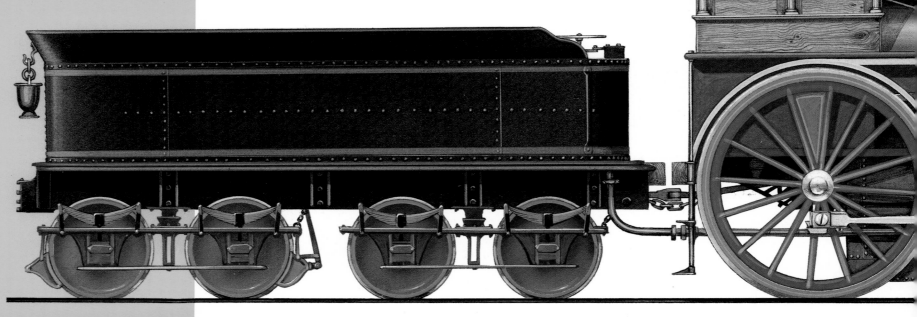

Left: These Chinese laborers on a hand-cart pause for the benefit of the photographer. Their capacity for work amazed even the Irish 'navvies' who formed the bulk of the work force and were noted for strength.

Right: This gang of construction workers was photographed in Wyoming during the 1870s. The little girl is believed to be the daughter of the foreman.

Below: 'Up the Pole', literally. A gang of men keep the telegraph lines open and under repair – essential work. The telegrapher at each station or 'depot' often acted for Western Union as well.

Above: Sidney Dillon, another of the Central Pacific's investors. Railroad stock became much in demand once the East and West were joined. The venture also inspired unscrupulous barons to speculate and some made fortunes.

added to passenger comfort, but encouraged more people to travel or emigrate West.

The railroads were not without their share of critics. In Missouri there was a general dislike of the so-called 'barons' who obtained 'right of way' through farmland and drove off the settlers. It was this behavior that put many people on the side of the likes of the James brothers whose train robberies infuriated company presidents and delighted others. But government controls eventually put paid to speculators and by the late nineteenth century the railroad was an accepted social asset, for without it the West would have remained 'wild' for a lot longer than it did.

Above: Edward H. Harriman, a Wall Street broker, one of the 'industrial giants' who succeeded the legendary Cornelius Vanderbilt. He strove to make transportation more efficient which did not please some of his rivals and the public.

THE CATTLE TRAILS

In 1890, Stuart Henry, who was later to write *Conquering the Great American Plains*, which told the story of Abilene, one of the most famous cowtowns of them all, was taking a summer's day buggy ride when he found himself on a part of the old Chisholm Trail that had escaped the plow ... still there 'defying time'.

The cattle trails later became part of various highways, but their original routes inspired old men to reminisce, to weep and to remember how it was when the longhorns headed north to the cowtowns.

Above: *The Texas 'longhorn' cow was the state's savior following the Civil War.*

1866
Goodnight–Loving Trail opens. Charles Goodnight also invents the mule-drawn chuck wagon

1867
The Chisholm Trail opens

1876
The Western Trail opens west of the Chisholm, going directly to the rail head in Dodge City

Artifacts courtesy of Buffalo Bill Historical Center, Cody, Wyoming

Cattle were driven up from Texas to eastern and western markets prior to the Civil War, but it was not until the immediate postwar years that beef would prove to be so important to the economic survival of the state. The end of the war, the growth of the railroad systems, and increased immigration from Europe into the Eastern states prompted a demand for meat that could not be met locally. In Texas, where the native longhorn cattle had run wild during the war, many thousands of them were ready to be rounded up in the brush country, but the problem of shipment remained.

In 1866 drives were resumed on the Shawnee Trail to Kansas City, Missouri, and as far as Baxter Springs, Kansas, on the border of both states. During the same year, Charles Goodnight and Oliver Loving ran cattle up as far as Fort Sumner and Colorado, but the Texans were more interested in a direct route to a railroad. Elsewhere we have noted that Joseph G. McCoy established Abilene as the first of the so-called 'Kansas Cowtowns', but the place would not have achieved its glory but for the railroad and the cattle trail. The 'Chisholm Trail' is by far the most famous of them all. Many believe that it ran all the way from Texas to Abilene, but that is not so. Jesse Chisholm, a half-breed Indian trader based at Wichita, Kansas, used to travel back and forth to Texas by a direct route that took him through the 'Nations' or 'Indian Territory' down as far as San Antonio and beyond. By the time the Texans had followed his trail north, it extended as far as Brownsville, and branched off to the main cities of San Antonio, Austin and Houston, before merging at Waco to head north. At Wichita, where there was no rail link until 1871, the trail then became the 'Abilene Trail' or 'McCoy's Addition'.

Among the other trails were the Abilene–Watersville extension; the Texas Cattle Trail (to Ellsworth); the Western Trail (to Dodge City and on to Ogallala, Nebraska); and the Wichita–

Right: The Kansas Pacific Railway was among several which produced 'Guides' and maps for the use of the trail herders. These gave details of water and grazing and suitable places to ford rivers.

Above and right: A fine Winchester rifle, model of 1873 in .44-40 caliber. This factory engraved rifle was once the property of Charles Goodnight, which is reflected in the steer's head inlay on the stock. Accompanying it, is a good example of the famous lariat or 'lassoo' long associated with the Texas cowboy and his Mexican counterpart. They were about thirty or more feet in length.

Below: Once a herd reached the cattle town, it was held some miles outside where it was grazed (to add a little weight to the 'critters') before they were driven to the pens alongside the railroad. The massive long horns (sometimes seven feet from tip to tip) were a problem, and were frequently sawn off prior to loading.

Newton Trail. A glance at the map will show how they merged in places then diverged. But regardless of the trail, they each had hazards of their own. The constant flow of cattle beat a mud-packed 'road' that was sometimes six hundred yards wide. Another problem was the sparse grazing caused by such a vast number of animals. In an effort to encourage the drovers and ease their problems, many of the railroads produced 'guides' which suggested good grazing and watering places. At a place called Turkey Creek, on the Texas Cattle Trail, the guide published by the Kansas Pacific Railway noted:

Trail from Red Fork over rolling prairie, with timber skirting east side, Small stream. Good camping ground, with plenty wood and water. Take wood from here for camping purposes. No wood at Hackberry. Supply store at this point.

Driving the cattle north to the railheads was a perilous business. Moving at a pace that covered perhaps fifteen miles or so a day, with stops for grazing and watering, and the ever-present stench of the cattle, flies, heat and dust, made the cowboy's life a chore. And then there was fear of a stampede, caused by sudden lightning flashes, sounds or simply something that spooked the cattle, which meant hours spent in rounding them up, or the terror of being thrown under their hooves if one's mount were to stumble and fall. And there was the bad food, primitive living conditions and the constant change in climate that led in later years to chronic lung and stomach complaints, hernias and 'rheumatics' that crippled many an old cowman. But in hindsight, many of those who survived the trail-driving days remembered the open range, freedom of movement with nostalgia if not romanticism.

Above: Charles Goodnight who, with Oliver Loving, blazed a trail from Texas to Fort Sumner and on to Colorado. Loving was killed by Indians, but Goodnight survived to become one of the great and legendary cattle 'kings' of his day.

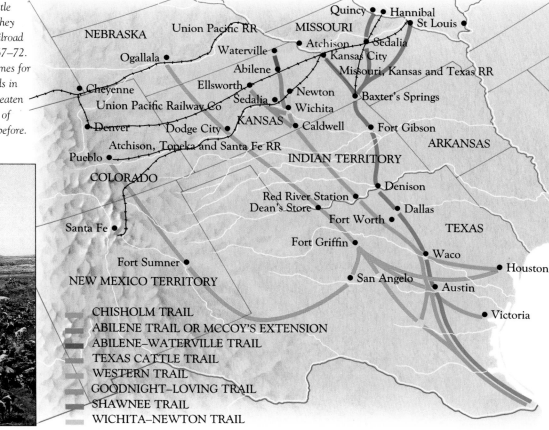

Right: The Texas cattle trails depicts them as they were with only few railroad links in the period 1867–72. They extended sometimes for up to six hundred yards in width, their surfaces beaten hard by the thousands of hooves that had gone before. The trail was tough.

NEBRASKA
Union Pacific RR
MISSOURI
Quincy Hannibal
St Louis
Ogallala
Waterville
Atchison Sedalia
Kansas City
Abilene
Missouri, Kansas and Texas RR
Cheyenne
Ellsworth
Newton
Union Pacific Railway Co
Sedalia
Baxter's Springs
Wichita
Denver
Caldwell
Dodge City
KANSAS
Fort Gibson
Atchison, Topeka and Santa Fe RR
ARKANSAS
Pueblo
INDIAN TERRITORY
COLORADO
Red River Station Denison
Dean's Store Dallas
Fort Worth
Santa Fe
TEXAS
Fort Griffin
Waco
Fort Sumner
Houston
NEW MEXICO TERRITORY
San Angelo
Austin
Victoria

CHISHOLM TRAIL
ABILENE TRAIL OR McCOY'S EXTENSION
ABILENE–WATERVILLE TRAIL
TEXAS CATTLE TRAIL
WESTERN TRAIL
GOODNIGHT–LOVING TRAIL
SHAWNEE TRAIL
WICHITA–NEWTON TRAIL

Above: Jesse Chisholm the half-blood Indian trader whose trail from Wichita down through the 'Nations' or 'Indian Territory' to Texas was to become world-famous as the 'Chisholm Trail', shown shortly before his death in 1868.

'Trail Herd to Wyoming', by W.H.D. Koerner (1878–1938)
(Buffalo Bill Historical Center, Cody, Wyoming)

THE COWBOY

President Chester A. Arthur, in his annual message to Congress in December 1881, referring to the recent violence in Arizona Territory, declared that 'armed desperadoes known as "Cowboys"' were a menace to the peace of the territory. Many people shared his opinion. Stuart Henry, a boy during Abilene's cowtown period, believed that they 'had little or no respect for law and order, religion or God'. But thanks to Buffalo Bill who 'sanitized' him and featured him in his Wild West, the cowboy's image today is that of a 'knight of the plains' who is idolized world-wide.

The origin of the cowboy in America has long been disputed. The word itself was in use during the Revolutionary period when in 1766 the Stamp Act and the Anti-Rent Rebellion in the New York colony led to a great deal of resentment. The local landed gentry (known as 'patroons' in what was at the time a Dutch-colonized area) called their rebellious tenants 'cow-boys' as an insult. By the time the whites had settled much of Texas, some of them became members of wild bands who made life miserable both for the Indians and the Mexicans. Ewan Cameron, one of their most prominent leaders, rejoiced in the knowledge that his men were known as 'Cameron's Cowboys'. Later, of course, when the whites vied with the Mexicans in the skill necessary to round up, brand and generally handle the half-wild longhorn cattle that infested the brush country, the word 'cow-boy

Right: A rare moment for relaxation: cowboys at the turn of the century eye the camera, perhaps not realizing that their free ranging days were numbered.

Below: This ornate, heavily tooled California saddle has stirrups fitted with tapaeros to protect the rider from thorns and cactus.

Bottom: Cowboys 'shooting craps' in between chores. The life was hard, the hours long, the food bad, and an all-weathers existence meant poor health in later life.

Above: *The quintessential symbol of the West: a cowboy has roped a calf ready for branding.*

1865
The Civil War ends, releasing thousands of men onto the job market. Although Texans and Mexicans are deemed the natural coboys, they are joined by immigrants, blacks, itinerant workers

1866
Charles Goodnight and Oliver Loving cut their trail from Texas to Cheyenne, Wyoming Territory

1886
Devastating winter follows drought, destroying 60 per cent of cattle in Montana

Artifacts courtesy of Buffalo Bill Historical Center, Cody, Wyoming

Above: The 'lassoo' or 'lariat' played an important role in a cowboy's life. Its uses were many and varied. A skilled 'roper' was considered to be a 'top hand' as was a good 'bronc buster'. The illustration depicts a rider holding a steer in check.

(the hyphen later disappeared) became synonymous with 'herder' or 'stock driver' and other terms before 'cowboy' dominated and remains in use today.

Skill in the handling of cattle was imported from Spain, and was a particular forte of the Mexican *vaquero* whose experiences predated those of the Texans. Much as the Texans might have detested the Mexicans (generally called 'greasers', they in turn referred to the whites as 'gringoes'), they had to admit they learned a great deal from them.

Many of the young men who rode the trails up from Texas to Kansas were 'unlearned and illiterate' ex-Confederate soldiers who understandably detested the 'Yankee' peace officers, who in turn expressed a mutual dislike and distrust. In fact, it was not until the 1880s, when Buffalo Bill Cody introduced the cowboy to the world as a romantic horseman of the plains, did he lose his image as a hell-raising, gun-toting roustabout who lived on a diet of whiskey and tobacco. Old-timers recalled that they were clannish, and imagined slights or insults could bring a swift reaction: pistols were freely used, and anyone who had upset a Texan had better watch out, for they were also prone to shoot from ambush. Rot-gut whiskey played a big part in such

Below: An artist's impression of an American cowboy and a Mexican vaquero may be a little 'clinical', but he does indicate how each character dressed. The woolen 'chaps' were not as popular as the leather version most Texans wore for protection against sharp brush and thorn.

'Waiting for a Chinook
(The Last of 5000)',
by Charles M. Russell (1864–1926)
(Buffalo Bill Historical Center, Cody,
Wyoming. Gift of Charles Ulrick and
Josephine Bay Foundation Inc.)

LAST OF 5000

Left: J. B. Stetson established a fashion with his wide-
brimmed hats. Flat or round,
high or low-crowned, they
became the acknowledged
'cowboy' hats and still are.

Below: Roping, pegging and
branding was all in a day's
work, and cowboys learned to
live with the dust, mud and
constant changes of climate.
But few of them would
change jobs.

behavior, for under normal circumstances they
were quiet and well-behaved 'decent and
honorable men'. But under its influence, they
became very dangerous.

The life of a typical Texas cowboy (and indeed
one should include those from other states) was
that of a laborer, the big difference being that it
took some skill and courage to handle the Texas
longhorn cattle. These animals were unpredic-
table. They came to accept a man and a horse as a
single being, but once the two became separated,
the man ran the risk of attack, which could mean
goring or trampling to death. Understandably,
after three months on a cattle trail, the cowboy

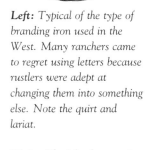

Above: The branding iron was
red hot; as it singed through
hide and skin, the smell of
scorched fur and burnt flesh
stung the nostrils. But it was
the quickest means of marking
cattle. The pain was
momentary, but the brand was
permanent.

Left: Typical of the type of
branding iron used in the
West. Many ranchers came
to regret using letters because
rustlers were adept at
changing them into something
else. Note the quirt and
lariat.

Right: The 'chuck wagon'
followed the herd, and the
cook (sometimes an old or
crippled cowboy) was an
important member of the
crew. His culinary skills
could make or mar the morale
of the hard-riding, hard-living
cowboys.

was anxious for a good time. He had a fistful of dollars and an insatiable desire to 'let rip' among the gambling and prostitution emporia. A few drinks, an invitation to dance, and the painted whores ('soiled doves' or 'nymphs du prairie' as the press tactfully called them) seen through an alcoholic haze seemed almost beautiful. But many a young man learned later that his passion had dissolved into a pox, and his hard-earned money ended up in the hands of those who preyed upon him and his kind.

Needless to say, the romantic side of the cowboy is the one that has survived. The brilliant horseman, gaudily dressed in a broad-brimmed sombrero (around the brim of which one could take a 'day to travel'); red or blue flannel shirt, brightly colored neckerchief or 'bandana', hand-tooled leather vest or 'waistcoat' and corduroy pants thrust into knee-high boots with high heels – the latter to prevent the feet from slipping through the large wooden stirrups on their saddles – a pair of jingling Mexican spurs and one or two Colt's pistols holstered on to a waistbelt completed the image of the 'knight chivalric of the plains'.

The predominence of 'white' cowboys has been questioned many times. For apart from the Mexican *vaquero*, black cowboys also rode the cattle trails north, many of them ex-slaves whose skills with cattle had long been ignored. During the immediate post-war years, the whites and Mexicans predominated, but by the early 1870s black cowboys were a common sight on the trails. The Texans had little liking for either of the two other races, but if asked would have expressed a preference for the blacks with whom they could identify, whereas the Mexicans were still considered the 'enemy', following the war with Mexico.

Whatever his faults, the skill, romanticism and appearance of the cowboy has endeared him to generations, and long ago he became an established figure in American folklore.

Above: *Cowboys of the W.D. Boyce Cattle Company prepare to bed down in Kansas. The celebrated 'bunkhouse' was fine for winter months, but most cattlemen (during summer months) preferred to bed down under the stars.*

Below: *'Chow time' was always welcome, even if it was a diet of 'beef and beans' yet again. The poor diet and primitive life of the cowboy left many of them with digestive problems that plagued them in their later years.*

Above: Negro cowboys comprised about one third of those who rode the cattle trails, but they were not so numerous until the early 1870s. During the drive they were better treated than their Mexican rivals, the *vaqueros*, called 'greasers' by the Texans.

Below: *A typical chuck wagon that was the social center of any cattle drive. 'Cookie' could also be relied upon for medical assistance on occasion.*

THE COWTOWNS

To the cowboy, the 'cowtown' or 'cattle town' as purists preferred to call it represented an oasis in a desert of dust and desolation masquerading as the Kansas prairie. Here he could quench his thirst and ease a need for physical contact with women. That they might infect him with something more than joy never crossed his mind. That thought came later. Others, however, saw the cowtown either as an economic miracle or simply as a reincarnation of Hell. But whatever the reaction, they were exciting and sometimes dangerous places.

Above: A quiet moment in a busy Western town: Front Street, Dodge City, circa 1878.

1867
Abilene becomes the 'first' of the Kansas cowtowns

1871–2
Newton and Wichita share the cattle trade with Abilene and Ellsworth

1875
Dodge City becomes 'Queen of the Cowtowns'

1880
Rivaled by Caldwell

1885–90
The era of the cowtown ends

Artifacts courtesy of Buffalo Bill Historical Center, Cody, Wyoming

The story of the cowtowns (or 'cattle towns' as purists prefer to call them) is a part of a colorful era in the epoch of the so-called 'Wild West'. Cowtowns provided the backdrop against which was set a romantic drama that, long after it became a part of history, continues to attract a wide audience.

The cowtown came about because of the need for beef in other parts of the Union, especially in the Eastern states. Even prior to the Civil War, cattle had been driven or shipped by sea to eastern and some west coast markets, but it was expensive and tedious. For a time cattle were driven up into Missouri to Sedalia where there was a rail link, and later Baxter Springs, Kansas. But problems with Jayhawkers and the fear that the dreaded 'Texas fever' (a disease found in tics carried by the longhorns who were immune) might affect domestic cattle, led to a disruption of the trade. But early in 1867, Joseph G. McCoy set out to find a place with access to the railroad and preferably one where settlement was sparse.

McCoy talked with several railroad companies, but had little success until he reached the small hamlet of Abilene, Kansas, on the route of the Union Pacific Railway Company (Eastern Division) then building across the state toward Denver. He approached the president of the company and, with the promise of five dollars commission on every carload of cattle shipped East on their tracks, McCoy purchased land at Abilene and built shipping and cattle pens. In turn, the UPED built a 100-car 'switch' (or 'siding') and McCoy was ready. It took some time to persuade the Texans to head their herds due north, but the first carload of cattle was shipped east on 5 September 1867. McCoy was in business and by 1869 there was a well-beaten trail up from Texas to the Abilene railhead.

Abilene was the first of the so-called cowtowns built for the purpose, and her neighbors and rivals followed its general layout. The railroad ran right through the center of town, and the residential and business areas were to the north and the less desirable establishments to the south or on the

Right: An early view of the stockyards at Abilene. Here the cattle were kept in pens (and some left to graze on the prairie to await their turn) before being loaded into the 'freight cars' to endure a hard trip east.

Above: Ivory dice were a common sight in most cowtowns where gambling and whoring was a way of life, and Lady Luck prevailed.

Right: A view said to be of the Pearl Saloon at Abilene circa 1871. The place is typical of the false-fronted era.

Below: Abilene about 1882; the cattle trade has long gone, but the buildings are still reminiscent of the days of the longhorns and cowboy chaos.

Below right: Newton in its infancy. The railroad tracks, seen in the foreground, separated the Texans and the saloon population from 'respectable' people.

'wrong side' of the tracks. The cattle pens were situated some distance from the main thoroughfares. Great care was taken to keep the cattle under control when moving them to or from feeding pens to load aboard the freight cars. Once, in 1871, a steer broke loose and stampeded down Texas Street, causing general panic until Marshal Hickok stepped into the street and shot it dead.

Understandably, the noise and the smell of the cattle was a constant irritation to residents, as were the activities of the gamblers and prostitutes. In July 1871, the 'respectable' ladies of Abilene petitioned the mayor to remove the 'evil in our midst' and the prostitutes were moved to another part of town. But the proprietors of the gambling establishments and the brothels thoughtfully laid on an 'omnibus' service for the benefit of their clients! Newton was another place where, to avoid conflict with the more prudish citizens, the 'ladies of the night' were housed in an area generally called 'Hide Park'. And like Abilene, most of the other cowtowns went through a period of lawlessness and 'depravity' that outraged their citizens. Fines and high-priced licenses did little to deter the gamblers and prostitutes. In fact, few

Above: 'Rowdy Joe' Lowe, photographed some years after his cowtown days. His 'duel' with Edward ('Red') Beard at Wichita in 1873 led to Red's death and a bartender being blinded by a shot across the bridge of his nose. Such were the risks in cowtowns.

Below: An Ethan Allen-type single-shot percussion pistol popular in the early 1850s, and a typical 'hand' at cards.

city councils would have dared destroy the trade completely, for the fines helped pay for the police force and other social needs that otherwise would have had to come out of the ordinary citizens' pockets.

Violence being common to all the cowtowns, they each had their own ideas on how to combat it. It is a part of Western tradition that the cowtowns were tamed almost single-handedly by two-gun marshals who brought order out of chaos simply because they were quicker on the draw than their cowboy opponents. The facts are that such men and others did play a part in establishing law and order, but it was the citizens themselves who voted for it. Local ordinances, backed by federal and state laws, were implemented by the police whose responsibility it was (and still is) to enforce such laws.

Abilene had no legal status until she was incorporated as a third-class city in 1869. Up to that time the place relied upon a couple of constables and the county sheriff. But two years of Texan violence led to a plea for 'incorporation' and once this was granted the city held elections

Above: 'Timberline', a typical Dodge City prostitute. All manner of names were found to disguise their occupations, but some tongue-in-cheek census-takers found delight in describing them as 'ceiling experts', 'horizontal workers' and other versions.

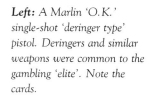

Above: Another Dodge City 'watering place': this one is the St James saloon, a typical narrow room with a bar and mirror on one side.

Left: A Marlin 'O.K.' single-shot 'deringer type' pistol. Deringers and similar weapons were common to the gambling 'elite'. Note the cards.

Below: A typical roulette table, complete with a deadly assortment of 'gamblers' friends' of various makes.

Above: 'Squirrel-tooth Alice' and 'friend'. She was one of the better class of 'sisters in sin' that populated the cowtowns and gave comfort (or something else). Many of these ladies gave up their profession, married clients and settled down.

Left: *Dodge City in its heyday. The Long Branch saloon is at the left (bearing no resemblance at all to its famous T.V. namesake!). Note the motley collection of characters.*

Below right: *Playing cards were the means of quick riches for some, or a quick death for others. Cheats could expect no mercy if caught out.*

Below left: *Ellsworth in 1872. At right is the famous Drover's Cottage, an hotel-cum-meeting place that was built at Abilene in the late 1860s. When the cattle trade moved on, it was dismantled and shipped to Ellsworth, where it was rebuilt.*

Above: David 'Prairie Dog Dave' Morrow was a colorful frontiersman who has sometimes been confused with Mysterious Dave Mather. It can be safely assumed that those who knew both men, in Dodge City at least, did not have that problem.

and voted in its own police force. Tom Smith, the first Marshal or 'Chief of Police', was appointed in May 1870. He did an excellent job, but his murder in November left the town without a police chief. Several men were hired as temporary police until the town held its first election early in 1871. McCoy was elected mayor and his first act was to hire Hickok (with the approval of the council), who in turn hired his own policemen.

A similar situation existed in other places. Some of them, such as Ellsworth, were incorporated prior to the arrival of the cattle trade, but in each place, local ordinances, a strong police force and large license fees and fines kept the Texans, gamblers and prostitutes under control. Ironically, only when the cattle trade had departed did the townspeople appreciate its economic importance. Up until that point they had concerned themselves only with violence and 'moral and social corruption'.

By the early 1900s, the cowtown was a memory, kept alive by the very people who had once condemned the trade and those who were connected with it. But as time passed so did many of the prejudices. Today, the places that lived through and survived the era of the cowtown hold celebrations in remembrance of the days of the cowboy and his battles with the legendary two-gun marshals who helped tame him.

Cowtown police forces tended to be geared to demand. If the season was particularly busy, extra men were hired and fired according to the number of cattle outfits in the town at any one time.

Above: James Masterson, younger brother of Bat. His gunfighting career surpassed Bat's, but he never had a reputation to match it. He was involved in the arrest of the Doolin gang. He died in 1895 in Guthrie, Oklahoma, where he had been a peace officer.

GUNS IN THE WEST

The gun in all its forms played a significant role in the civilization of the West. In fact, its importance has often been obscured by an over exposure in movie and T.V. Westerns. In his classic *The Great Plains*, Walter Prescott Webb stated: 'It enabled the white man to fight the Plains Indian on horseback' at a time when such as the Texas Rangers were hardpressed to compete with the Comanche Indians who were able to loose off several arrows to the Ranger's one shot. And as a weapon of offense and defense, the revolver was in a class of its own.

The gun has long played an important role in America's social and historical development, and its part in the exploration and civilizing of the West is essential to any explanation of the continuing fascination for firearms. As with all facets of historical and social expansion, guns were used for practical purposes rather than as symbols of power. Only later did the 'power of the pistol' assume a significance during the period when 'civilization' imposed itself upon the so-called freedom of earlier days.

By 1800, weapons had undergone a number of changes and included the introduction of the rifled musket. In England Major Ferguson had aroused much interest in his breech-loading flintlock rifle. But the flintlock system proved a hindrance, and a search for something better continued. This was left to a Scotsman, the Reverend Alexander John Forsyth, an amateur chemist and keen sportsman. His use of fulminates led eventually to the percussion cap and, by the 1820s, arms makers the world over were turning to cap rather than flint for ignition.

Revolving arms of various types had been known since the sixteenth century, and by the early 1800s several successful longarms and multi-shot pistols using revolving chambers were known. But it was Samuel Colt's development of a

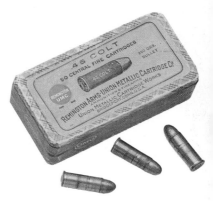

Above: A box of .45 caliber cartridges for the Colt revolver. This one was made by Remington and was interchangeable with their own weapons in similar caliber.

Below: A fine engraved 1849 Model Pocket pistol. These pistols were produced in various barrel lengths and were ideal 'hide-out' guns. More than three hundred thousand were made between 1848 and 1873.

Bottom: Freund's Gun Store at Laramie, W.T., in 1868. The 'Buffalo Bill' lookalike is armed with what looks like a plains rifle.

Above: Winchesters and shotguns were issued to Wells Fargo guards such as these two confident individuals.

1807
Forsyth's percussion system

1820s
The percussion lock replaces flintlocks

1835
Colt's 'revolving breeched pistol' makes its appearance

1873
The Colt Peacemaker and the 1873 Model Winchester rifle are introduced

Artifacts (pistol) courtesy of Buffalo Bill Historical Center, Cody, Wyoming; (cartridges) Gene Autry Western Heritage Museum, Los Angeles, California

Left: These two Arizona Rangers are literally 'armed to the teeth' with Colt revolvers and Winchester rifles. Of particular interest are the 'double' cartridge belts that bristle with 'shells' for the rifle and pistol.

Below: An illustration from the Winchester catalogue of 1867. The rifles were chambered for .44 rim-fire.

Bottom: Ed Schieffelin, whose discovery of silver led to the establishment of Tombstone. Dressed in a typical 'miner's outfit', Schieffelin is 'toting' a Sharps rifle, and what appears to be a Smith & Wesson revolver on his left hip. Note the cartridge belt.

Above: Samuel Colt, from a photograph made circa 1858. Sam never claimed to have 'invented' the revolver, merely to have improved upon existing ideas. But his pistol and means of manufacture by machinery changed the industry worldwide.

practical means of turning a 'revolving breech' and locking it into position ready for firing that proved to be the most successful. Once he had secured backing for his invention, Colt's 'revolving pistol' (as he described it) was soon in great demand. By the middle 1850s he had a large factory in Hartford, Conn., and one in London from which he supplied several thousand revolvers to the British government and parts of Empire.

The revolver more than any other weapon contributed to the wellbeing of individuals who relied upon it, and its effect in the hands of trained troops or such as the Texas Rangers against hostile Indians was remarkable. Single-shot slow-loading pistols or muskets were no match against a Comanche lance and a shower of arrows fired by well-mounted warriors, but the introduction of the revolver proved to be the turning-point.

By the middle 1860s and early 1870s, improvements in ammunition (the gradual change from rim-fire to center-fire cartridges) and mechanisms revolutionize warfare. Such improvements were not lost upon frontiersmen: the cowboy, outlaw, marshal or soldier who used a revolver swore by its potential for sorting out an enemy, whether it was a hostile Indian or a bandit.

Among the most popular pistols produced by Colt were the small Pocket models in .31 caliber; the two Navy pistols in .36 and several Army revolvers in .44. Following Colt's death in 1862, the company stagnated for some years because of the patent held by Rollins White for bored-through cylinders which he had assigned to Smith & Wesson. But when the patent expired in 1869, Colt, Remington and others produced weapons that rivaled or surpassed existing cartridge revolvers. Colt's single-action .45 caliber Army revolver (known as the 'Peacemaker') and its companion in .44 caliber ('The Frontier Six-Shooter') proved to be very popular, as did Remington's and Smith & Wesson's own 'frontier' or 'army' pistols.

The use of weapons in the West, necessitated by circumstances and as a means of survival, has achieved a status that none of those who used them could possibly have foreseen. Legend now asserts that it was neither the pioneer spirit nor the growth of the railroads and the onward push of civilization that civilized the West, but rather that the West was 'won' by the gun.

Above: Oliver F. Winchester, who found guns more profitable. He skillfully employed a number of good men with talent to work on his weapons, among them John Browning, a genius in his own right, who drastically improved the Winchester actions.

Interior of Sawtell's Ranch, Fremont
City, Idaho, by William Henry
Jackson. Guns displayed include
Spencer and Sharps carbines,
Remington and Colt revolvers

THE GUNFIGHTERS

The potency of the gunfighter inspired poets. In his *Dodge City The Cowboy Capital*, Robert M. Wright quoted from 'The Two Gun Man' published originally in the Denver *Republican*.

One day, rode forth this man of wrath,
Upon the distant plain,
And ne'er did he retrace his path,
Nor was he seen again;
The cow town fell into decay;
No spurred heels pressed its walks;
But, through its grass grown ways, they say,
The Two Gun Man still stalks.

Above: *Portrait of James Butler Hickok, taken from an 1858 family tintype.*

1865
Hickok–Tutt duel at Springfield, Missouri

1867
Hays City, Kansas, opens the original 'Boot Hill'

1874
A character known as 'Cemetery Sam' describes himself as a 'gunfighter'

1900
'Gunfighter' has replaced 'Mankiller' or 'Shootist' in a generic sense

Artifacts courtesy of Buffalo Bill Historical Center, Cody, Wyoming

The gunfighter is as instantly recognizable as is the cowboy, the Indian and the cavalryman, and has long been an established figure in American folklore. But unlike the others, he is not as easily defined, for the gunfighter is a complex character. No two were alike, yet all shared one common trait: they were killers. Some killed 'to see a man kick'; others killed under provocation (usually associated with a reputation) or in the line of duty when fulfilling an official function. Consequently, it is important to remember these facts in any consideration of the characters themselves.

It is traditional to describe the law-abiding or law-orientated individuals as 'gunfighters' and the outlaw or homicidally inclined as 'gunmen', a subtlety that endured into the Western films when the good guys wore white hats and the bad men wore black. In their time, however, the men who

Right: Benjamin ('Ben') Thompson, the English-born Texas gunfighter. His Yorkshire origins perhaps accounted for his 'stubborn streak' and a bull-dog-like tenacity when in a fight. He was also a good gambler and pistol shot.

Below: Bartholomew Masterson, the Canadian-born gunfighter who in later life changed his name to William Barclay Masterson. Generally called 'Bat', he became renowned on the frontier as a peacekeeper, and later as a newspaperman.

that such a relationship could not last, and he bids a sad farewell and rides off into the sunset. This lack of commitment would be viewed by most people as a basic immaturity and fear of responsibility. But the gunfighter of legend is not a normal person. Rather, he is the principal character in what would best be termed a modern 'morality play', and for him to succumb to normal human needs and desires would destroy his whole purpose. Therefore, his audiences are prepared to ignore his weaknesses because they know that his strength lies in his ability with a gun and the courage to fight evil in order that good can prevail. And they would not have it any other way. For the gunfighter represents the survival of good in an increasingly evil world.

On a historical level, of course, gunfighters (on both sides of the law) were an accepted part of Western society, and the better known are the ones whose exploits have been told and retold and now form a part of the 'Western myth'. But it was the gun that gave them purpose and continues to help perpetuate the legends. Some, like Hickok, achieve reputations as shots and 'quick draw' artists, and their various *modus operandi* in that direction has long intrigued historians.

In the early period (about 1850 until the early 1870s) the percussion revolver dominated. Good powder and caps were not always easy to come by, so it became commonplace for men to carry two pistols, or extra loaded cylinders. Most wore their pistols butts forward for a 'reverse' or plains 'twist and draw' or for a cross draw. This was the safest means of carrying a pistol. Only later, when it became customary for pistols to be carried butts to the rear in conventional hip holsters, did a careless individual run the risk of shooting himself in the leg or foot if his thumb slipped off the hammer when the pistol was drawn.

The gunfighters, whether on the side of law and order or against it, have for so long been depicted as the Old West's 'civilizers' that it is difficult to convince people otherwise. But history and legend have always gone hand in hand and if it means that in order to keep history alive a certain laxity in factual reporting is permissable, then the gunfighter will always have his niche in history.

lived and died by the gun were generally regarded as 'man-killers', a name that carries greater emphasis than 'gunfighter' which, although in use as early as 1874, did not gain prominence until the early years of the twentieth century.

One of the basic problems faced by any researcher into the origin and true status of the gunfighter as a character is the tendency among historians, novelists, and those responsible for the Hollywood version to set him apart from his fellow beings. Something that attracts today's audiences to the gunfighter is his reluctance to form any long-term emotional or physical relationships. Time and again he is depicted as a loner who appears from nowhere, has no visible means of support, and yet his presence is felt to be providential. Even when he has been accepted into the community, he remains aloof. Occasionally, however, an old flame might be rekindled, or there is a brief affair with a local dance-hall girl or perhaps a 'school marm'. But once his task is over, the gunfighter makes it plain

Above: David ('Mysterious Dave') Mather, whose feud with Tom Nixon led to him killing Tom one dark night, for which he was tried and acquitted. Robert M. Wright recalled him as 'a very wicked man, a killer of killers.' Dave's demise remains a mystery.

Above: Clay Allison, another character whose real and imaginary exploits have long fascinated historians. In 1878 he described himself as a 'shootist' and meant 'gunfighter'. Ironically, he died when a wagon rolled over his neck when he fell under it.

Above: Joseph Thomas Lowe was best known as 'Rowdy Joe' Lowe. He and his common-law wife 'Rowdy Kate' ran several dance halls-cum-brothels in Ellsworth, Wichita, Newton and later in Texas before splitting up. They rowed constantly.

Above: *A fine example of the early .45 caliber Colt 'Peacemaker'. It is nickel-plated with wooden stocks. Note the well-worn holster and cartridges.*

CRIME AND PUNISHMENT

Retribution, revenge and restitution seem to sum up the concept of crime and punishment, not only in the Old West but in other areas of society. The forces of evil pitted against the good have fascinated people and the priesthood for generations. But rarely does one encounter the sort of characters thrown up by the Old West that inspire so much adulation or anger. And when confronted by 'instant' or inevitable justice, an audience is guaranteed.

The Old West's attitude to crime closely followed that of eastern states, the difference being that in the East a man might be flogged, fined or imprisoned for horse-stealing, but out West, where a horse or mule (and cattle) were a means of survival, those who were caught rustling other people's livestock invariably found themselves dangling from the end of a rope. Some ended up in jail with time to reflect upon their crime, or, perhaps, plan a different approach when they got out.

Lynching, generally understood to mean 'illegal hanging' (in fact anyone shot, stabbed or even beaten to death by a mob was said to have been 'lynched') was a feature of the West that has long disturbed historians and sociologists anxious to explain why such drastic action was deemed necessary. In short, most lynchings, backed by vigilante action, were the result of a desperate need for law and order in lawless societies. San

Right: Judge Roy Bean, 'the Law West of the Pecos', photographed at Langtry, Texas. His verdicts were often humorous, racial and controversial. One man who killed an unfortunate Chinese was hauled up before the judge who ruled that 'the statoots don't mention anythin' about killin' a heathen Chinee – case dismissed!'

Below left: Sometimes executions were held in the privacy of the prison yard – hence the 'invite' – but most of them were exposed to public view.

Above: *Doom and gloom . . . stern glances from the bench of Tombstone's courthouse.*

1857
James Copeland, 'Mississippi Misfit' and killer, is executed

1863
Vigilantes deal out justice to the Plummer gang in Montana

1870
Murder of 'Bear River' Tom Smith, one of the first marshals of the 'cowtown' era

Artifact courtesy of Buffalo Bill Historical Center, Cody, Wyoming

Mr *James Stirling. Ex Sheriff*
You are hereby invited to be present at the execution of
GEORGE A. BLACK,
which will take place at the Court House, in Laramie, Wyoming Territory, on the 26th day of February, 1890, at the hour of 11 o'clock, A. M.
Not transferable.
CHARLES YUND,
Sheriff Albany County.

Francisco's vigilante experience in the early 1850s (in the East some compared it with the 'Committee of Public Safety' of the French Revolution) was brought about by intense frustration and an increasingly lawless population. Once law and order was established, the vigilantes disbanded. Similar situations existed in Montana, Texas and Kansas. And on one memorable occasion in 1834, when a man in Iowa Territory murdered a companion, those who tried him had doubts concerning their legality. Although at the time Iowa was a part of the original Missouri Territory, a request to the governor was met with a suggestion that they approach the President, Andrew Jackson. He replied that since United States laws had yet to be extended to the territory he felt powerless to act. The decision was theirs – they hanged the man!

All over the West the people demanded protection from speculators, outlaws, land-grabbers and others whose anti-social activities aroused anger and resentment. Squatters' courts, citizens' courts and, of course, vigilance committees, endeavored to bring some order out of chaos, and punishments were made to fit the

Center right: 'An invitation to a hanging' did not always mean that the individual was to be the guest of honor at a 'necktie party'. For it was customary to invite prominent people to attend such functions. At Judge Isaac Parker's court, for instance, a number of men went through the trap at the same time which cut costs!

Right: The last public execution to take place in Arapahoe County, Colorado, in the bed of Cherry Creek (now a salubrious part of Denver). The gallows are slightly right of center; the crowds that such events attracted speak for themselves.

crime. Curiously, during the height of the 'wild' part of the West (1854–90), there were few legal hangings. In Kansas for instance, despite some well-publicized killings (among them the murder of Marshal Tom Smith of Abilene by McConnell and Miles), the death penalty was not imposed. Lengthy penitentiary sentences were passed instead. Other states, however, were not so lenient, and hanging was common, particularly in the court of Judge Isaac Parker who presided over Indian Territory. Few convicted murderers escaped with their lives when put on trial in the 'hanging judge's' court.

Eighteenth-century justice, which apart from death sentences including branding and flogging, later took the more frequent form of lengthy terms in jail, so that by the middle and late nineteenth century justice might not have been perfect, but it was swift, and those who defied the law knew exactly what would happen if they were caught. It is ironic, therefore, that in the one hundred years since the frontier officially ceased to exist, law and order is no longer seen to be done; for what once took weeks to resolve can now take years.

Above: Chauncey B. Whitney was sheriff of Ellsworth county in 1873 when he was gunned down by Ben Thompson's homicidal brother Billy on 15 August. Billy escaped (with Ben's help) but was brought back in 1877 and put on trial. He got off on a technicality.

Above: Thomas James ('Bear River Tom') Smith, reputed to be a New York policeman who moved west in the mid-1860s and for a time worked for the Union Pacific Railroad. He led a riot at Bear River, Wyoming, and served for a short period in the state penitentiary.

107

JESSE AND FRANK JAMES

On 12 April 1882, the Kansas City *Times* noted that the New York *Herald* reported that the 'outlaw James is regarded in some quarters as a first class hero, and his relative [sic] who killed him as a dastard and a traitor of the vilest sort; and this view seems to be held by persons not brought up on dime novels. . . .' The *Herald* also reviewed Jesse's career and concluded: 'The most cowardly killing of such a fellow is not more cowardly than his daily life.' Frank James managed to avoid the bullet, dying in bed an elderly and reformed man in the early twentieth century.

Throughout history outlaws have been controversial figures. The establishment views them as criminals or social misfits, whereas the 'common herd' often regards them as heroes, Robin Hood-like figures that right wrongs and look after the poor. In reality, of course, such romanticism is misplaced. The likes of Jesse and Frank James were not at all romantic. They were products of the era that spawned the pre- and post-Civil War guerrilla, whose exploits on either side were remembered with horror by most of those who experienced them.

Right: The James family farm at Kearney, Missouri, c. 1877. Frank and Jesse were born here and much of the original home still stands. The brothers hid out here after the Civil War, and in later years visited their mother when they were able. Frank James died here in his bed in 1915, surviving his more wayward sibling.

Following the war, many of the guerrillas and militiamen who joined unofficial outfits were pardoned, but some of those who had followed the black flag of Quantrill or 'Bloody Bill' Anderson were not – and the James family claim that Jesse's problems started because he was refused a pardon. Perhaps – but it was not reason enough to start robbing banks, stopping and robbing trains and organizing several gangs of criminals.

Jesse, like so many of his ilk, was an enigma. He married, had a family and at times settled to an orderly existence; but when the urge came, he would plan and execute more robberies. Frank, his elder brother, seemed happy to go along with his plans.

By many of the people of post-war Missouri, Jesse and Frank were regarded as heroes when they robbed banks and stopped trains owned by the 'robber barons' who had forced people from their homes on the pretext that the railroad had right of way through their property. There is some evidence that this was true, but with time the

Above: *Jesse Woodson James photographed in Nebraska in about 1874 or 1875.*

1847
Jesse Woodson James born on 5 September

1866
With the Youngers, the James brothers rob the Clay County Savings Bank of $60,000

1875
The James farm is attacked, possibly by Pinkertons. Their mother is badly injured

1882
Jesse murdered at his house by Bob Ford on 3 April. Frank will survive him by more than thirty years

Artifacts courtesy of Gene Autry Western Heritage Museum, Los Angeles, California.

Left: *Frank James at about the time he and Jesse were busily robbing banks and stopping trains. He had ridden with Quantrill when he sacked Lawrence. Later, he was to follow his brother into outlawry, but never served a prison sentence.*

Right: *Robert ('Bob') Ford who followed the James star and ended up by shooting Jesse in the back on 3 April 1882. He is recalled today as 'the dirty little coward that shot Mr Howard [Jesse's alias], and laid poor Jesse in his grave'.*

Above: Thomas Coleman ('Cole') Younger was regarded as one of the deadliest of the Younger clan. He followed the 'black flag of Quantrill' and was present when he sacked Lawrence. He was wounded during the Northfield raid of 7 September 1876.

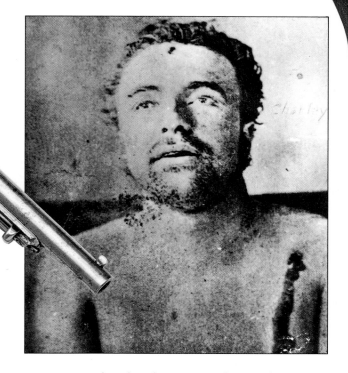

Above: *Frank's leather gunbelt and holster. Included are some .45 caliber Remington 'shells' for his pistol. The holster was worn on the right hip for a butt forward or 'reverse' draw. Below is Frank's 1875 Model Remington .45 Army six-shooter. These pistols were similar to the Colt 'Peacemaker' but were not quite as popular.*

Right: *Clelland ('Clell') Miller was killed on the Northfield raid. He should have realized that his hero worship of Jesse James was ill-advised.*

Above: Robert ('Bob') Younger, the 'youngest' of the brothers. Bob envied his elder brother his adventures as a guerrilla. He, too, was wounded at Northfield and jailed. But unlike Cole, he did not fare so well in jail, and he died in the state penitentiary.

government legislated against such speculators, so that by the late 1870s there was no longer any excuse for the James brothers to continue their life of crime on that pretext. But public sympathy was extended to them when the Pinkerton Detective Agency persuaded the government to issue them with a bomb containing what some described as 'Greek fire'. This was tossed into the family home in January 1875, and as a result Jesse's young half-brother was killed and his mother lost an arm. The Pinkertons denied that they used a bomb, and its actual type only came to light in recent years when Ordnance Department records were discovered authorizing its use.

Jesse was the subject of many reward offers, and in April 1882 two gang members, Robert and Charles Ford, set out to claim one of them. On the 3rd, at St Joseph, Mo., where Jesse was living under the alias of Howard, Bob took his Colt .45 and shot Jesse in the back as he adjusted a picture. Some claim that a $10,000 reward had been offered, but if one takes into account that those involved in the hunt for the brothers took a cut, then Bob and Charley were probably lucky to receive $600 each.

Frank James surrendered to the state governor and following several aborted trials was released and died in 1915 in bed. But the legendary Jesse James continues to ride the owlhoot trail, and he remains as heroic as he is controversial.

Above: James Younger, the most inexperienced of the gang. He was also wounded at Northfield and was sent to the state penitentiary. Prison life did not suit him, and when he was paroled in 1901 he could not settle down. He committed suicide in 1902.

OUTLAWS AND GANGS

In 1918 in his Preface to *Beyond the Law*, Emmett Dalton wrote: 'To the average American of to-day, surrounded by all the luxuries and improvements which time and science have brought to his aid, the stories of frontier days . . . the cattlemen, or cowpuncher, the bank or train robber, seem like some strange phantasmagoria conjured by a fertile imagination . . . to one who played an important, if not praiseworthy, part in the making of that history, a calm and silent retrospect brings back events startling in their nature which to-day seem like a dreadful dream.'

Above: *Emmett Dalton in his Hollywood film-making days. He acted as advisor on Western film sets.*

1876
In September the James and the Youngers ride into Northfield, Minn., to rob the bank. The James boys escape; the Youngers do not

1892
The Daltons try – and fail – to rob two banks at once in Coffeyville, Kansas. The town resists and only Emmett Dalton survives the raid

1896
Bill Doolin, leader of the 'Oklahombres' and often associated with the Daltons, meets his end at Lawson, Oklahoma

Artifacts courtesy of Gene Autry Western Heritage Museum, Los Angeles, California

'The Daltons! The Daltons – they're robbing the bank!'

That cry was soon taken up, and the citizens of Coffeyville, Kansas, on that morning of 5 October 1892 found themselves confronted by desperate men whose reputations for violence had become a household word. Not only were they robbing the Condon Bank, but the First National Bank as well! But once alerted, the townsfolk armed themselves and launched into a deadly gunfight that ended with the death of the city marshal Charles Connelly and three other people. And of the Dalton gang, which consisted of Bob, Grat and young Emmett, accompanied by Dick Broadwell and Bill Power, only Emmett, badly wounded, was to survive. He was later sentenced to life imprisonment. But the Dalton legend was such that, when he was released from prison fourteen years later, he became a celebrity; he appeared in early Westerns and later acted as technical historical adviser for a film about the raid (actually filmed at Coffeyville). He later went to Hollywood where again he acted as an adviser for Western pictures.

Unlike the James brothers, the Daltons had little reason to take to crime. Their elder brother Frank was killed when serving as a deputy U.S. Marshal in Indian Territory (Oklahoma). Although Bob and Grat also served as deputies after his death, their careers were short-lived – Emmett later claimed that they found they were being fleeced by the administration of monies owed to them, so they quit. Other sources suggest that they were engaged in a little cattle rustling on the side. Whatever the reason, their careers, and that of Emmett, deteriorated until they were, to quote Emmett, 'beyond the law' and in the company of the likes of Bill Doolin.

William M. Doolin was the leader of a gang of outlaws known as the 'Oklahombres'. He was associated with the Daltons and only by a fluke was not a member of their Coffeyville raid. His turn came later when he was killed by a posse in 1896. And there were many others (including the Wild Bunch) who rode the outlaw trail during the last years of the nineteenth and early twentieth centuries. The old days of freedom from pursuit in rough country were gone thanks to the telegraph and the telephone; but a man could still get lost in parts of Texas and Wyoming until the heat died down.

The Youngers, associates of the James boys, were of a similar ilk. They accompanied the James brothers on their abortive raid on Northfield, Minn., on 7 September 1876. Jesse and Frank escaped, but Bob, Cole and Jim were wounded and captured. Bob died in prison while the other two served their time and were paroled in 1901. Despite a brief notoriety as a member of a 'Wild

Right: *The Condon Bank at Coffeyville (which is still in business), one of the two banks the Dalton gang planned to rob at the same time. Half the gang was in this bank when the alarm was raised.*

Below: *Emmett Dalton's gunbelt and holster. The buckle is typical of the period. Note that the holster drops over the belt. He was carrying this ornately engraved pearl-handled Colt .45. The leg irons (complete with key) were carried in pursuit of Doolin's gang and no doubt were used.*

Bottom: *The aftermath. The bodies of (left to right) Bill Power, Bob Dalton, Grat Dalton and Dick Broadwell, lie handcuffed outside the Coffeyville jail. The local photographer sold many prints of this scene.*

West Show' in partnership with Frank James, Cole realized that his day was gone. And as the old time outlaws slipped into obscurity and the grave, a new breed took their place – the Chicago gangsters and racketeers. Their kind of lawlessness, however, was born out of greed and a lust for power, and a total disregard for human life. With a few exceptions, Western 'badmen' could excuse some of their actions. They were also well aware what their fate would be if caught. But like Robin Hood, there were always those ready to romanticize their deeds on the grounds of social unrest and deprivation.

Above: Emmett Dalton as he appeared at the time of the Coffeyville raid. He always maintained that the brothers were driven into crime and were credited with the deeds of others. But evidence to the contrary was overwhelming. He died in 1937.

Above: Bill Doolin, cohort of the Daltons, who led a gang of cut-throats known as the 'Oklahombres'. He was ambushed by a posse in 1896, and as he lies on a mortuary slab, his features still register surprise at his sudden end. 'Morgue' shots were popular.

Above: Roy ('Arkansas Tom') Daughtery, hailed from Missouri, and was a well-known gunfighter, who rode for a time with the Doolin gang. He spent much of his life on the run, and survived until 1924 when he was killed at Joplin, Missouri.

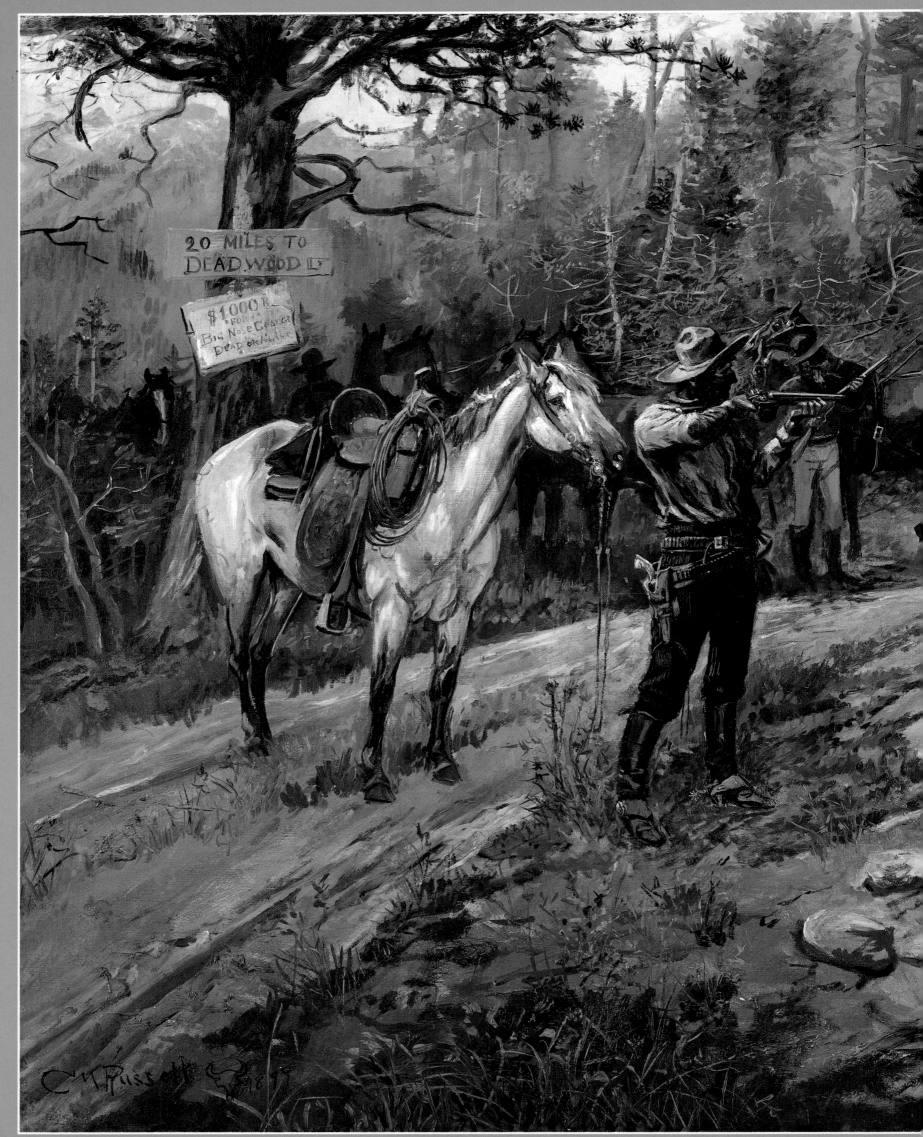

'The Hold Up', by Charles M. Russell (1864–1926)
(Oil on canvas, 1899. Courtesy Amon Carter Museum, Fort Worth)

'WILD BILL' HICKOK

'I say, Bill, or Mr Hickok how many white men have you killed to your certain knowledge?' He replied, 'I would be willing to take my oath on the Bible tomorrow that I have killed over a hundred . . .' 'What made you kill all those men; did you kill them without cause or provocation?' 'No, by Heaven! I never killed one man without good cause.' When Henry M. Stanley put those questions to Hickok in 1867, he did not realize that his leg was being pulled. Unfortunately, others believed it, too, and Hickok's reputation as a prolific 'man-killer' was born.

Above: *James Butler Hickok taken from a family portrait from around 1873.*

1837
Born at Homer, Illinois (the place was later renamed Troy Grove)

1856
Emigrated to Kansas Territory

1863–5
Provost Marshal's detective; scout and spy in Missouri and Arkansas. Now known as 'Wild Bill'

1867–9
Scout for Custer; deputy U.S. Marshal; acting sheriff of Ellis County, Kansas

1871
Marshal of Abilene

1876
Wednesday 2 August, murdered at 4.10 p.m., in the No. 10 Saloon, Deadwood, Dakota Territory

Artifacts courtesy of Gene Autry Western Heritage Museum, Los Angeles, California

W ild Bill Hickok . . . it is a name to conjure with, and is probably the most apt monicker of any 'Wild West' character, for it epitomizes the time and the place. As for Hickok himself, the image is that of a long-haired, buckskin-clad figure, or, perhaps, dressed in a long frock coat and sporting a fine waistcoat surmounted by a boiled white pleated shirt and bow tie. Add a low-crowned hat and a pair of pistols and the portrait is complete.

Hickok crammed more into his thirty-nine years than did most people who lived twice as long. From his birth in Illinois in 1837 until his death in 1876, Hickok either witnessed or was involved in some of the most dramatic events of the mid-nineteenth-century West. He left home in 1856 and went to Kansas where he soon became involved in the territorial disputes over the issue of slavery. He served as one of four village constables at Monticello before moving on in 1858 to working as a teamster. In 1861 he joined the Union army as a wagonmaster, later transferring to scouting and spying behind enemy lines. And at the end of the war he had won the name 'Wild Bill' (for an undetermined reason). During 'Hancock's Indian War' of 1867, he served as a scout and courier for the Seventh Cavalry, and later as a deputy U.S. Marshal. Further service as a scout in 1868–9 was followed by a brief period as acting sheriff of Ellis County, Kansas, and later, in 1871, as Marshal of Abilene.

Many claimed that Hickok was the best pistol shot on the plains, but it was his reputation as a 'man-killer' that interested most people and irritated Hickok himself. Although his tally was less than ten known victims, his own leg-pulling of journalists and the deliberate lies of others upped the ante to 'considerably over one hundred'. Of his reputation he declared that 'I am called a red-handed murderer, which I deny', adding that he had only killed men in self-defense or in the line of duty. But he always made sure no one got the 'drop' on him!

Right: Wild Bill, circa 1863–4. He served both as a wagon-master and provost marshal's detective before becoming scout and spy.

Below: A Colt's 1851 Navy pistol allegedly owned by Hickok. The backstrap read originally J.B. Hickok 1869, but the second 'C' was removed later. Serial numbered 138813, the cylinder number is 13 digits apart, suggesting it might have been one of a pair. Note its open top holster, and 'Aces and Eights'.

Bottom: Deadwood in 1877. Founded in April 1876, the place attracted hundreds of wouldbe goldseekers.

Bottom right: Alvin Smith's statue of Wild Bill, erected over his grave in 1903, was destroyed by souvenir hunters.

As a person, people found Hickok courteous, friendly and very knowledgeable concerning the plains. Aware as he was of his snowballing reputation, Wild Bill did little to exploit it. Indeed, many found him self-effacing, inclined to avoid publicity and much at ease when pushed into the limelight. Others, of course, claimed that this was an act; that the smile and courtesy merely presaged the sudden move, the sound of a shot and yet another victim to add to his tally. But as has been stressed elsewhere, any 'pistoliferous' behavior within city limits or any other place where there was access to lawmakers or a coroner's court involved an appearance and a plea of self-defense, which would preclude some of the more bizarre allegations made concerning Hickok's 'triggernometry'.

As a peace officer, Wild Bill was effective, but limited (as were most of his contemporaries). His function was to keep the peace not control the local morals. Indeed, his presence was usually enough to quell even the most boisterous Texan who, having taken on board too much 'tanglefoot' ran the risk of arrest or worse if he unlimbered his artillery and opened fire. Most of the time Wild Bill was given a wide berth, and his reputation did much to preserve law and order.

When, in 1873, Buffalo Bill Cody persuaded Hickok to join him in his Combination as one of the 'Scouts of the Plains', he agreed to do so on the understanding that it would be for one season only. As it turned out, Hickok lasted eight months before quitting – he made it clear to Cody that he regarded acting as a sham.

Above: Polly Butler Hickok, the mother of Wild Bill. The Butler family claim kin to Gen. Benjamin Butler of Civil War fame, and also to President George Bush who bears a resemblence to Polly. She died in 1878, still mourning her youngest son.

Above: William Lorenzo Hickok, father of Wild Bill. He was very aware of his youngest son's independent nature. His death in 1852 robbed the family of a God-fearing influence. William thought of entering the church, but took up farming instead.

Following the discovery of gold in the Black Hills and the frantic rush to the place, Hickok joined the goldseekers in June 1876, leaving his wife Agnes Lake Thatcher (whom he had married in March) back in Ohio. On 2 August, as he sat playing cards in Nuttall & Mann's No. 10 saloon, John (alias 'Jack') McCall walked up behind him and shot him through the back of the head. McCall was later hanged for murder.

Across the West, eulogies abounded, although some of Hickok's critics sought to blacken his name. Among those who had known Wild Bill, there was a genuine sense of loss, for despite his controversial reputation, Hickok had many friends. And a century after his death, the legend of 'Wild Bill Hickok' is still very much alive.

Above: This portrait adorns the Old-Style Bar at Deadwood and is alleged to be Jack McCall who murdered Wild Bill and was later hanged. But the man bears no resemblence to the 'cross-eyed', 'low-browed', creature described by the contemporary press!

LAW AND ORDER

On 17 July 1886, the editor of the Coolidge, Kansas, *Border Ruffian* defined a city marshal as 'having the skin of a rhinoceros, a bullet-proof head, who can see all around him, run faster than a horse, and is not afraid of anything in hades . . . a man who can shoot like [Captain A.] Bogardus, and would rather kill four or five whisky-drinking, gambling hoodlums before breakfast than to eat without exercise. Such a man can get a job in this town at reasonable wages, and if he put off climbing the gold stair for a few years may get his name in a ten-cent novel.'

Above: *Victims of a lynch-mob swing in the breeze. Justice – swift and to the point.*

1851
San Francisco policed by Vigilante Committee

1861
Kansas achieves statehood. Texas Rangers disbanded

1866
Law and order begins to spread across the West in the wake of the Civil War

1876
The invention of the telephone. Communication used in fight against crime

Artifacts courtesy of Gene Autry Western Heritage Museum, Los Angeles, California

Once people began to migrate into the Western wilderness, they also yearned for some sense of civilization; but above all, they desired law and order. During the early period, before and after the Civil War, the change from territory to state invariably meant the introduction of both state and federal law, together with local ordinances. It was a slow process but, given time and patience, it worked. During the territorial periods of most states, United States district courts flourished and were backed either by the army or United States marshals. Although strictly concerned with federal crimes (desertion from the army, theft of government property or murder upon an Indian reservation), the marshals nevertheless proved very effective in controling some of the violent characters that abounded. Vigilante justice (as we have noted elsewhere) was often effective if not always welcome, and sometimes the people themselves rounded up villainous characters and handed them over to the authorities. Whatever the means at hand, the message was plain: law and order must prevail.

Right: *George W. Campbell, an early marshal of El Paso, who fell foul of politicians. He got killed in error by Dallas Stoudenmire.*

Far right: *Dallas Stoudenmire, whose courage, aided by a pair of .44 Smith & Wessons, tamed El Paso. Alcohol and his temper proved his undoing.*

Below: *Danish-born Chris Madsen was one of the 'Three Guardsmen' who helped establish law and order in early Oklahoma.*

Inset: *A 'Special Police' badge. The five- and six-pointed star symbolized the legal status of city or U.S. Marshals.*

Above: Alexander Davis, the 'miners' judge', a tough opponent of the 'ungodly'. He once issued a warrant for the arrest of Jack Slade (himself more feared than the 'almighty') for upsetting a milk wagon, who talked him out of it.

Above: Lawrence E. Deger, a mountain of a man who once served as Dodge City's marshal and later as its mayor. He was one of the so-called 'Reformers' who claimed to be in opposition to the 'Gang' (that included Bat Masterson) who ran the saloon businesses.

Above: William Smith, who served as marshal of Wichita in the early 1870s, and later as county sheriff. He was born in England and emigrated to the United States at an early age. He was regarded as a 'tough' customer and a good law enforcer.

Below: A .45 Colt and belt and holster once owned by George Gardiner, cowboy, 'Wild West' performer and later lawman in the 1890s.

Inset above: Yet another variation of the lawman's 'star'. The Texas Rangers' version was identical to this but in silver.

The American legal system was based upon English law, and similar officials such as sheriffs and marshals were elected or appointed by county and city officials. A sheriff was elected to a county and had an under-sheriff (a term rarely used today) and several deputies. A marshal or chief of police was elected or appointed by a city council, and his jurisdiction extended only to the limits of that town. He was expected to enforce both local and state laws or call in the sheriff or federal officers if need be.

The law, like government, followed in the wake of emigration and was only enforced when there were sufficient people in an established location to vote for it, or request it. Once this was achieved, and good communication was established between cities and townships (from the 1850s and 1860s by telegraph and from the 1870s by telephone), law and order prospered. Where once outlaws and others on the run could disappear into a wilderness, improved communications soon narrowed their field of operations and tightened the noose.

The use of firearms was always a problem. The free use of the revolver in personal disputes was frequently condemned, but for those whose survival might depend upon a weapon the revolver seemed the best means at hand. Men who engaged in pistol fights (both legally and otherwise) who fought in towns or other settled places, ran the risk of a court appearance unless it could be proved that they fired in self-defense. This also applied to the police who had to satisfy the city council or coroner that their actions were justified. But efforts to curtail the use of the revolver and other weapons were doomed to failure, for, despite state and local laws against firearms, disarming the citizenry was practically impossible. The compromise was to impose severe fines or prison sentences.

The attitude toward law land order in the Old West was that of a largely God-fearing population brought up to respect family values and, despite lapses among the frontier 'types', they also displayed a greater moral sense than is the case today. What may seem harsh by our standards was the norm; a situation understood by all and ignored at one's peril.

U.S. MILITARY 1872–1900

By the early 1870s the army, in particular the cavalry regiments, were spread over many parts of the West. While a number of infantry regiments were also based at various frontier posts, it was the cavalry that bore the brunt of the ongoing hostilities between the Indians and the whites. Although these troops were designed for combat on horseback, they were also trained to fight on foot, a facet rarely considered by those used to European traditions. Therefore, the U.S. cavalry could also be described as 'mounted infantry, making them unique 'horse soldiers'.

Above: Mounted black troops shown at drill on the Plains in the 1880s.

1866
Four new regiments of cavalry formed. The Seventh and Eighth are 'white' while the Ninth and Tenth are 'black'

1868
Battle of the Washita; Custer's troops victorious in a dawn attack on Black Kettle's camp

1876
Custer's Last Stand; victory for the Sioux and Cheyenne at the Little Big Horn

1890
Battle of Wounded Knee. Many Indians die in what some claim was a revenge attack by the Seventh for Custer

Artifacts courtesy of Buffalo Bill Historical Center, Cody, Wyoming

In the aftermath of the Civil War, and with the commencement of the Indian wars of the 1870s, the United States army faced a species of challenge unlike any it had confronted before. It had to shift from conventional war on a massive scale to a largely guerrilla form of conflict, in which the foe was seldom seen, almost never stood to fight face-to-face battles, and usually disappeared before the soldiers could react to the most recent depredations. Moreover, the natives were operating in their own territory. Unlike the army, the Indians could subsist on next to nothing, and had the added psychological advantage of fighting for their homeland.

It was a thankless duty. Most of the officers were holdovers from the Civil War, many of them somewhat resentful – like George A. Custer – that they had been reduced in rank as the military shrank in the 1870s. The enlisted men, on the other hand, ranged from misfits fleeing settled society, to men on the run from the law, to newly freed blacks, and a smattering of career soldiers. Life for them was hard, a mix of boredom in garrison duty, and hot, exhausting, and very frustrating campaigning against an enemy they could rarely bring to bay. Worse, all too often they found themselves bested by a combination of resourceful opponents and inept officers of their own. They paid with their blood and their lives for the slowness with which all too many commanders learned the new rules of warfare on the Plains.

Of the nearly one quarter-million natives in the West, about 50,000 stood at one time or another in open hostility. Against them, the army rarely fielded more than 20,000 soldiers, and those lay dispersed over half the continent in food, equipment, and fire power, though some tribes, especially the Nez Perce, proved themselves to be more skilled with rifles than the soldiers. Contrary to popular mythology, not all of the bluecoats were cavalrymen. Several infantry regiments were stationed in the region, and often went on campaign riding in wagons to increase speed and spare the men's energies. More and more, however, authorities learned that mounted men offered the best chance of catching the Indians.

In the quarter century ending in 1890 and the

Right: Troopers of the Tenth Cavalry. When on Plains service, during the winter months they wore buffalo robe coats which prompted the Indians to dub them 'buffalo soldiers'. Both the Ninth and Tenth regiments served in the West.

Below: A Springfield Model 1884 breech-loading rifle and bayonet for infantry use. Also illustrated is a Model 1881 canteen, a Tenth Cavalry officer's kepi (as issued in 1874) and a fine pair of riding gauntlets made of kid leather.

Above: George Armstrong Custer, from a photograph by Brady depicting him in his self-designed general's uniform. Custer was one of the youngest men to reach such a rank (by brevet) and revelled in the title of 'The Boy General'.

quelling of the Ghost Dance movement, the frontier army met the Indian in at least 1,000 engagements of greater or lesser size, and in most emerged at least tactically victorious, though their definition of winning and an Indian's were often contradictory. Sadly, there were a few in which no one could argue the point, as with the Sand Creek massacre of Black Kettle's Cheyenne, or the massacres at Fort Phil Kearney and Custer at the Little Bighorn. Victory, like so much else on the frontier, could be very personal, determined not by who held the field, but by who lived and who died. At least 2,000 were casualties of the Indian wars, yet they accomplished their task, slowly, sometimes blunderingly, but also humanely when possible.

Above: In 1883 the army was issued with a new cap and a jacket with only five buttons. It was generally called a 'sack' because it was loose-fitting. A typical army bugle is shown below with tassles.

Left: This dramatic illustration depicts Custer's dawn attack on Black Kettle's village on the Washita River in November 1868. An estimated 103 warriors, women and children were killed, and about 53 women and children taken captive.

INDIAN WARS: PLAINS

Quanah Parker, Kicking Bird, Satanta, Black Kettle, Dull Knife, American Horse, Roman Nose, Red Cloud, Crazy Horse, Gall, Kicking Bear, Sitting Bull, Rain-in-the-Face, Man-Afraid-of-his-Horses; Chivington, Custer, Benteen, Grattan, Fetterman, Reno, Keogh; Sand Creek, Powder River, Beecher's Island, the Washita, Slim Buttes, Little Bighorn . . . On 7 Steptember 1877, Crazy Horse, who had never surrendered to the whites, died on a guard's bayonet: 'My father, I am bad hurt. Tell the people it is of no use to depend on me any more now.'

Above: *Quanah Parker, who led the Kwahadi Comanche against a group of buffalo hunters at Adobe Walls in 1874.*

1862
Revolt of Santee Sioux led by Little Crow, in Minnesota

1864
Sand Creek massacre, Colorado

1868
Fort Laramie Treaty. U.S. government agrees to abandon forts on the Powder River

1877
Death of Crazy Horse

Artifacts courtesy of Buffalo Bill Historical Center, Cody, Wyoming

Nothing in the previous experience of white American prepared them for the scale, ferocity, or nature of warfare on the Plains. It was a vast expanse of hundreds of thousands of square miles, settled chiefly by nomadic hunters who were masters of horsemanship, of fighting on the run, and who practiced a species of guerrilla warfare ideally suited to the land. Moreover, many of them were peoples with highly developed warrior societies, who glorified the manly virtues of battle, and whose only fear of death was if it should come with dishonor. While they often did not feel the same intimate sense of ownership of the land of the tribes east of the Mississippi, they looked on all the vast West as their domain. They were bound to resent the incursions of the whites, and to express that resentment with violence.

The Plains Indians skirmished with whites almost from their first encounters. When Texas was settled, immigrants immediately came into clashes with the Comanche and others. As white civilization jumped the Mississippi and spread across Missouri and began to trickle on to Kansas and Colorado, and on to the Plains from Oklahoma to Montana, more and more outbreaks of violence occurred. The first formal warfare, however, waited until 1854 when settlers in future Wyoming complained of Sioux cattle thefts. An

Right: *Little Crow's wife and children, photographed in captivity at Fort Snelling, Minnesota, in 1863. Little Crow was the Sioux chief who had led his frustrated warriors in the massacre of whites in Minnesota in 1862.*

Below left: *Headdress of bald eagle feathers (it had no trailer) belonging to the Northern Cheyenne. Note the use of red trade cloth, beads and ribbon. After a treaty in 1851 the Cheyenne split into northern and southern bands.*

Bottom: *A Sioux encampment in winter. Note the external use of lodge poles. Winter on the northern Plains was harsh; early tipis were made of buffalo skins, later to be replaced by canvas as the buffalo were mercilessly hunted to near-extinction by whites.*

army detachment foolishly confronted the supposed offenders and opened fire on them, precipitating a massacre of the soldiers that inevitably led to reprisals.

In the following months the Sioux began raiding travelers on the Oregon Trail and other isolated routes, and the army just as steadily tried to contain them, to little avail. Finally an expedition as far north as the Black Hills of future South Dakota induced the Indians to accept peace terms, but only grudgingly. The next year, in 1856, their kinsmen the Cheyenne found themselves involved in a similar war after soldiers killed some of their number in a dispute over a horse. The following spring Cheyenne and soldiers met in pitched battle on the Platte River, with the Indians taking flight but striking back later in the kind of hit-and-run raids for which they were famous. Meanwhile the Kiowa and Comanches engaged in a running conflict with authorities in Texas that would last up to the Civil War, and continue sporadically while the whites took time out to fight among themselves.

The first major Indian war on the Plains came in 1862, when the northern Sioux rose in Minnesota in a fruitless attempt to evict the whites from the territory. The Indians went on a killing rampage that killed 400 whites in its first day, and more in the days to follow. Soon they laid siege to Fort Ridgeley before volunteers rushed to arms to meet the threat. Only quick reaction and retaliation put an end to the uprising that saw almost 1,000 whites dead before the Sioux gave up and saw their leaders tried and

Above: Kicking Bird, chief of the Kiowa of the southern Plains. After the Medicine Lodge Treaty of 1867 he left the Fort Cobb agency north of the Red River for the Staked Plains in Texas. He died in 1875, having selected Kiowas for exile to Florida.

Left: Refugees of the Indian massacre of whites in 1862, these fortunates had been aided in their escape by friendly Sioux.

Right: Sioux pipe tomahawk with wooden handle and iron axehead. Note the beaded and fringed buckskin attachment.

Below: November 1862, Fort Snelling, Minnesota, where about 1700 Sioux spent the winter in captivity after the earlier outbreak.

Above: Shakopee was, with Medicine Bottle (see below), one of the leaders of the Sioux uprising of 1862. Four young men from his band had started the troubles by killing four white settlers. He was eventually hanged at Fort Snelling in 1863.

Above: Medicine Bottle, another leader of the uprising in Minnesota. His capture and execution with Shakopee had been engineered cunningly by the whites. Drugged and bound, they were spirited out of Canada and ended up on the gallows.

'Bringing Home the Spoils', by Charles M. Russell (1864–1926)
(Buffalo Bill Historical Center, Cody, Wyoming. Gift of William E. Weiss)

Above: The great war chief Satanta of the Kiowa. Dee Brown's *Bury My Heart at Wounded Knee* describes him as 'a burly giant with jet black hair reaching to his enormous shoulders'. He died in 1878, wasting away in a prison hospital in Texas.

Above: *The log house trading post owned by François La Bathe, which was used as a courthouse after the Sioux revolt of 1862. Blanketed Sioux sit huddled in the foreground.*

Right: *On 26 December 1862, the mass hanging took place of thirty-eight Sioux who had participated in the revolt. President Lincoln had reprieved two hundred and sixty-five other intended victims.*

Left: *An exquisite medicine shield of the Sioux. Made of hardened buffalo hide and covered with buckskin, adornments included on the shield are gathered feathers, among them those of the bald eagle, beadwork and trade cloth.*

Above: Colonel John Chivington, the former Methodist minister whose irreligious behavior made him the villain of the piece at the Sand Creek massacre of Cheyenne in 1864. For his brutality he faced a Congressional investigation.

executed. Others continued their hostility along the upper Missouri through 1863 and 1864 until General Alfred Sully quelled the uprising at the Battle of Killdeer Mountain.

To the south, meanwhile, Colonel John Chivington conducted barbarous raids on the Cheyenne, fomenting renewed fighting on the central Plains in Kansas and Colorado. Finally in November 1864, at Sand Creek, Colorado, he attacked a village of Cheyenne who had come to surrender and killed more than 200. The outrage induced the Sioux to join with the Cheyenne in raiding and threatening on the Colorado frontier the following year, and after the Civil War ended, several of the Plains peoples amassed a force of 3,000 or more that raided with impunity before retreating up the Powder River in the face of an ineffectual army campaign.

The following decade was one of frustration and disaster for the army. In 1866 Crazy Horse of the Sioux led a massacre of eighty soldiers near Fort Phil Kearney. At the other end of the decade Crazy Horse again, along with Sitting Bull's Hunkpapa Sioux and other groups totaling 2,000

or more, led the attack in the greatest defeat ever suffered by the Indian fighting army. On 25 June they struck Colonel George Custer and portions of the 7th United States Cavalry along the Little Bighorn River in Montana. Not a man of the soldiers immediately with Custer survived, while the rest of his column was badly battered and barely held out.

Of course the army could not accept that, and during the ensuing five years it relentlessly pursued Sioux and Cheyenne until Crazy Horse was dead, and Sitting Bull and the other chiefs finally surrendered, to be sent to prison or reservations. There for several years they languished, feeling the anger of losing their hunting lands and the humiliation of defeat. Younger warriors arose to demand that they redress their wrongs. Mysticism gained a foothold among the young men, and in 1889 there appeared a Paiute shaman named Wovoka, who began to tell a message that won wide acceptance on the Plains. He performed a frenzied ritual dance that, in a trance, allowed him to see the future, all of the Indians' slain ancestors reunited, and the white men pushed out

Above: Sitting Bull of the Hunkpapa Sioux. His refusal in 1876 to leave the Powder River country to register at one of the agencies sparked off a new war with the army, which culminated in the victory of combined Plains tribes at the Little Bighorn.

Above: *The annihilation of Custer's command at the Little Bighorn prompted many interpretations of the conflict, such as this 'artistic' and imaginative Anhauser-Busch lithograph.*

Right: *A pictograph of the same battle from an Indian point of view. Stylized and direct in its imagery, it depicts the greatest Indian victory in decades of war on the Plains against the army.*

of their homeland for good. Others quickly seized on his message and adapted it to their hatred and resentment, and turned the Ghost Dance into a means of whipping up emotions for another war with the whites. Convinced that blessed 'Ghost shirts' would repel the soldiers' bullets, the Sioux especially answered the call. Authorities led by General Nelson Miles, veteran of so many Indian campaigns throughout the West, quickly gathered to quell any outbreak, but in the process Sitting Bull was killed and several of his people left their reservation to seek refuge in the high wilderness. But there was nowhere they could go that the army, more numerous and better equipped, could not follow, and the Ghost Dance inevitably ended in the bloody snow of Wounded Knee, and with it extinguished what some say was the last spark of resistance of the Plains peoples.

Below: *Arapaho from Fort Washakie, Wyoming, with the Paiute Wovoka, prophet of the Ghost Dance whose influence reached the Plains.*

Above: Red Cloud of the Oglala Sioux. The eponymous Red Cloud War led to the abandonment of three forts – including Phil Kearney and C.F. Smith – and the closure of the Bozeman Trail. Peace was restored in 1868 with the Fort Laramie Treaty.

GEORGE A. CUSTER

General Custer described the Plains Indians as 'savages in every sense of the word', yet romanticized over their 'strange customs, and fantastic culture', expressing wonder at their horsemanship and hunting skills. Custer himself was a contradiction: his bravery and courage were never questioned, but his ego was such that during the Civil War he felt the need to dress in gaudy, self-designed uniforms, and on the Plains he emulated his scouts by appearing in buckskins. However the complexities of his character keep his legend alive.

Above: *Tom Custer, his brother, stands behind George and his wife Libbie.*

1861
Custer graduates from West Point – bottom of his class

1861–5
Cavalry leader, national hero and renowned as the 'Boy General'

1866
Appointed Lieutenant Colonel of the newly formed Seventh Cavalry Regiment

1876
25 June, makes his 'Last Stand' at the Battle of the Little Bighorn

Artifact courtesy of Gene Austry Western Heritage Museum, Los Angeles, California

Any attempt to evaluate Custer both as a man and a fighting soldier is fraught with problems. To some he was a headstrong egomaniac anxious for glory regardless of the cost in lives. Others, however, see him as a misunderstood, devoted soldier who regarded his duty as paramount. Obviously, the real man exists somewhere between both extremes – as indeed does any individual who has made an impact upon society or history.

In Custer's case, however, emotion plays a great part. Born in 1839, he went to West Point where he graduated bottom of the class in 1861, following a number of misdemeanors and with a resentment of authority. But during the Civil War, Custer rose from the rank of a lowly lieutenant to captain, Brigadier General of Volunteers, and Brevet Major General, U.S.A. During the conflict his 7th Michigan Brigade distinguished itself on numerous occasions, and newspapers were full of stories extolling the exploits of the 'gallant boy general', as he was known.

With the close of the war, Custer was reduced in rank, but retained his brevet rank for the remainder of his career.

In 1866, Congress authorized the organization of four new cavalry regiments, and Custer was given the lieutenant colonelcy of the Seventh, then being organized at Fort Riley, Kansas. Joining him in the months to come was his brother Thomas, twice awarded the Congressional Medal of Honor during the Civil War.

Once the regiment was organized they needed some action, and in 1867 they were ordered into the field against hostile Indians in Kansas. Placed under the command of General Winfield Scott Hancock, who had a force consisting of 1500 men, the Seventh soon learned that fighting Indians was nothing like the straightforward engagements of the recent war. They proved evasive and only attacked when the advantage was with them. Despite a number of Delaware Indian scouts, and notables such as Hickok, Comstock and Guerrier, Hancock failed to catch his prey.

Right: *President Abraham Lincoln confers with General McClellan and staff in 1862. To the right is Custer. Already he has an air about him of one anxious to be noticed. As commander of the Seventh Michigan Brigade he achieved his object.*

Far right: *This fine pair of Smith & Wesson Model No. 2 .32 caliber Army revolvers was presented to Custer in 1868. The stocks are pearl.*

Below: *Custer and his Indian scouts (kneeling to his right is Bloody Knife, his favorite). The pistols are nickel-plated Peacemakers. He also loved dogs.*

In 1868, at the request of General Philip Sheridan (who had long supported Custer), Custer was recalled to service and during a winter campaign against the Indians led his troops into an engagement remembered as the Battle of the Washita. Accusations of deserting men in the face of the enemy and the killing of women and children were to plague Custer for years, but he appears not to have let it affect him.

By 1874, having established his reputation as an Indian fighter and the author of a number of magazine articles and a book, Custer led an expedition into the Black Hills of Dakota Territory, at that time Sioux land. On his return he reported 'gold in the Hills' and started a stampede that led eventually to the Sioux war of 1876. In June that year, in the midst of a full-scale campaign against the Sioux, Custer and more than two hundred Seventh Cavalry troops were killed in his now legendary 'Last Stand'.

George Armstrong Custer remains a controversial figure, a man one either admired or hated. There seems to be no middle course. But in the eyes of the general public who tend to ignore their heroes' faults, his image remains that of a cavalier in buckskin at the head of his troops, guidons fluttering and the band playing 'Garry Owen' as they prepare once more to gallop into the fray at the sound of the charge.

Above: The 1874 expedition massed and ready for the march. It consisted of over 1,000 men; 1,900 horses and mules, and 300 beef cattle and 110 wagons.

Below: Seventh Cavalry officers at Fort Abraham Lincoln. Custer is third from the right, and his wife Elizabeth is third from the left. Tom also appears.

Above: The youthful Custer photographed in his West Point Cadet's uniform, circa 1859. His period at the academy was marked by frequent brushes with authority and he was often 'on report'. But he survived and passed out in 1861.

Above: Thomas Custer, George's younger brother, served in the Civil War (where he won *two* Medals of Honor!) and later on the Plains as a captain in the Seventh Cavalry. He idolized 'Autie' (as George was known to his family), and died with him.

'The Custer Fight', by William Herbert Dunton (1875–1936)
(Buffalo Bill Historical Center, Cody, Wyoming. Gertrude Vanderbilt Whitney Trust Fund Purchase)

INDIAN WARS: CALIFORNIA

The war between Indians and whites focuses in this section on the struggle between the Modoc and the army in the northern corner of California. The key figure of resistance to white encroachment into Indian lands was Captain Jack, whose father had been killed by whites in 1852. In 1873 he inpired Modoc resistance at the Battle of the Lava Beds, but the ultimate story of such resistance against great odds, surrender but not capitulation, then execution, was to be repeated in California, as elsewhere, as Indians increasingly were overwhelmed.

Above: *Tenino Indian scouts from the Warm Springs Reservation who helped to track and pursue the Modoc.*

1872
In November, Company B of 1st U.S. Cavalry rides into the Modoc camp. Shots are exchanged, the Modoc flee, war breaks out

1873
(April) Brigadier General Canby is murdered by Captain Jack during negotiations for a settlement

(January) Fierce resistance by the Modoc; it continues into the spring as they defend their position in the Lava Beds

(October) Captain Jack (Keintpoos, Kintpuash) is executed

The story of Indian wars in California focuses largely on one tribe. In northern California, where the remains of once-active volcanoes created a lava moonscape around the Klamath Lakes, a hardy, fierce, and often predatory people calling themselves the Modocs clung to life in the barren wastes. They survived by hunting and gathering, and by preying occasionally on more peaceful tribes closer to the coastline. They even practiced slavery, trading captured natives of other tribes to eastern Indians for horses. From the first incursions of whites into their domain in the days following the Gold Rush, they showed themselves hostile.

For a number of years no declared warfare broke out. Instead, Modocs and occasionally Klamaths joined with their cousins the Snakes or Northern Paiutes to raid miners' encampments, and always army efforts to track the perpetrators seemed futile. Authorities complained that one Indian could occupy ten soldiers in the chase, and that every one actually killed cost $50,000 or more to the government. Still, by the end of the Civil War soldiers in northern California had subdued the Shasta, Klamath, and Hupa.

That left the Modoc. Following the subjugation of the Paiute after the Civil War, only the Modoc remained intractable. Their numbers were few, probably between 400 and 800, but their fierce independence and the impenetrable terrain they inhabited made them formidable foes. By the 1870s their more warlike braves followed the lead of Kintpuash, nicknamed Captain Jack by miners with whom he had once been friendly. He had signed a treaty in 1864 and allowed himself and followers to be relocated on a reservation, but life there proved intolerable and they left for their ancestral home once more. Fearful whites in the region demanded that the Modoc be removed.

The task fell to General E. R. S. Canby, a long-time veteran of Indian fighting in the West, and a distinguished army commander during the Civil War. In the summer of 1872 he began preparations to track down Captain Jack and his followers, and in November had located the

Above: *A quirt said to have belonged to Captain Jack, formerly owned by August Berggren, a Swedish-American banker.*

Above right: *Donald McKay (center) and two of the Modoc who helped capture Captain Jack, having agreed with the army to track down their leader in exchange for an amnesty.*

Right: *From the left, Shacknasty Jim, Hooker (Hooka) Jim, Steamboat Frank and the white rancher Fairchild. Hooker Jim betrayed Jack after the Lava Beds battle and defected to the army.*

Below: *Army personnel fighting the Modoc during the battle of the Lava Beds. In this inhospitable terrain, Captain Jack's band was able to hold off its attackers with great success before escaping and prolonging the struggle.*

Modoc camp and demanded Captain Jack's surrender. The Modoc met the demand with shooting, retreating after half an hour to join another band in a seemingly impregnable natural fortress called the 'Stronghold', that someone likened to a huge crashing ocean surf frozen into stone.

There in January 1873 Canby's forces approached once more, and there followed an inconclusive 'battle' in which the soldiers got the worst of it. The Modoc knew their lava fortress so intimately that the soldiers were almost helpless against them. Frustrated, they settled down to a siege while conducting month-long negotiations with Jack, whose own people vacillated between resistance and surrender. The standoff went on into the spring, with the Modocs even more divided, and Captain Jack actually more moderate now, beginning to favor capitulation, and resisted by the militant Hooker Jim and Curley Headed Doctor. Finally Jack agreed to meet with Canby in April between their lines. When he announced his intention to talk of peace, militant Modocs humiliated him until he agreed to go along with a plan to kill the negotiators and continue

resistance. On 11 April Canby and his negotiators, with two interpreters, met Jack and his party. During their talks, Captain Jack suddenly stood up, drew his pistol, and shot Canby in the head. Other Modocs brought out their weapons and almost massacred the whole commission, killing two and leaving a third for dead.

It was a foolish bit of treachery. Canby had been a very popular officer, widely respected, and one with a comparatively benevolent attitude toward the native peoples he was charged to subdue. In the face of his murder, Washington reacted with predictable vehemence, virtually giving its commanders in the region *carte blanche* to do as they wished in suppressing the Modoc uprising. 'Any measure of severity to the savages will be sustained', came the word from headquarters. Yet Captain Jack and his people just heaped embarrassment on to humiliation. After a three day assault by the soldiers, the Modoc left the Stronghold and retreated deeper into the lava barrens. Several days later they ambushed and almost wiped out a fifty-man scouting party, leaving twenty-five of the soldiers dead, and then a few weeks afterward completely eluded their pursuers. The Modoc were beginning to break up, as one faction decided it had had enough and left to surrender. Its leader Hooker Jim offered to help capture Captain Jack in return for amnesty, and led the soldiers to Willow Creek near Clear Lake. On 28 May they sent in a demand for Jack to surrender. Knowing that he would be killed if captured, Jack and his people scattered, being captured one-by-one in subsequent days. Finally on 3 June soldiers took Captain Jack himself.

General William T. Sherman, commanding the United States army, had hoped that Jack and all the others would be killed rather than captured. He wanted to disperse the survivors among reservations in the East so that, as he put it, 'the names of Modoc should cease'. But the capture required that Jack, Hooker Jim, and others be turned over to the courts. In the end Jack and one other were hanged, while the pitiful 155 survivors of the Modoc were sent to the Indian Territory to be assimilated into the Cherokee and other tribes. The Modocs were gone and almost the only reminder of their existence would be their name on a county in northern California.

INDIAN WARS: BASIN

'It is cold, and we have no blankets. The little children are freezing to death. My people – some of them – have run away to the hills and have no blankets, no food. I want to have time to look for my children, and to see how many of them I can find; may be I shall find them among the dead. Hear me, my chiefs; my heart is sick and sad. From where the sun now stands, I will fight no more forever!' These are said to be the words of Chief Joseph of the Nez Perce, spoken after he and his people had been chased and caught by the army some forty miles short of refuge in Canada.

Above: Hein-mot Too-ya-la-kekt, better known as Chief Joseph of the Nez Perce, in 1901.

1877

(June) Battle of White Bird Canyon: seventy Nez Perce warriors rout a column of U.S. Cavalry

(August) Battle of the Big Hole: the massacre of more than eighty Nez Perce men, women and children

(September) Battle of Bear Paw Mountains: the Nez Perce, fleeing from the army, are forty miles from the Canadian border

(October) Chief Joseph surrenders; Nez Perce resistance ends

Over 200,000 square miles of the West constitute the Great Basin, that vast expanse between the Rocky and Sierra Nevada Mountains. It includes most of the states of Nevada and Utah, as well as parts of California, Wyoming, Idaho and Oregon. A host of Indian tribes lay scattered through the region, from the Western Shoshoni and Paiute to the west, to the more imposing Bannocks and Northern Shoshoni and Utes in Utah. The last group were more hostile toward whites, leading to repeated military operations against them during 1863, producing a series of treaties.

The greater problem centered in the northern part of the basin. In the Oregon country the Nez Perce also concluded a treaty in 1863, but the Western Shoshoni in Idaho held out against the white advance and joined with small elements of other tribes to continue raiding. Moreover, a portion of the Nez Perce never accepted the 1863 treaty and refused to settle within the reservation lands prescribed for them. Instead they banded around their Chief Joseph and clung to their lands in Oregon and Idaho. When he died in 1871, they gave their allegiance to his charismatic son and namesake. He successfully argued that they had never signed the earlier treaty and therefore had not yielded claim to their lands in the Wallowa Mountains of Oregon, and in 1873 Washington agreed and created a separate reservation for them in their old homeland. Two years later, unfortunately, the press of white settlers led the government to renege. In spite of this, for a time the Nez Perce attempted to coexist peacefully with the settlers who began to come

Right: The Shoshoni chief Washakie's village, near the Sweetwater River, Fort Stambaugh, Wyoming, from a photograph by W.H. Jackson on the Hayden Survey in 1870. Like their neighbors the Crow, the Shoshoni were friends to the army.

Far right: Typical handiwork – a twined basketry water jug, waterproofed with pinon pitch, from the Pyramid Lake Reservation of the Northern Paiute.

Bottom: A group of Ute Indians. The Utes were Rocky Mountain people from Colorado who were, in 1881, marched out of Colorado into new reservations in Utah.

Below right: This photograph shows the prophet Smohalla (center, clothed in white) with members of the Dreamer cult. Smohalla preached that the dead would eventually arise and push the whites from Indian land once and for all.

into their home. Well-intentioned authorities then attempted to buy the land from them in return for their removal to the reservation. Chief Joseph refused, and months of negotiations could not change his mind, until he saw columns of troops moving into the Wallowa. Then, at least, he saw he had no choice.

Before the Indians could go to the reservation, scattered outbreaks of violence resulted in dead settlers. Then Joseph decided to try to lead his people east to the Great Plains and their Sioux cousins. When the army caught up to them at White Bird Canyon, Joseph handed them a humiliating defeat. In the days that followed the Nez Perce handed the bluecoats more defeats,

most of them in spite of being outnumbered, and only increased General Oliver O. Howard's determination to track them down in order to save his waning reputation. In July at Clearwater Creek, though forced to retire, the Indians again largely outfought the whites, drawing grudging praise even from Howard.

Now Joseph and his other chiefs decided to head for Montana, there to join with the Crow, or perhaps even move into Canada to join the Hunkpapa Sioux and wait until the current furore subsided. After they started on the long trek, Howard and the army followed, launching one of the most fabled of all Western sagas. Through the rest of July and on into August Joseph led his

Above: After the abortive flight of the Nez Perce to the Canadian border, Chief Joseph was sent to Indian Territory – miles from his Oregon homeland – where he remained until 1885. He died in 1904 in Washington State, worn down by sorrow.

Above: General Oliver Otis Howard, the One-Armed-Soldier-Chief who was sent in 1877 to clear all Nez Perce from the Wallowa Valley. In May of that year he summoned Joseph to Lapwai to discuss the removal of the Nez Perce from their ancestral lands.

Above: Colonel John Gibbon, who in August 1877 led an attack on the Nez Perce camp on the banks of the Big Hole River. Following orders from Howard to head off the fleeing Nez Perce, Gibbon's action led to the massacre of some fifty women and children.

Left: *Nez Perce woman's buckskin legging decorated with beadwork.*

Above: *Nez Perce warrior on horseback. He wears a Plains style eagle feathered warbonnet. The large tipi in the background is made of canvas.*

Below: *Four Nez Perce parfleches, with a small comb. Parfleches were large folded rawhide cases, usually painted with geometric designs.*

people northeastward until they reached Montana, tired, hungry, broken down. Unfortunately, they stopped to rest and forage, and that gave the soldiers time to mount a pursuit. On 9 August some 200 soldiers led by Colonel John Gibbon caught up with them and attacked. The Indians resisted for two days and then retreated, but not before leaving a third of Gibbon's command killed or wounded. Once again the Nez Perce had outfought the soldiers.

Moving with lightning swiftness despite their condition and their wounded, the Nez Perce turned west and crossed into Idaho trying to evade pursuit. Howard came after them as fast as he could, but by mid-August was always one day behind, and still the Indians, fighting rearguard actions, retarded his progress and inflicted embarrassing casualties. Then on 22 August the Nez Perce entered Yellowstone National Park, terrifying tourists while Howard's exhausted men halted and begged to stop the chase. Washington refused, and instead issued orders for other commands in the region to start to converge on the beleaguered Indians. Time after time Joseph either eluded his pursuers, or else turned and handed them stinging rebuffs while his people pressed on.

By late September the Indians were heading toward the Canadian border. They crossed the Missouri River, and then halted once more to rest. It was a fatal mistake. At last several of the columns pursuing them approached, and on 30 September the soldiers, now commanded by General Nelson Miles, launched an attack on their camps in the Snake Creek Valley, just forty miles short of the Canadian border. For the next five days Joseph held Miles at bay, inflicting substantial casualties. Then Howard and his column arrived, and the Indians realized that this time they might not fight or maneuver their way out. Some argued that it was time to negotiate, and Joseph decided to talk with Miles. The general offered generous terms, promising to allow them to return without reprisals to the Idaho reservation.

Joseph accepted, and returned to his ragged people to declare his intention to 'fight no more forever'. Some 800 Nez Perce had struggled 1,700 miles across rivers, mountain ranges, past numberless columns of soldiers. In the sad aftermath of their heroic trek, the authorities reneged once more on Miles' promise, and sent them first to Kansas, where many sickened and died, and then on to the catch-all Indian Territory. Even Miles became enamored of Joseph's cause, and in later years helped him plead his case for a return to the Wallowa. The closest he got was a reservation in Washington, where he died in 1904 widely revered by white and Indian alike.

While the Nez Perce war attracted much of the country's attention, the Ute and Bannock went hostile again in 1878–9, and only the assembly of some 4,000 soldiers impelled the Indians to come to a negotiated rather than a military settlement. When they did so, the Great Basin Indian wars came at last to an end.

Left: *Looking Glass, a Nez Perce chief, in a camp of his friends the Mountain Crow. He died at the Bear Paw Mountains in 1877.*

Right: *A Nez Perce bag, leather with a beaded, geometric design similar to those exhibited on the parfleches (left).*

Below: *The caption 'Home of Chief Joseph at Nespelem, Wash.' tells nothing of the sad exile of Joseph and his people after their brave struggle.*

Above: Colonel Nelson Miles pursued the Nez Perce to within forty miles of the Canadian border. His terms of surrender to Joseph were clear: 'If you come out and give us your arms, I will spare your lives and send you to your reservation.'

"Home of Chief Joseph" at Nespelem Wash.
W.J. Moorhouse

INDIAN WARS: S'WEST

The surrender of the Chiricahua leader Geronimo in September 1886 effectively marked the end of Indian wars in the United States. Before that, the Southwest had witnessed a violent struggle on the part of the Navajo and the Apache to resist the influx of whites into their lands. By 1864, the Navajo had succumbed to the scorched earth policy of General Carleton and suffered through starvation and depredation in the 'Long Walk'. The Apache fought on, their struggle personified by Geronimo. When he finally surrendered, he was sent first to Florida, then to Oklahoma.

Among the bitterest and longest lasting conflicts between the United States army and the native peoples were those in the southwest, in western Texas, the New Mexico Territory, and surrounding areas. There lived the Navajo, the Apache, and allied tribes, spread across an arid desert dotted with bare mountains, hidden canyons, and the kind of rugged, flinty terrain that suited ideally their sort of hit-and-run guerrilla style of fighting.

The Southwestern peoples came late to conflict with the spread of American civilizations from the East, yet they were among the first to clash with the Spanish as they settled Mexico and spread northward into California. By the time people from the United States began to filter into the region following the end of the war with Mexico in 1848, the Southwestern peoples knew all too well what to expect.

Only a year passed from the end of that war before the Navajo began to raid American settlements in 1849, leading to immediate reprisal and an initial treaty that failed to last. In 1851 Washington ordered Colonel Edwin V. Sumner to launch a campaign against the Navajo, Ute, and Apache, intended to root them out and so punish them that they would never raid settlers again. Sumner's campaign failed, but while in New Mexico he began the construction of the chain of remote forts that would be the foundation of frontier defense for the rest of the century.

Genuine warfare against the Navajo finally came in 1858, precipitated when a distraught Indian trader at Fort Defiance took out his frustration by mortally wounding a slave boy. All that fall an expedition of mounted riflemen and

Above: A Navajo cap, from 1898. By this date the Navajo were firmly established in a large reservation within their old ancestral territory.

Right: A Navajo warrior, posing for a studio photograph. Antagonism had been smouldering for some time between Navajo and the army before all-out war broke out in 1858.

Below: Three Navajo warriors. They called themselves Dineh – 'The People' – and possessed, when the army annexed their lands in 1849, a fearsome reputation.

Above: Apaches photographed in 1886 by the celebrated Camillus Fly of Tombstone, Arizona.

1861
Attempted (and failed) capture of Cochise leads to guerrilla warfare between Apache and the U.S. in the Southwest

1863–4
Destruction of Navajo and enforced march to Fort Sumner: the 'Long Walk' of the Navajo

1868
Treaty with the Navajo and creation of Navajo Reservation

1886
Surrender of Geronimo ends warfare against the Indians in the United States

Below: Navajo bowcase attached to a quiver, made of mountain lion skin, shown with bow and four steel-tipped arrows.

Above: Brigadier-General James Carleton, who was responsible for the campaign of 1863-4 which saw the forced removal of over 8,000 Navajo to the Bosque Redondo in New Mexico. Many Navajo never learnt of Carleton's 'peace initiative'.

Left: A Navajo war captain. He wears a war hat made of tanned leather and carries a lance and a shield made of rawhide.

infantry chased after the culprit. When they rode through a deep canyon, Navajo on the heights on either side fired arrows down at them and dropped boulders. Later the Navajo launched a small attack of their own, to no effect, and up to Christmas soldiers and Indians continued to snipe at each other until a peace treaty put an end to the little campaign. A year of peace followed before an escalated war broke out, with 1,000 Navajo attacking Fort Defiance itself, one of the very few instances in which native peoples assaulted an army installation. Almost miraculously, soldiers repulsed the attack with scant losses, then launched a retaliatory campaign that achieved little militarily, but which in almost two years gradually persuaded the foe to sue for peace once more. By 1861 the Navajo were quiet again.

Sporadic raids continued as the Civil War raged in the East, and finally in 1863 General James H. Carleton determined to end the Navajo as a menace forever. He ordered all the chiefs and groups who wanted peace to leave their land and move to Bosque Redondo, near Fort Sumner, where the army could watch them. Those who did not go he would root out ruthlessly. That summer Carleton ordered Colonel Christopher 'Kit' Carson to lead nearly 1,000 soldiers on a

Above: 'Kit' Carson, who was commissioned by Carleton to round up the Navajo and move them to a new reservation in east-central New Mexico. Following his commander's instructions, Carson systematically destroyed the Navajo's economic base.

Above: Chato was an ally of Geronimo's for a short time but changed his ways in 1884 to scout for the army. He later received a medal for his help but it was not enough to stop him being sent to prison in Florida with other renegade Apaches he had betrayed.

Above: The Mimbres Apache Victorio. He took his band on the rampage in the southwest after the army moved his people to San Carlos. The items shown below were collected from his band by the Swedish-American soldier Major Charles Steelhammer.

Right: Geronimo of the Chiricahua with some of his band of renegades, photographed in 1886. Apache tribes had no recognized leaders, but bands and groups did. Geronimo – intelligent, resourceful and daring – exerted enormous influence upon his band and upon the entire southwest until his final surrender in 1886. That said, he was one of many notable Apaches.

campaign that killed few Indians, but ravaged their crops and herds, reducing them to near-starvation. Weakened thus, the Navajo also fell prey to raids by rival native tribes. Finally some 8,000 or more gave in and went to Bosque Redondo on the Pecos River. It was a disaster for them with disease and hardship wearing them down so severely that in 1868 the authorities let them go back to their homeland. But the Navajo would never again make war on the whites.

Not so their Apache neighbors. By nature more warlike, the several Apache groups – Mescalero, Jicarilla, Chiricahua, Coyotero, and Gila – totaled some 8,000 perhaps, but wreaked a havoc with authorities that belied their limited numbers. Throughout the 1850s they raided settlers, especially along the Santa Fe Trail, and in 1854 handed army regulars a sound defeat with twenty-two dead near Taos, New Mexico. For the rest of the decade the army and the Apache sparred with each other, the Indians suffering casualties but usually disappearing into their remote fastnesses. Most of the troubles came with the Jicarilla, who were the first subdued, and the Mescalero. The Coyotero were more agricultural, less reliant on hunting and raiding, and the Chiricahua at first seemed inclined to be peaceful. But in 1860 when a settler wrongfully accused Cochise of the Chiricahua with kidnapping a half-breed boy, a scuffle broke out that led to a fourteen-year war. The wily chieftain baffled the soldiers at almost every turn, meeting brutality with brutality. Meanwhile the Mescalero yielded, but the Gila, led by chief Mangas Coloradas – 'Red Sleeves' – raided and killed widely. Soldiers killed Red Sleeves after he was captured, but the Gila maintained their resistance for years.

Thereafter it would be chiefly two Apache who would dominate the confrontation in the Southwest. Cochise's war with the whites lasted for some fourteen years. In spite of 137 skirmishes and battles between 1866 and 1870 alone, the scale of Cochise's raids never lagged. Finally, thanks largely to Cochise's friendship with Indian agent Tom Jeffords, the Chiricahua made a truce for a time. But after Cochise's death in 1874, his successors squabbled over war and peace, and soon

Right: A well-armed group of Apache scouts in Arizona. Apache scouts were first recruited at Camp Apache in 1871.

Below right: Cavalry leaving Fort Bowie, in southwestern Arizona. The fort was built to help control Apache Pass in the difficult early days.

Below: Saddle, stirrups and whip, possibly from the band of the Mimbres Apache Victorio, collected at Fort Craig, New Mexico.

Above: After the death of Victorio in 1880, Nana, although elderly at the time, took over leadership of the remaining Mimbres renegades. He had escaped the slaughter by Mexican soldiers of seventy-eight Apache which had claimed Victorio's life.

a new specter arose in the shape of Geronimo, who would become the most feared Apache of them all. Along with Victorio of the Warm Springs faction, Geronimo would set the Southwest trembling for more than a decade.

Victorio himself became hunted both by United States forces and Mexican troops alike for he raided on both sides of the border. Finally in 1880 he fell to a bullet. Geronimo, however, led a more charmed life. Intelligent, daring, resourceful, he remained ever one step ahead of his pursuers. In fact, he was not a chief, but only a charismatic warrior to whom others gave allegiance. In 1882 when he helped lead a bloody raid along the Arizona–New Mexico border, the army immediately pursued, and for the next five years

skirmished with the elusive raider. Frequently Geronimo slipped into Mexico for safety, then raided back north, with General George Crook relentlessly pursuing. Geronimo surrendered in 1883 and went to a reservation for a time, but then broke out once more two years later. He led Crook a merry chase until March 1886 when once more he surrendered, only to run off soon afterward. General Nelson Miles took over the pursuit and finally caught him for good, sending him to Florida and then Oklahoma for the rest of his days. The end of Geronimo's resistance called a virtual halt to Indian warfare everywhere except for the last gasp of the Sioux in the Ghost Dance in 1890, when they would respond to the prophecies of a Paiute shaman named Wovoka.

Above: Geronimo (Goyathlay) ended his days in Oklahoma. Mourning his homeland and his lost freedom, he said: 'There is no climate or soil equal to that of Arizona. It is my land, my home, my father's land . . . I want to spend my last days there.'

Left: Apache prisoners in transit to prisons in Texas and Florida, 1886. Geronimo is seated third from right, front row.

Below: Geronimo (hand on hat) in imprisonment. Exiled to Florida with other Apache, he died in 1909 in Oklahoma, far from his beloved Arizona.

Below: A beaded Sioux vest, collected by Major Walker. Records indicate that this garment was once the property of Geronimo.

Above: Brigadier General Crook held council with Geronimo in the Sierra Madre in March 1886. Ten years before, he had led companies of cavalry into the Powder River area of the northern Plains against Sitting Bull and his Cheyenne allies.

RANGE WARS

It seems strange to this generation that with so much land available, much of it for the taking, Westerners should fight and kill each other. But out West that is just what did happen. And when a man put his 'brand' on land or cattle he expected to keep it. Water rights, grazing and the eternal wrangling between 'cattlemen' and 'sheepherders' was a surefire way to start a row that soon led to a fight and then a long-standing feud. And the added ingredient of so-called 'sodbusters' or 'homesteaders' incited both sides into open warfare and violent death.

Above: Philip (Doboy) Taylor, one of many involved in so-called range wars; he was murdered in 1871.

1878
Lincoln County war erupts in New Mexico Territory

1886
The Pleasant Valley war between the Grahams and the Tewksburys begins to smoulder in the Tonto Basin, Arizona Territory

1892
Outbreak of the Johnson County war in Wyoming. Its effect is to break the power of the cattle barons, many of whom are bankrupted and disgraced as a result of taking the law into their own hands

Artifact courtesy of Gene Autry Western Heritage Museum, Los Angeles, California

Man's greed for power, possessions, and a lust to own land were the main ingredients in the events that led up to some of the more bizarre incidents in frontier history – range feuds. Many reasoned that the land was there for the taking anyway. So thought the white man and, despite the presence of the Indian, an estimated sixty million buffalo and other wild animals, civilization slowly crept from sea to sea and a wilderness became a republic. There were also those who sought land for other purposes than civilization and the betterment of mankind; these were the cattle and sheepmen who made fortunes, and convinced others (notably in England and Scotland) that there was a valuable return, particularly in cattle.

The great cattle ranges of Texas, Montana and Wyoming were living proof of the profit in beef, but they also witnessed bitter rage feuds that led to wars between factions that went on sometimes for so long that no one was really sure what started them in the first place. It became a way of life to some, and the likes of John Wesley Hardin, one of the most homicidal of the old Texas 'badmen'

Right: Sheep graze on the Powder River Bandlands circa 1884. Many cattlemen alleged that their presence made it impossible to graze cattle on the same land.

Below: This ramshackle building is the old Graham Ranch in Pleasant Valley as it looked at about the time of the deadly feud.

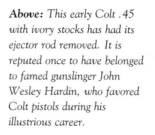

Above: This early Colt .45 with ivory stocks has had its ejector rod removed. It is reputed once to have belonged to famed gunslinger John Wesley Hardin, who favored Colt pistols during his illustrious career.

Right: The Tewksbury cabin was the scene of bloodshed on 2 September 1887, when the Graham faction shot dead John Tewksbury in revenge for the murder of one of their own kin.

relished his part in the Sutton–Taylor feud (he sided with the Taylors who were 'kin'), and was active during some of its more violent periods.

People took second place to cattle in the eyes of many of the cattlemen, which accounted for a number of bloody conflicts. The land on which the cattle or sheep were reared was well grassed, watered and was arable. In fact, its value could be compared to today's obsession with oil. Men were prepared to fight to keep it or gain a part of it. Under the Homestead Act of 1862, a man could claim so many acres of land and, if he worked it for a set period, it was his. But the cattlemen regarded such individuals as 'sod-busters' or 'nesters' and bitterly fought to keep them away.

The Johnson County war was the result of such feeling and led to the invasion of the county by a bunch of 'Regulators' or 'gunfighters' hired to keep down the nesters. This failed, but the bitterness lasted for years. Similarly, the Lincoln County, New Mexico, war of the late 1870s was a dispute over land owned by John Chisum and the local ring or businessmen anxious to take over both the county's economic and political potential. Chisum himself had reputation for pre-empting public lands, which only served to alienate many of the small ranchers, some of who had switched their allegiance to the so-called 'ring' led by James J. Dolan and Lawrence G. Murphy, a pair of ruthless, hard-headed business men who in their turn resented the cattlemen.

Billy the Kid's involvement in the Lincoln County war has kept it alive in popular legend, but it was as sordid as the Johnson County war. In keeping with this kind of tradition, the sheep war in Pleasant Valley, Arizona, between the Grahams and the Tewksburys was just as bad. In all instances, greed, money and power went before people and prosperity. The result was bloodshed, tears and misery that lasted for generations.

Above: Tom Pickett, a noted Texas hard case, had a varied career as a cattle rustler, cohort of Billy the Kid and 'hired gun' during the Pleasant Valley war. He dodged bullets and avoided becoming too involved, and died at Pinetop, Arizona, in 1934.

Above: The legendary John Chisum, one of the most famous cattlemen of them all. He once employed Billy the Kid and sided with McSween against the 'Ring' led by Dolan and Murphy. His death in 1884 helped end the Lincoln County war.

Above: Thomas Graham, leader of the Graham faction. He did his best to break the feud, but finally had to make a stand. He was murdered in 1892 by Ed Tewksbury and John Rhodes who escaped justice on a technicality. With Graham's death the feud was over.

JOHN WESLEY HARDIN

Recalling post-Civil War Texas, and his feelings about blacks, John Wesley Hardin wrote: 'In those times if there was anything that could rouse my passion it was seeing impudent Negroes lately freed insult or abuse old, wounded Confederates who were decrepit, weak, or old . . .' One such bully he 'tamed' with the threat of a bullet to heaven, and noted that to 'be tried at that time for the killing of a Negro meant certain death at the hands of a court, backed by Northern bayonets . . .' We may not condone his and others' views or behavior, but we can understand it.

It was said of him that his pistol had 'forty notches' cut into its stock. The notches are fictional but the tally is probably correct, for John Wesley Hardin ranks as probably the most homicidal of all the noted Texas bad men. Born in 1853, he was still a child when the Civil War broke out, yet its effect upon the South and particularly Texas following the defeat of the Confederacy in 1865 was marked. Like many of his contemporaries, Hardin hated blacks, and when the Union army, backed by politicians and later the detested State Police, employed them to keep the peace, trouble was inevitable.

Hardin's first recorded killing was that of a former slave named Mage who incurred his wrath during a visit to an uncle's ranch. Wes claimed that Mage had threatened him, so he ambushed and killed him. Later, he killed three black soldiers who were ordered to bring him in.

By the late 1860s, Hardin was noted for his quick temper and readiness to use a pistol to settle an argument rather than discuss it. When he came up the Chisholm Trail to Kansas in 1871 as a member of Columbus Carroll's outfit, he killed a number of Mexicans who crossed him, and by the time he left Abilene some months later, eight men had died at his hand! In Abilene he met up with Wild Bill Hickok who made it plain that he would tolerate no nonsense. In his posthumously published autobiography, Wes claimed to have

Right: According to family sources, this photograph of Wes was made at Abilene in 1871. The nearest photographer was A.P. Trott at Junction City which is where we believe this was made. The original is a tintype or 'mirror' image.

Below: Hardin's .41 caliber 'Thunderer', a nickel-plated ivory-stocked version. These were Colt's first double-action revolvers. The actions were unreliable. The playing card was 'autographed' by Wes just over a month before his death. Note Hardin's business card.

JOHN W. HARDIN Esq.
ATTORNEY AT LAW

OFFICE:
200½ El Paso
Wells Fargo Bldg.

PRACTICE IN
ALL COURTS

Below: El Paso, the famous border town on the Rio Grande, in its early years. Here Hardin was murdered in 1895.

Above: John Wesley Hardin, jaw set firmly, stares at the camera, and looks mean.

1853
John Wesley Hardin born Bonham, Texas, the son of a Methodist circuit preacher

1871
Hardin shoots two black state policemen in Smiley, Texas, one of whom survives

1877
Hardin arrested on a train at Pensacola, Florida, by Texas Ranger John Armstrong. Imprisonment follows

1895
Hardin shot dead in the Acme Saloon, El Paso, by John Selman

Artifacts courtesy of Gene Autry Western Heritage Museum, Los Angeles, California

worked the 'border roll' on Hickok as the marshal reached for his pistols, but no one believed that. In fact, Hardin wrote to his wife expressing his admiration for Hickok, and there are those who believe that he idolized Wild Bill.

Back in Texas, Wes went from scrape to scrape, and even found time to involve himself in the Sutton–Taylor feud (on the Taylors' side), before disappearing to Florida where he was arrested by the Texas Rangers in 1877. Imprisoned at Huntsville, Wes spent much of his time studying law and eventually passed his bar examination. In 1894, he was parolled and moved to Gonzales, Texas, and later to El Paso. Wes had quietened down, but he drank too much and was often in trouble. His reputation as a gunfighter and an excellent shot (he 'autographed' a number of playing cards with his six-shooter) made him a character to be avoided. But on the night of 19 August 1895, as he stood drinking at the bar of the Acme Saloon, John Selman, a policeman and himself a noted gunfighter, stepped up behind him and shot him in the back.

Any study of Hardin reveals a very complex character. Depending upon one's view, he emerges as a homicidal maniac or a misunderstood individual who used violence rather than debate to settle personal disputes. His present-day reputation (outside Texas, at any rate) is not good, but one is left with the feeling that had circumstances been different, and had his aggressive tendencies been channeled in the direction of the law at an early age, he could have become a much respected advocate. Instead, it is his reputation as a killer that is remembered.

Right: John Selman's .45 with its barrel cut back to 5 in., to make it easier to hide and draw. A number of the old-timers used short-barreled pistols which they often carried in their coat or hip pockets.

Below: The murder of Hardin was widely condemned by Wes's friends and the drawing shows the layout of the Acme Saloon that night.

Above: A photograph reputed to be of Jim Taylor, who killed Bill Sutton. But some believe that it is a photograph of a man with the same name, Jim 'Fancy Jim' Taylor who was also a friend of John Wesley Hardin's. The 'Jim Taylor' was killed in 1875.

Above: John Armstrong, who looks more like a banker than a Texas Ranger, pursued Hardin to Florida and arrested him on a train at Pensacola. Wes's pistol got caught in his suspenders, otherwise his 'tally' would have been increased.

Above: John Selman, the man who gunned down John Wesley Hardin without giving him a chance for his life. Selman was himself killed a year later by George Scarborough, who survived until 1900 when he was killed by rustlers.

BILLY THE KID

His photograph shows him to be buck-toothed, slack-jawed and with an expression that suggests he might have been mentally retarded. But what Billy the Kid might have lacked in looks, he more than made up for in animal cunning. So much so that for more than a century he has captivated historians, folklorists and songwriters, all anxious to pore over the mystique of a 'two-bit hoodlum' who became a legend and continues to arouse bitter controversy. And, as historian Robert Utley remarks, 'few people from the past have so profoundly stirred the human imagination'.

The myth of Billy the Kid is one of the more enduring of the Old West legends. In folklore, Billy is portrayed as a young rebel (which may account for his youthful appeal) whose involvements in the Lincoln County cattle war did much to perpetuate both his own and the feud's reputation. Yet his place in folklore still exacerbates some of the more cynical historians and buffs. In truth, the 'Kid' did little to justify his myth. He was born in New York City in 1859, and his real name was Henry McCarty. In later life he went under the name of William H.

Right: Pat Garrett dressed in the mode of the time, a far cry from the 'cowboy image' so beloved of fiction writers.

Below: Two famous participants in the Lincoln County war. Seated is James Dolan and standing is Robert ('Bob') Ollinger who was blasted to death by Billy the Kid.

Above: Pat Garrett, the 'slayer of Billy the Kid', a reputation he came to hate.

1850
Patrick Floyd Garrett born in Alabama, spending his early adult life as a buffalo hunter and cowboy

1859
'Billy the Kid' born Henry McCarty in New York

1878
The murder of the Englishman John Tunstall touches off the Lincoln County war in which the Kid becomes involved

1881
The Kid kills deputy sheriff Bob Ollinger while making his escape from jail. Three months later, he himself is shot dead by Pat Garrett

Artifacts courtesy of Gene Autry Western Heritage Museum, Los Angeles, California

Bonney, or Henry Antrim (the name of his stepfather). His father is believed to have died when he was very young, and his mother moved via Indiana and Wichita, Kansas, to Silver City, New Mexico, where she died in 1874.

In his 'teens Henry proved to be a handful, and is reported to have been in trouble several times with the local law. He was nicknamed 'Kid' Antrim, and his later use of the name 'William' or 'Billy' led naturally to his legendary tag 'Billy the Kid'. A blacksmith named Cahill is reported to have bullied the boy and received a bullet in return which did not prove fatal. Arrested, the Kid escaped, and fled to Mesilla and from there to Lincoln County where he worked for a time for John Chisum. Here he also met the Englishman John Tunstall, whose later murder at the instigation of Lawrence G. Murphy, one of the leaders of several individuals who were determined to dominate both the county and the cattle business. Alexander McSween, who had sworn to avenge Tunstall's death, welcomed the Kid to his ranks, and soon the 'war' was raging.

Billy the Kid's reputation as a killer abounded, and it is a part of his myth that he killed twenty-one men – one for each year of his life – but the true figure is probably closer to six. However, such a reputation soon gained him notoriety in high places. When McSween was killed in a five-day siege of his home (the Kid barely escaped with his life), his faction, now without a leader, was regarded as the losers and perpetrators of the original feud, and a territory-wide hunt was on for them. By 1879, however, even the governor

Above: James J. Dolan was a ruthless, hard-headed businessman who cared more for cash than he did for people. An active supporter of the so-called 'Santa Fe Ring' of Republicans, he sought to control the economic life of New Mexico.

Left: This case was designed to hold the nickel-plated Merwin & Hulbert .38 caliber double-action revolver with Garrett's name engraved into the ivory stock. Garrett used a .45 caliber Colt Peacemaker when he killed the Kid.

Above: Lawrence G. Murphy was able to gain control of government contracts for Indian beef and he had other irons in the fire of political and economic ambition. For a time he and his partner controlled law enforcement in the territory.

Left: Lincoln, New Mexico, from a photograph taken in 1885. It shows a number of buildings important to the events of 1878, notably the stores owned by Dolan and Tunstall.

Right: This letter is addressed to deputy U.S. Marshal Bob Ollinger and is dated 5 April 1880, advising him that warrants had been issued for 'Kid Antrim' and others. The letter also indicates how confused even his contemporaries were over the Kid's real name.

(General Lew Wallace, at that time engaged in writing his best-selling novel *Ben Hur*) called a truce and a meeting was arranged between him and the Kid. A pardon was promised if the Kid would testify in the case of the murder of a lawyer named Chapman. He agreed, but when Chapman's alleged murderers escaped Billy did the same.

There were reports of other killings, and this time the governor was determined that the Kid should be brought in and placed on trial. In an effort to achieve this, he ordered Pat Garrett, newly elected sheriff of the county, and a man who knew the Kid personally, to bring him in. Patrick Floyd Garrett was born in 1850 in Alabama, but spent his adult life in the West where he became a buffalo hunter, cowboy, and other occupations before becoming sheriff of Lincoln County and the nemesis of Billy the Kid.

Garrett captured the Kid and some companions at a place called Stinking Springs, about twenty-five miles from Fort Sumner. Placed on trial, the Kid was convicted and sentenced to be hanged. But before sentences could be carried out he made his escape by overpowering one of his guards and shooting the other one, Bob Ollinger, with a shotgun as he ran toward the jail. The Kid then casually mounted a horse and was gone. But not for long. Garrett was again on his trail and during the night of 14–15 July 1881, while he was hiding out at Pete Maxwell's house at Fort Sumner, Garrett surprised him as he entered Maxwell's bedroom. Seeing a figure in the dark, Billy called out: 'Quien es?' ('Who is it?') and was answered by a bullet. He was dead before he hit the floor.

Pat Garrett lived to become the favorite of politicians (among them President Teddy

Above: John Tunstall, the young Englishman whose death sparked off the Lincoln County war, arrived in New Mexico in 1876. Born at Dalston, London, in 1853, he was one of many British-born entrepreneurs in the American West.

Above: Alexander McSween, from a photograph believed to have been made at Topeka, Kansas. As a fledgling lawyer he had hung out his shingle at Eureka, about 55 miles from Wichita, where in 1871 young Henry McCarty spent some of his formative years.

Above: Sheriff William Brady, who is alleged to have been implicated when Tunstall was ambushed and killed following the attachment on his stock following allegations of rustling (never proved), was himself murdered by the Kid from ambush.

Right: This Whitney-Kennedy .44-40 caliber carbine is alleged to have been given by the Kid to deputy U.S. Marshal Eugene V. Patten.

Right: Henry McCarty, alias 'Kid' Antrim, alias William H. Bonney, alias 'Billy the Kid'. The original is a tintype so the image has been reversed to lose the mirror effect. The Kid wears his pistol on his hip, as was the custom of the time.

Below: The Pete Maxwell house where the Kid was shot to death during the night of 14–15 July 1881.

Left: The Murphy–Dolan store, c. 1884. Among the crowd is John W. Poe who was with Garrett the night he shot the Kid. Lincoln, like Tombstone, has hardly changed over the years.

Right: The fine silver cased watch presented to Garrett by grateful citizens of Lincoln County after the shooting.

Roosevelt who appointed him collector of customs at El Paso, Texas, in 1901) and to be reminded frequently that he was the slayer of Billy the Kid. In 1908 he was murdered. There were reports of financial problems and that he was having rows with Carl Anderson and Wayne Brazel. Both men are credited with his murder (their accounts are confusing), but some claim that the notorious arch assassin Jim Miller may have been the killer. But whoever it was who pulled the trigger on Pat could not wipe out the fact that he will always be remembered as the man who killed Billy the Kid. The irony is, of course, that few people know much about Pat Garrett, but Billy the Kid is world famous.

Below: Almost overnight, the Kid became a dime novel hero and in time came to symbolize the 'rebel' in the eyes of youth.

Above: John William Poe, from a photograph made in 1881. He waited until 1919 to write his own memoir of the event that led to the shooting of the Kid, and it differs from Pat Garrett's version. He later succeeded Garrett as sheriff of Lincoln County.

PRICE, 25 CENTS.

BILLY THE KID.
A ROMANTIC STORY OF LIFE IN THE GREAT WILD WEST.
Founded Upon the Play by Walter Woods and Joseph Santley.
ARDA LA CROIX, Author.

"I LOVE YOU, NELLIE, I HAVE ALWAYS LOVED YOU."
As Played by LEROY E. SUMNER, Young America's Favorite Actor.
Management of CHAS. H. WUERZ.

WYATT EARP

The 'Gunfight at the O.K. Corral' was one of the most controversial of such encounters in the history of the Old West. Wild Bill Hickok's shoot-out with Dave Tutt at Springfield, Mo., in 1865, when both men opened fire as they walked toward each other, established the 'walk 'n draw' duel, but the Earp–Clanton confrontation was more than a personal settling of accounts: there are hints of behind-the-scenes disputes involving local politics and economic rivalries.

B y the early years of the twentieth century, Wyatt Earp and Doc Holliday were remembered as characters from another era. Doc was long dead and Wyatt was occasionally written up in a magazine or a newspaper, his most prolific fan being none other than Bat Masterson, himself one of the Old West's famous characters. By this time, of course, Earp was an old man in his seventies. But the name still commanded some interest and, living in California as he then was, it soon put him in touch with the likes of William S. Hart and later Tom Mix, two of the cinema's most popular cowboy stars. Later, Earp was to meet a journalist named Stuart N. Lake who, following Wyatt's death in 1929, wrote a biography of his hero that is as controversial today as it was when it was first published. As a result, the real Wyatt Earp remains something of an enigma.

The Earp brothers formed part of a large family: besides Wyatt there was Virgil, Morgan, James, Warren, a half-brother named Newton, and a sister Adelia. Wyatt, Virgil and Morgan earned reputations as gunfighters, gamblers, saloon-keepers, miners and peace officers. They were a clannish family, whose exploits did not always endear them to their contemporaries, but thanks to Lake (and Walter Noble Burns) their lives and adventures were widely publicized – and sanitized

Below: Allen Street, Tombstone, at about the time of the October 1881 'Gunfight at the O.K. Corral'. It was while he was sitting in a barber's shop on Allen Street that Sheriff John Behan heard that the Earps and Holliday were on their way to the corral to 'arrest' the Clanton faction. This photograph graphically depicts the raw frontier town.

Above: *'Doc' Holliday, photographed some years before his lifestyle, and tuberculosis, killed him.*

1848
Wyatt Earp born in Monmouth, Illinois

1876
Earp becomes a policeman in Dodge City; he resigns in September 1879

1879
Virgil, James and Wyatt Earp arrive in Tombstone, Arizona Territory

1881
Gunfight at the OK Corrall goes down in history. The Clantons and McLaurys suffer at the hands of the Earps and Doc Holliday

1882
Morgan Earp is murdered while playing billiards in Tombstone

Artifacts courtesy of Gene Autry Western Heritage Museum, Los Angeles, California

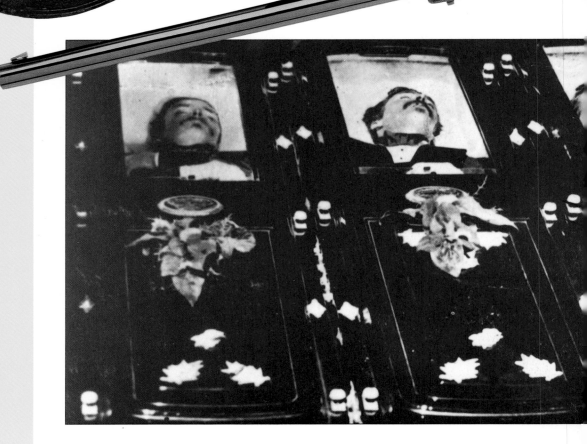

for public consumption.

Like most of the well-known Western gunfighters, the Earps emerge either as noble upholders of the law or vicious, unprincipled thieves, conmen and frauds, depending upon whose side the writers are on, or how much attention has been paid to factual reporting. Wyatt has been singled out as the main character, although Virgil is thought to have been the real leader of the bunch. Nevertheless, it was Wyatt's exploits that inspired the adulation or controversy that has surrounded the family for generations. He served as a constable at Lamar, Missouri, in 1870 (beating his half-brother Newton in the election). He married, but lost his wife to typhoid fever. Wyatt then drifted into Indian Territory where he was arrested for horse-stealing, but escaped to Kansas where he worked as a buffalo hunter. He

Above: Wyatt Berry Stapp Earp, whose reputation as a gunfighter was established at the O.K. Corral. Before then, his exploits in Kansas, where he had proved to be a useful police officer, had not convinced the public of his 'killer instinct'.

later appeared at Wichita where he served briefly as an assistant marshal. But problems with the city council (James's wife was fined for operating a brothel), and a falling out with the city marshal, Bill Smith, led to his dismissal. From Wichita, Wyatt went to Dodge City where he achieved a good reputation on the police force. From Dodge City Wyatt moved on to Tombstone, Arizona Territory, then the center of attention for its silver deposits. Here he was joined by Virgil and Morgan and the redoubtable Doc Holliday.

John Holliday was born in Griffin, Georgia, in 1851 and was reared into the genteel traditions of the South. In 1872, he graduated from the Pennsylvania College of Dental Surgery, but when he learned that he was suffering from tuberculosis (and also a bad reputation for trouble-making), Holliday went West for his health. Soon he had made a reputation as a 'bad man to fool with' and was generally called 'Doc'. He continued to practise dentistry and set up in business at Dodge City where he met Wyatt. The unlikely pair became friends and, when the Earps moved to Tombstone, Doc followed them.

Wyatt's political ambitions, a falling out with the local 'rustlers' and other problems led eventually to the celebrated Gunfight at the OK Corral in which Wyatt, Morgan and Doc, deputized by city marshal Virgil Earp, shot it out with the Clantons and McLaurys on 21 October 1881. The Earp faction was exonerated following a lengthy court of enquiry, but their reputations suffered. Morgan was murdered soon after the O.K. Corral shoot-out and Virgil was ambushed and crippled. Wyatt subsequently killed one of the alleged assassins. Doc died from galloping consumption in 1887. In later years, Wyatt achieved a reputation as a gambler and speculator, and in 1896 he refereed the controversial Sharkey-Fitzsimmons boxing fight. A spell in the Klondyke and other ventures kept Wyatt occupied until late in life. The adulation heaped upon him in his last years probably caused him some ironic amusement. His fame, nonetheless, was assured.

Above: Morgan Earp, Wyatt's younger brother whose participation in the O.K. Corral fight led to his death from ambush as he played pool in a saloon. Normally a 'pleasant outgoing' sort of man, he was nonetheless known to be a hothead.

Left: A Colt .45 'Peacemaker' with a 16 in. barrel, complete with a factory supplied holster and a metal 'skeleton' stock to turn it into a rifle. It was claimed that in 1876 Ned Buntline presented such a weapon to Wyatt Earp.

Left: Laid out in ornate glass-fronted coffins are Tom McLaury, Frank McLaury and Billy Clanton, described by some as 'murdered on the streets of Tombstone' by the Earps. This notorious gunfight has become probably the most famous shoot-out in the history of the Old West. No matter how one views the evidence, it remains controversial among pro- and anti-Earp protagonists.

Right: This diagram of the 'O.K. Corral Gunfight' was drawn by Wyatt Earp in later years. During the hearing that followed the fight, he was allowed to read from a prepared statement concerning what happened.

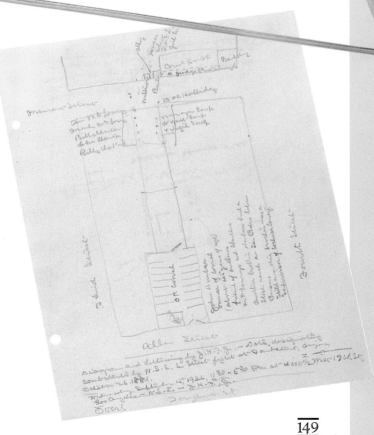

Above: Virgil Earp, regarded by many as the true leader of the Earp faction. He was city marshal of Tombstone at the time of the shoot-out, and also held a commission as a deputy United States Marshal. His action in deputizing his brothers had met with criticism.

INDIAN TERRITORY

'Indian Territory', that piece of land on the Chisholm Trail that separated Texas from Kansas, has long been a focal point when discussing outlawry in the Old West. Here men on the run from the law sought sanctuary and for a long time escaped justice. But when Judge Parker's merry band of deputy U.S. Marshals started riding into the territory to seek them out, shoot-outs between good and bad, Indian and white became common. Parker used white, black and Indians to uphold or impose law and order, and a number of them died trying to do their duty.

In the early nineteenth century, as the pressure for Indian land became greater, and Indian resistance repeatedly broke out in the form of uprisings and massacres, especially in Alabama, the government sought a solution in treaties like the Dancing Rabbit agreement of 1830 in which whole tribes agreed to leave their ancestral homes in return for substantial gifts, monetary concessions, and a large new homeland west of the Mississippi. There lay an unsettled wilderness south of Missouri and north of Texas, and to it authorities sent scattered portions of some tribes, and then wholesale the Five Civilized Tribes – namely the Creek, Chickasaw, Choctaw, Cherokee and Seminole. At Tahlequah the Cherokee established a capital for their new domain, and there they ruled more or less without interference from Washington for many years. Indeed, the native Americans lived relatively undisturbed until the Civil War, when both North and South courted them, and in the end the tribes split their allegiance.

More or less true to its word, Washington protected the Indians in their new land, and tried honestly to prevent whites from illegally moving in and settling on Indian land. But after the war pressures began to grow increasingly strong. Arkansas had already been made into a state before the Civil War, leaving the Indian Territory now pinched between two Southern states full of land-hungry farmers. Moreover, in the aftermath of the war, the lawless element North and South

Right: Ned Christie, shown in death, was a Cherokee who had worked as a blacksmith, gunsmith, whiskey runner and horsethief. When he shot a deputy U.S. Marshal, he was a wanted man. He was killed in 1892.

Far right: Crawford Goldsby, alias 'Cherokee Bill', who was part white, part Cherokee and part Mexican, and displayed the worst traits of all three races. At his hanging he declined to make a statement.

Bottom: The Rufus Buck Gang who carried out 'thirteen days of terror' before being apprehended by a posse of U.S. Marshals and Indian police. The jury hardly deliberated over their verdict. They were hanged in 1896.

Above: Judge Parker, known as 'the hanging judge', sent many a man to meet his maker.

1803
The Territory becomes a part of the United States

1819
Spain and the United States agree on the Red River as the international border

1830
'The Indian Removal Act' enables the government to force the Five Civilized Tribes to relocate in the territory

1907
Indian Territory becomes the state of Oklahoma

Artifacts courtesy of Buffalo Bill Historical Center, Cody, Wyoming

Above: Bass Reeves, one of a number of blacks who became famous as deputy U.S. Marshals in Indian Territory. An estimated sixty-five black, red and white deputies died in the territory when attempting to enforce law and order. Bass survived into old age.

Above and left: A Winchester 1873 .44 caliber saddle carbine. Note how the action cocks the hammer and ejects the 'shells'. A box of cartridges is below it.

Below: A hanging in 'the Territory'. Westerners had a fine sense of the macabre on such occasions. Even the condemned man seems impressed.

Above: Henry Andrew ('Heck') Thomas was one of the great early day Oklahoma marshals. He learned a lot from Longhaired Jim Courtright, and later Bill Tilghman. He was serving as chief of police at Lawton, Ok, when he died in 1912.

began to take refuge west of the Mississippi. Texas teemed with bandits, gunfighters, cattle rustlers, and more. To escape the law in white society, such men often escaped into the Indian Territory, which became a murky no-man's-land. Law of a sort prevailed, but more in name than fact, and such desperate characters as Ned Christie, Cherokee Bill, and more, lived a remote life in hiding until their next sally out.

To protect the Indians and maintain some kind of order, the government built Fort Gibson and stationed a small garrison of soldiers there. Moreover, at Fort Smith, Arkansas, Washington established a territorial court and appointed Judge Isaac Parker to preside. Quickly known as 'the hanging judge', Parker exerted virtual one-man rule, meting out the harshest sentences for the most minor infractions. Operating on warrants from his court, federal officers went deep into the Indian lands to track malefactors and bring them back. The mere theft of a horse or cow could bring a sentence of death from Parker, though in one case when the rustler turned out to be over seventy years old, the hanging judge simply told him to go home and stop acting like a foolish old man.

The Indian Territory remained largely a lawless place until late in the century. The settlement of lands to its west in the Cimarron and other land 'runs' brought whites in by thousands, and with them came pressure for more formalized law and order. Finally their new territory and the old Indian Territory were joined into one – under white domination, of course – and in 1907 they became the state of Oklahoma.

Above: William ('Bill') Tilghman, who first made his name at Dodge City and later in the Territory and early day Oklahoma. He was one of the most respected of the state's early peace officers. He was murdered at Cromwell, Oklahoma, in 1924.

OKLAHOMA LAND RUSH

Interest in Indian Territory for settlement was not sudden, for in the early 1870s there had been those who thought that it would eventually end up either as a separate state or perhaps tacked on to Texas or Kansas. But its destiny lay in self-determination as a state – Oklahoma. Remembering how quickly 'treaties' were broken or 'interpreted', cynics might be forgiven for thinking that it was yet another government ploy to steal Indian land. But the land made available was not a part of the Indian grants. And once the signal was given to move in, the rush was on.

Above: Guthrie in 1889, the opening of the Cherokee strip. A makeshift town grows.

1875
The government encourages Plains Indians to move into the Territory

1885
About fifty Indian tribes are represented in the Territory on land once promised to the Five Civilized Tribes

1887
Arrival of the Atchison, Topeka and Santa Fe Railroad en route for Fort Worth and beyond

Americans approached an emotional and psychological crisis as the end of the nineteenth century neared. For almost 300 years there had been an inexhaustible supply of cheap land, always over the horizon. But now the continent had been bridged and girdled by railroads, cut up into dozens of states, the natives contained, the prairies fenced. The 'frontier' was about to be a thing of the past, and with it the inexpensive land that had always been the symbol of opportunity that, itself, symbolized the West.

The last opportunity for cheap land seemed to reside in the Indian Territory, that large expanse once given to the Five Civilized Tribes because presumably no one else wanted it. The area was heading toward statehood, bringing with it a huge tract of acreage not part of the Indian grants, and still public land. Interests in Washington pressed for opening this land to the public, even though technically some 2 million acres of it still belonged to the Indians but had been taken away in punishment for their siding with the Confederacy during the Civil War. Congress settled the issued by keeping the land, paying the Indians $1.25 per acre for it, and then prepared to open it to settlement in a very distinctive fashion.

On 22 April 1889, a portion of the land would be made available for homesteading claims on a first-come, first-served basis. Wouldbe claimants must assemble at a starting-point, and when an official fired a signal gun, they would race to drive their stakes, setting off their claims. Some 50,000 gathered for the first of several 'runs', to open the Cimarron or 'Panhandle' strip. Upon instructions, they swarmed around three sides of the area to be given away, it having already been surveyed into plots. Then as the gun went off, so did they, some on foot, others in buggies, on horseback, even bicycles. Not a few decided to leave nothing to chance; they stole into the Territory early to locate plots they wanted. There they illegally drove their stakes, and on 22 April simply raced for those spots and seemingly had their claims made sooner than others. They gave a name to Oklahomans, ever-after to be known as 'Sooners'.

Right: This poster is dated 1879, and is graphic evidence of the interest already being shown in the Indian Territory. Note the reference to 1866 purchases from Indians.

Below: Wouldbe settlers gather for the land rush. An estimated 50,000 people joined in the race when the signal gun was fired. The army watched out for 'Sooners' jumping the gun.

Below: The scene at noon on 22 April 1889, when the signal was given for the rush to begin. Settlers who had lived on land for seven years kept it free.

The first 'run' lasted less than a day, but there would be several to follow. Other Oklahoma land was parceled out by lotteries, and large portions of the opened land soon found itself organized into the Oklahoma Territory, named for an Indian word that meant 'red man'. Later it merged with the Indian Territory still owned by the Cherokee and others, and became the state of Oklahoma. In the wake of the 'runs' whole towns appeared almost overnight, populated by 'sooners' and others, and filled with the inevitable entrepreneurs who came to profit by selling goods to the new farmers. By 1890 the land rushes were done and most of the government acreage had been staked. With almost poetic fittingness, the last of the frontier had been not conquered but dealt out almost like a casino game, going in the end to those who were a little faster, a little smarter, or a little more willing to bend the rules.

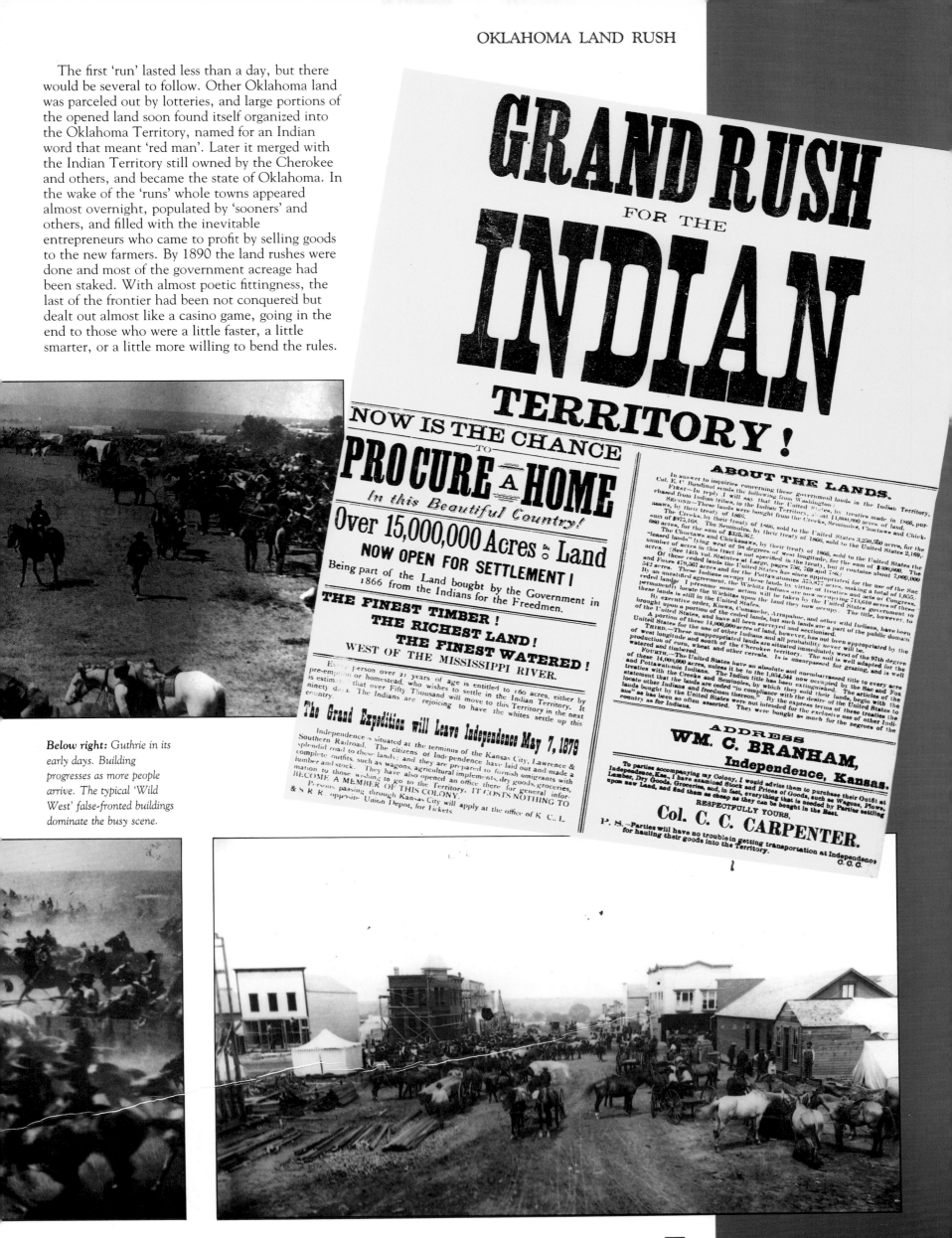

Below right: Guthrie in its early days. Building progresses as more people arrive. The typical 'Wild West' false-fronted buildings dominate the busy scene.

'Oklahoma Land Rush', 22 April
1889, by H. Charles McBarron
(Courtesy Peter Newark's Western
Americana)

TOM HORN

Few Western characters have stirred up as much controversy as has Tom Horn, not for what he did, but more in the manner of his going. For a man who worked for the Pinkerton Detective Agency, tracking down bank robbers, mine company payroll thieves and other criminals, his purported role as a bushwacking assassin in range wars and ultimately as the alleged murderer of a fourteen-year-old boy, conflicts with his other exploits as an army scout and interpreter. And his death at the hands of the hangman left many questions unanswered.

Above: Tom Horn sits in jail, a study in patience (or anticipation?), a self-made hemp rope in hand.

1860
Tom Horn born in Memphis, Missouri

1875–86
As a scout, Tom Horn helps to track down Geronimo and other militant Apaches in the Southwest

1890
Horn enlists as a range detective with the Wyoming Cattle Growers' Association

1901
Fourteen-year-old Willie Nickell is found shot dead. Horn is blamed and subsequently imprisoned for murder

1903
In November, Tom Horn is hanged in Cheyenne for Nickell's murder. A century later, his name is cleared

Artifacts courtesy of Gene Autry Western Heritage Museum, Los Angeles, California

In 1993, ninety years after Tom Horn's death, a court re-examined the evidence (some of which had not been presented at the original trial) for which he had been found guilty and hanged all those years before. This time he was found not guilty. Tom Horn, ex-cowboy, bronco buster, army scout, mule packer (for the Rough Riders in Cuba) and (according to some) hired gunman for the big cattle outfits in Wyoming, would probably have smiled ironically at the verdict. For in the weeks before, during and after his trial, he had been frustrated by the way things were going. When he learned, on 23 October 1903, that his reprieve had been turned down, he wrote to John Coble, a former employer and one of the many cattlemen who had befriended him, and remarked that his friends had 'made a gallant fight and lost. I knew in my own mind that they would loose [sic] from the time that I first came to trial. I don't know what can be done now and from what the lawyers told me I guess I am in the last ditch . . .' He also urged those who could save him to tell the truth, but for whatever reason no one did, and on 20 November (on the eve of his forty-third birthday) he was hanged.

This was a sad and sordid end for a man who, in the opinion of many of those who knew him, deserved much better. Born in 1860, Horn led a varied life until 1875 when he met Al Sieber, chief army scout at the San Carlos Indian reservation. Horn's ability to speak Spanish, and his early grasp of the Apache language, impressed Sieber who soon took advantage of his linguistic and tracking abilities. From 1875 until 1886, Tom Horn was on the trail of Geronimo and other warlike Apaches. Tom even claimed that he was the man who set up the famous leader's final surrender to General Nelson A. Miles in Skeleton Canyon. Some army officers, however, disputed his claim, while others defended it. Envy probably played a part in the reaction of his critics, for like many frontiersmen Horn attracted much attention, which was often bitterly resented.

There is evidence to suggest that he was involved in both the Graham–Tewksbury sheep war and the Johnson County cattle war. He was

Below: Handcuffs were the 'bracelets of brigands' and their use led to a number of refinements. This pair is believed to be circa 1894 and are of a basic design.

Above right: Tom Horn, despite his pending date with the hangman, looks strangely at ease. By now he was reconciled to his fate and faced it bravely.

Right: The street scene when Tom Horn was hanged. The troops were called in in case of any civil disturbance, but in the event there were no demonstrations.

Right: Following his sentencing, Tom made one bid to escape, but was recaptured. Here he is being returned to jail accompanied by a crowd anxious to see him. The photograph also shows how times had changed. Small boys now ride bicycles instead of ponies, and the place looks like any other small town of the day.

Above: General Nelson Miles, who replaced General Crook in the pursuit of Geronimo. His chief of scouts, Al Sieber, employed Tom Horn as a scout and interpreter who proved his worth and tracked the wily Chiricahua leader to his lair.

an expert horseman, and his experience with cattle led to him winning the steer-roping contest held at Phoenix in 1891. But it was his ability with a gun that is best remembered. Unlike most gunfighters, Horn was not noted for his quick trigger finger but for his marksmanship. Rumors abounded linking him with range killings on the orders of various cattlemen. He was said to 'ambush' alleged 'rustlers' with a high-powered rifle, and his trade mark was to place a couple of rocks beneath his victim's head to guarantee his six hundred dollar fee.

Most of the allegations made against Tom Horn were hearsay but no one doubts that he was a killer. What is not clear, however, is whether his killings were planned or provoked. And, of course, there was his drinking. Periodically, Tom would leave for Denver and spend time whooping it up in saloons and telling outrageous stories about himself. When, in 1901, Willie Nickell, a fourteen-year-old boy, was found murdered, Tom was implicated. Later, it was alleged that he had boasted about it. Joe Lefors, a lawman, was ordered to bring him in. He found him in his usual haunts at Denver. Pretending friendship, Lefors got him drunk and claimed that Horn confessed to the killing. He was arrested, placed on trial and, despite an able defense (furnished by his cattlemen friends), the jury believed his 'confession' and found him guilty.

The recent (1990s) re-enactment of his trial was the culmination of controversy over his alleged guilt that has raged since his death.

Above: This photograph is reputed to be that of Willie Nickell, the fourteen-year-old boy allegedly murdered by Tom Horn in a drunken 'confession'. Willie was the son of Kels P. Nickell, who was in dispute with Tom's boss, and friend, John Coble.

Above: Joseph Lefors, whose reputation as a lawman was suspect according to some, and to others he was the ideal choice to bring in Tom Horn. Lefors' ploy was to convince Tom that he was a friend, and then get him drunk enough to 'confess' to the killing.

JOHNSON COUNTY WAR

According to *Frank Leslie's Weekly* of 2 June 1892, the 'expedition of the large cattle-owners in northern Wyoming is an event that has attracted attention throughout the entire country'. The report then suggested that a 'professional exagerator' had stirred up interest in what was a common event – that 'men who had for years suffered from the depredations of thieves should at least organize with a determination to exterminate the outlaws, is nothing new or strange'. But to the innocents among the so-called 'rustlers' it was a matter of grave concern.

Above: The 'Regulators' in this rarely seen photograph get ready to destroy the rustlers.

1862

Homestead Act allows an individual to claim up to 160 acres of public land. This proves an early upset to the cattle barons who believe they own the range

1886

A bitter winter in the northern states wipes out huge numbers of cattle, prompting cattle owners to reassess their approach to stockraising. Sodbusters move onto the range

1892

Forty-six 'Regulators' employed by the Wyoming Cattle Growers' Association gather at Casper to combat so-called rustlers. 'Local heroes' Nick Ray and Nate Champion are killed

Artifact courtesy Buffalo Bill Historical Center, Cody, Wyoming

The range wars, as we have noted elsewhere, tended to revolve around greed, power and possessions. And if one were to pick on one single event (apart from the Lincoln County war) it would have to be the Johnson County cattle war of 1892. For it had all the ingredients beloved by novelists and film directors – cattle barons, cowboys, gunfighters, rustlers, nesters and even the U.S. cavalry.

The animosity between the cattlemen and settlers in Wyoming had been growing for some years, but it was Johnson County that bore the brunt of it. Situated about 250 miles northwest of Cheyenne, it was excellent cattle country. Its popularity meant that some of the larger outfits found themselves short-handed when their cowboys resigned and took advantage of the Homestead Act of 1862 which allowed an individual to claim up to 160 acres of public land, providing he worked it for a minimum of five years. Of course, one could claim it earlier, six months after possession in fact, but then it cost $1.25 an acre. This is a small sum compared to current rates, but for someone earning only $30 a month as a cowboy, it was a fortune. Even if one were fortunate enough to buy the land, and it was close to one of the large cattle outfits, that could mean trouble.

The Texas, Wyoming and Montana cattlemen were jealous of their possessions and wealth. Despite the legality of claims under the Act, some of them tended to think themselves above the law. Indeed, they were not called 'barons' or 'kings' for nothing. Their domain was an 'empire' and miserable 'sodbusters' or 'nesters' (although many of them preferred 'rustler') were unwelcome intruders. The majority of the newcomers were hard-working, but were regarded in the same light as those who, rather than work toward building a herd of their own, preferred to take in 'strays' from the bigger outfits. Naturally, if such people were caught, they were shot or hanged, or if they were very lucky, severely beaten up and their shacks burned and their own stock run off. This kind of treatment was often meted out in the name of the

Right: The man leaning against the wheel, second from right, is purported to be Nate Champion, photographed circa 1884 when he worked for the Bar C Ranch. He later worked for himself, which proved to be a fatal move.

Below: A page from the Wyoming Stock Growers' Association's Brand Book of 1885. A clever 'running iron' expert could soon change most brands, and some were good enough to fool the experts.

Left: Three prominent figures in the Johnson County war. Dudley Champion, Al Alison and, it is claimed, Nate Champion. According to most published accounts, during the siege of his cabin that finally led to his death, Nate wrote down an indictment against his attackers.

Right: A barn at Nolan's KC Ranch near Casper. On this ranch Nick Ray and Nate Champion were besieged by the wealthy stock owners' hired gunmen from Texas. Under the direction of Major Wolcott their bolt hole was set on fire. Ray was dead by then, but the flames drove Champion into the open, where he in turn was gunned down.

Above: James Averill, whose political ambitions did not sit well with the cattlemen. His repeated attacks upon their methods led finally to his death at the hands of the cattlemen who lynched him and his cohort and paramour 'Cattle Kate'.

rancher by his foreman or manager, for the man himself was probably an 'absent landlord' who may have lived as far away as England or Scotland. This feudal approach did not endear itself to friend or foe, and juries in particular were reluctant to convict alleged 'rustlers' of beef from absentee owners.

Determined to combat the real and alleged rustlers, the barons then hired 'detectives' to hunt them down. Until 1886 the Wyoming cattle ranges were overstocked. Then came two disasters that changed things for ever. First there was a great drought, followed in 1887 by a great blizzard that wiped out many of the herds. This called for a complete change of attitude. New herds were carefully controlled and care was taken with their grazing areas. It was then that the trouble really came to a head. Large numbers of 'sodbusters' moving in on what was regarded as 'open range'

Above: Ella ('Cattle Kate') Watson, whose alleged liaison with known rustlers led to her being lynched along with Jim Averill. The affair outraged the county, but nothing was done to avenge the pair. The 'sodbusters' were not yet strong enough to resist.

Above: The odious Frank Canton whose nefarious past as Joe Horner did not come to light until much later (he actually confessed who he was and received a pardon!). He was placed in charge of the 'Regulators' hired to sort out the so-called 'rustlers'.

Above: Major Wolcott, the pompous martinet who led the attack on the 'rustlers' of Johnson County. He had come to the territory some years before and at one time served as United States Marshal. He maintained that the cattlemen were in the right.

Above: Fred G. S. Hesse, who came to the territory in 1876 and entered the cattle business. As superintendent of the Powder River Cattle Company, he represented a number of English interests, and was himself considered a prominent stockman.

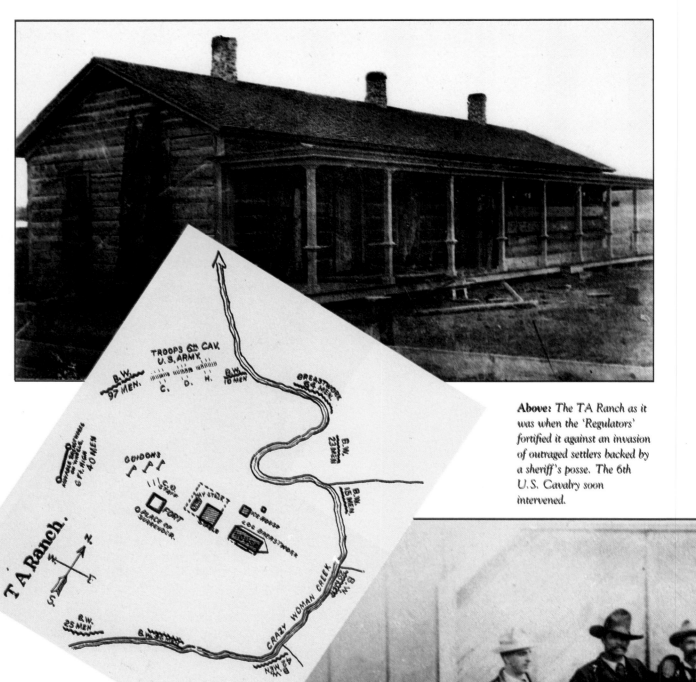

Above: The TA Ranch as it was when the 'Regulators' fortified it against an invasion of outraged settlers backed by a sheriff's posse. The 6th U.S. Cavalry soon intervened.

Above: A sketch of the TA Cattle Ranch where Major Wolcott and his gang retreated when they found themselves outnumbered by outraged settlers and the law, together with troops of the 6th U.S. Cavalry. The sketch shows the locations of the various participants during the 'holing up' of the 'Regulators'.

Right: The 'Invaders' or 'Regulators' (some called them 'Vigilantes') seated or standing for a group photograph. They look more like prosperous cattlemen than hard-bitten gunfighters. It is interesting to see that each man has been identified. Frank Canton is no. '34'. It is also noticeable that Major Wolcott did not deem it the right thing to do to be photographed with such a motley crew of characters and thus ensured he was omitted from the line-up.

caused much friction. Led by the powerful Wyoming Stock Growers' Association, whose membership included some of the richest and most influential of the cattle barons and local politicians, the cattlemen decided to make a stand.

To combat the rustlers, the 'maverick law' was invoked. This law allowed every unbranded calf found on a member's land to become his property. He was also permitted to sell these animals at prices too high for the average homesteader. High-priced gunfighters were then brought in to act as 'detectives'. Their incentive was $250 for each rustler caught and (if still alive) tried and convicted. Among this motley crew was the notorious Frank Canton, whose real name was Joe Horner, a one-time bank robber, rustler, gunfighter and, in later years, deputy U.S. Marshal and who also held several political positions.

When Albert Bothewell, a cattle baron, laid claim to land on which a woman named Ella ('Cattle Kate') Watson and James Averill had built their homes, both made it plain what they thought of him. He promptly had them strung up on the pretence that they were rustlers. This outrage led to open war, and word went out from the cattlemen for more gunfighters. These assembled at Paris, Texas, and headed for Cheyenne. On 5 April 1892, forty-six of them, now called 'Regulators' or 'Invaders' (vigilantes might better describe them), under the command of Major Frank Wolcott headed by train for Casper. Here the heavily armed band mounted up and set about some of the so-called rustlers. Nick Ray and Nate Champion defied them. Ray was killed early on, but Champion held out for some hours before being riddled with bullets as he tried to escape when the gang set fire to his cabin.

But the word was out, and the sheriff at Casper telegraphed the governor and hurriedly assembled a posse. He caught up with the gang at a ranch near Buffalo. In Cheyenne, the acting governor promptly ordered in the U.S. cavalry. Wolcott and his crew were all arrested and, despite attempts to get them placed on trial at Buffalo, they were escorted to Cheyenne. Placed on trial in January 1893, they were released through lack of evidence; so terrorized were the witnesses that they refused to testify. But retribution in the form of the cost of the invasion and legal fees broke many of the participants. The Federal government then sent in deputy U.S. Marshals to tackle the real rustlers, and things quietened down, but resentment festered between both factions for years.

Right: *This is how Frank Leslie's Weekly reported the Johnson County war. The affair received a lot of publicity and created much controversy across the entire country.*

Above: Wolcott got most of the publicity, but William C. Irvine, manager of the Ogalalla Land and Cattle Company was also considered to be one of the leaders of the 'Invaders'. He appears as no. 13 in the infamous line-up shown below.

E INVADERS"
CATTLE WAR, TAKEN AT Ft, D.A. RUSSELL
E. WARREN) MAY 4th 1892
NO. 22 Y.J. CLARKE
" 23 L.H. PARKER
" 24 TESCHMACHER
" 25 B.C. SCHULZE
" 26 W.H. TABOR
" 27 J.A. GARRETT
" 28 W.A. WILSON
NO 29 J. BARLINGS
" 30 MA. MCNALLY
" 31 MIKE SHONSEY
" 32 DICK ALLEN
" 33 FRED HESSE
" 34 FRANK CANTON
" 35 Wm LITTLE
NO. 36 JEFF MYNETT
" 37 BOB BARLINGS
" 38 S. SUTHERLAND
" 39 BUCK GARRETT
" 40 G.R. TUCKER
" 41 J.M. BENFORD
" 42 WILL ARMSTRONG

FRANK LESLIE'S WEEKLY.

302 THE WYOMING CATTLE WAR.
AN INTERESTING STATEMENT OF ITS CAUSES AND EXTENT

WOUNDED KNEE

'The world world is coming, a nation is coming' was how one Sioux Ghost Dance song told of Wovoka's promise. But the ultimate tragedy at Wounded Knee is perhaps best summed up in the words of Black Elk, a survivor of those grim days in the winter of 1890. 'I did not know then how much was ended. When I look back now from this high hill of my old age, I can still see the butchered women and children lying heaped and scattered . . . and I can see that something else died there in the bloody mud, and was buried in the blizzard. A people's dream died there.'

The last major battle between the United States army and American Indians was hardly a 'battle', but more of a one-sided skirmish, neither intended nor managed by either side. Yet at Wounded Knee Creek in South Dakota on 29 December 1890, almost three centuries of steady armed conflict between white man and red came at last to an end.

It arose out of a mystical movement called the Ghost Dance that started among the Plains peoples in the late 1880s. The Sioux especially heard its message of immortality, reunion with long dead loved ones, and immunity to white bullets. Nursing the resentment of two generations of losses to white advances, the Sioux saw in the Ghost Dance a promise of restoration of their lands and their honor. Naturally the military feared this resurgence, and the belligerent, even threatening, posture it encouraged in the Indians. By December 1890 the situation appeared critical. Military authorities, led by General Nelson Miles, ordered the arrest of the leading chiefs Sitting Bull and Big Foot, but in the confusion the former was

Right: Ration day at the Pine Ridge Reservation, 1891. Indians lined up to receive bacon, cornmeal, flour, coffee and sugar.

Below: On 13 November 1890, Indian agent Royer made a desperate plea for troops. Quickly deployed, they arrived in a week and here pose for the camera.

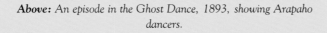

Above: An episode in the Ghost Dance, 1893, showing Arapaho dancers.

1889

In January Wovoka, a Paiute shaman, has a vision, the genesis of a religious movement to become known as the Ghost Dance

1890

In the spring, a delegation of Pine Ridge, Cheyenne and Rosebud Indians visit Wovoka in Nevada. They return to spread the word. On 15 December Sitting Bull is killed. On 28 December Big Foot's band is wiped out in what becomes known as the Massacre at Wounded Knee

Above: A Sioux Ghost Dance shirt collected at the Cheyenne River Agency by an Indian policeman. It has eagle feathers on the sleeves; the red paint on the fringes may have been some of Wovoka's special pigment from Nevada.

Right: Lieutenant Sydney Cloman of the First Infantry. Cloman accompanied the burial party which removed the dead from the snow in the days following the massacre, and he drew up the army's official map of the scene of the fight.

accidentally killed, and the latter and hundreds of his people escaped and fled their reservation.

Federal cavalrymen quickly rounded them up and began to escort them toward a new reservation. By 28 December they reached Wounded Knee Creek, and there, surrounded by 500 or more bluecoats, the 120 warriors were ordered to give up their arms. The next morning, while cannon trained on the Indian encampment, soldiers tried to disarm the Sioux. A few yielded their rifles, but most hid them, and cavalrymen started searching through their packs and lodges. Inevitably a trooper and a warrior scuffled when the latter refused to yield his gun, it went off, and a brief but brutal firefight followed.

At once the warriors revealed the rifles they concealed beneath their blankets and loosed a volley at the hated whites. Then red men and white rushed into hand-to-hand fighting, while Miles' troopers on the fringes began to open fire with their own rifles. Then when the cavalrymen extricated themselves and withdrew, Miles' cannon sent round after round of exploding shells into the Indian camp, indiscriminately killing and wounding men, women, and children, young and old. When at last the firing stopped, 150 Sioux lay dead, including Big Foot, and fifty more wounded. Of the soldiers, twenty-five had been killed and thirty-nine wounded. Many of the remaining Indians had run from the field and would have to be rounded up again, but any fight that had been in them fled as well, and the Ghost Dance would be seen no more. A snow storm that night covered the field, and many of the wounded Indians still lying on the ground would freeze to death in the darkness.

The army conducted an investigation afterward, concluding that it had not been a deliberate massacre, but a spontaneous accident in which neither side intended to fight, but matters simply escalated too fast out of control. Definitions mattered little to the Sioux, of course. For them it was the final coda on a century of unrelenting tragedy in their dealings with the white man.

Below: The medicine man dead at Wounded Knee. Mooney thought him to be Yellow Bird; others identified him as Sits Straight.

Below, right: One of the survivors of Wounded Knee, Blue Whirlwind, with three of her family. Two of her sons were wounded.

Right: A wooden Ghost Dance staff, collected by Mooney. It is adorned with red painted horns and a yellow cow's tail.

Above: Sitting Bull was considered a troublemaker by the U.S. government. He continued to practice the Ghost Dance on the Standing Rock Reservation, despite the agent's ruling and was killed during an attempt to arrest him in mid-December.

Above: Colonel James W. Forsyth carried the burden of the blame for Wounded Knee: 'Incompetency and neglect when found, should not pass unnoticed . . . Warnings and orders were unheeded by Colonel Forsyth' said Nelson Miles, his commanding officer.

Above: Major Samuel M. Whitside was responsible for apprehending Big Foot's armed band in late December. Big Foot was ill with pneumonia; Whitside insisted that he sleep in an army tent with a stove. It was to prove a futile gesture.

BUTCH CASSIDY

Thanks to a motion picture devoted to the exploits of Butch Cassidy and the Sundance Kid, the 'Wild Bunch' is known to a world-wide audience. But few people can name the other members of the gang who enjoyed a reputation for robbing banks, trains and anything that would reap a profit. At the height of their infamy, the police, railroad detectives, and various 'Pinkerton' type agencies had joined forces to hunt them down. But it proved to be a difficult task. Yet even the 'Wild Bunch' could not outrun the telegraph or the telephone, and the technological noose tightened.

Above: Kaycee, Wyoming, was a small town, the closest to the 'Hole in the Wall' country.

1866
Robert Leroy Parker, alias Butch Cassidy, born to devout Mormon parents in Circleville, Utah

1894
Butch Cassidy sentenced to two years in Wyoming State Penitentiary for rustling

1896
On his release he forms the Wild Bunch and rides with such men as Harvey Logan and Harry Longabaugh (the Sundance Kid)

1902
Butch and the Sundance Kid leave the U.S. for South America. Six years later, they supposedly meet their deaths at the hands of Bolivian soldiers

Artifact courtesy of Gene Autry Western Heritage Museum, Los Angeles, California

The 'Wild Bunch' are still remembered in the wilds of Wyoming as the 'Hole in the Wall gang' and for some of its more colorful members, notably Butch Cassidy and the Sundance Kid.

Butch Cassidy's real name was Robert Leroy Parker, but he adopted the name Cassidy in tribute to one Mike Cassidy who had influenced his earlier years and turned him toward cattle-rustling for a living. 'Butch' came from 'butcher', a trade he had very briefly engaged in. Curiously, Butch was never known to kill anyone, which is remarkable when one considers that the Wild Bunch consisted of some of the most notorious killers then at large.

The 'Wild Bunch' included such characters as Harry Tracy, perhaps the most dangerous member of the gang, and reputed to be a vicious killer; there was also Harry Longabaugh, known as the 'Sundance Kid' and Butch's particular 'pard'. Others included Ben Kilpatrick, 'the Tall Texan, Will Carver and Harry Logan, alias 'Kid Curry', the eldest of three brothers who fell foul of the law. But it was Harvey who achieved a reputation as a killer and was reputed to be the 'tiger of the Wild Bunch'.

Captured and sentenced to the state penitentiary in 1894, Butch was paroled in 1896; some sources claim that in return he promised never again to carry out robberies in Wyoming. True or not, he never did, but he did use the territory as a means of access to the 'Hole in the Wall' country, a remote, vast and picturesque region in the southeast corner of the Big Horn mountains in north central Wyoming. Inaccessible to man or beast except by way of the steep V-shaped notch or pass (the 'hole in the wall'), it was ideal for the likes of the Wild Bunch. The place had been the haunt of outlaws for many years and is today a tourist attraction.

Brown's Hole, which bordered upon the states of Wyoming, Utah, and Colorado, and stood in close proximity to the 'Hole in the Wall' region, was also another favored haunt of the outlaws. But once the telephone and telegraph established

Right: The Ghent cabin once owned by Alexander Ghent who built it in the 'Hole in the Wall' country during the time he rode the owlhoot trail with the likes of Kid Curry and other gang members. The present owner moved the cabin to Old Trail Town, Cody, in recent years.

In their time, there were a number of such places dotted about the area that harbored the various outlaw bands that infested the region. Access was limited and, with sufficient provisions, a man could hide out for months at a time.

Below: The 'Wild Bunch' photographed dressed in all their dandified finery. They are, left to right: standing, William Carver, Harvey Logan. Seated, Harry ('The Sundance Kid') Longabaugh, Ben ('The Tall Texan') Kilpatrick, and Robert Leroy Parker, alias Butch Cassidy.

Above: Butch Cassidy, a 'mug shot' believed made when he was an inmate of the Wyoming State Penitentiary. It is hard to believe, but true, that he himself never killed anyone even though he consorted with murderous cut-throats and thieves.

Left: This 4¾ in. barreled nickel-plated Colt .45 was once the property of Harvey Logan (alias 'Kid Curry'). This version was the 'Civilian Model'.

better communications between towns and states, the outlaw fraternity realized that its days were numbered. The Wild Bunch split up. Some were killed when pursued by possees, others escaped into obscurity, while Butch and Sundance set course for South America, where they were reported killed by soldiers in Bolivia.

For more than eighty years controversy has raged over that claim. Butch's sister was convinced that both he and Sundance returned secretly to the United States and lived in obscurity, but the evidence is by no means conclusive. Recent excavations into the grave sites of the village in Bolivia where the two men are reported to have been buried following their fight with troops have so far not revealed any evidence to support either theory. So Butch Cassidy and the Sundance Kid continue to enthral both the buff and the fan, for both might well be described as Robin Hood-like characters.

Below: A posse appointed by the Union Pacific Railroad to hunt down the Wild Bunch. T. Jeff Carr is believed to be the second man from the right.

Above: Harry Longabaugh, immortalized as 'The Sundance Kid'. He and Butch high-tailed it to South America when things got too hot in the States, first paying a visit to England where one of them had relatives living in Preston, Lancashire.

Above: Harvey Logan, better known as 'Kid Curry', might appear relaxed, but when aroused was one of the most dangerous of the Wild Bunch. Few people cared to tangle with him. He shot himself in June 1904 rather than surrender to a posse.

INDIAN RESERVATIONS

Until the Indian Reorganization Act of 1934, the reservation system – designed to relocate Indian tribes in places where they could not interfere with the white man's urge for acquiring land – had failed. It instead brought about poverty and the destruction of age-old ways. When the Act was passed, tribal governments re-emerged, loans were given to stimulate Indian economy and some 250 reservations were able to survive, most of them west of the Mississippi. The largest – created for the Navajo – comprised some 24,000 square miles and is today the most populated.

Above: Interior of a Crow home in Montana, 1910, showing an unidentified family.

1830
President Andrew Jackson signs the Indian Removal Act, relocating eastern tribes to a designated Indian Territory west of the Mississippi River

1838–9
The Trail of Tears – the forced removal of Five Civilized Tribes from their homelands in the east

1854
In an Act of Congress, a northern part of Indian Territory becomes Kansas and Nebraska territories

1862
The Homestead Act opens up more Indian lands in the territories to white homesteaders

From the first days when spreading white civilization clashed with Indians and the latter were forced to yield their lands, the conquerors, both good men and bad, argued over how best to deal with an aboriginal people in their midst. In the end the solution seemed to be two-fold. First they must contain the natives, whether in their midst or on the outpost of civilization. Second, they must break up Indian culture and society and reform it along white lines, thus to reduce the threat of resistance, and to facilitate limited assimilation into the new American society.

It was easier said than done. For one thing, politics governed Indian dealings, which meant that every four years policy could change with a new administration. Far worse, no one understood the psychological effects of reservation life, the virtual concentration camp nature of it that depressed spirits, reduced or eradicated self-esteem, and turned once-proud nations of independent peoples into hopeless wards of Washington. It hardly helped that those administering support services for the reservations, especially agents responsible for supplying food and goods, often profiteered corruptly at the expense of their supposed beneficiaries.

The first reservations were not called that. Groups like the Civilized Tribes relocated in the 1830s from the Old Southwest to the unsettled parts of Arkansas and the Indian Territory were simply given title to new land that no whites wanted, there to live unfettered under their own governance. It was not until the time of the Civil War that the reservation system really began to take off, as white expansion now pushed even those lands once given to relocated tribes. The government set up the reservations in return for Indian concessions of land, or agreements not to make war. Under authority from Congress, the president made the treaty with a tribe, and in the process pledged annual gifts of tools, weapons, clothing, food, and money. By the 1870s such agreements were downgraded from formal treaties, removing Congressional authority and oversight,

Right: Ration day at the San Carlos Agency, 1880, by Vincent Mercaldo. The people were mainly Western Apaches.

Below: Brulé Sioux outside their log cabin. Such accommodation was provided by the U.S. government following assimilation in to the world of the whites.

Bottom: Two Comanche women shown in a studio portrait at Fort Sill, Oklahoma Territory (formerly Indian Territory) at the end of the last century.

and allowing the president greater latitude.

The voracious white hunger for land would not leave the reservations alone for long, of course. Once valuable minerals or tillable land was found on Indian property, legislators started looking for loop-holes to regain the property. In 1887 Congress passed the Allotment Act that broke up over 100 reservations, giving each Indian a piece of property belonging to him alone instead of all of it being held communally, but at the same time some 90 million of 150 million acres of reservations lands were declared surplus and opened to white exploitation.

The reservation system failed in almost all its objectives, despite the good intention of many. Indians were reduced to poverty and almost complete dependence on the government, while they remained separate and apart and unassimilated into white society. Finally in 1934 with the Indian Reorganization Act the government started to attempt to redress the wrongs, encouraging native American culture and independence and enterprise, and promoting their crafts, languages, and traditions.

Above: Hat on Skin, or Bacon Rind, an Osage. This is probably the same Tom Baconrind who was a prominent spokesman for his tribe during their time of great wealth (created by oil) on their reservation land in Oklahoma in the 1920s.

Above: *'Map showing Indian Reservations within the limits of the United States, compiled under the direction of the Hon. W.A. Jones, Commissioner of Indian Affairs, 1899.' The reservations are shown in the darker color on the map; they sit like forlorn little islands in the vast expanse of the United States.*

Left: *Indians and whites on the Pine Ridge Reservation. The figure kneeling in the front row left of center is Major Burke of Buffalo Bill's Wild West. He was there to select Sioux for the show's forthcoming season.*

Above: Quanah Parker, principal chief of the Kwahadi Comanche and inspired war chief. He had never signed a treaty with the whites but he eventually led his people onto a reservation in 1875, knowing that the old days were passed.

WILLIAM F. CODY

Queen Victoria described Buffalo Bill as splendid, handsome, and gentlemanlike in manner. The cowboys were 'fine looking', while the Indians in their paint and feathers were 'alarming' and they had 'cruel faces'. But her reaction to the 'Wild West Exhibition' would have pleased Cody immensely, for he strove for realism. The London *Daily Telegraph* on 21 April 1887 remarked that this 'peculiar and antique show . . . is not acting or imitation of Western life, but an exact reproduction of the scenes of fierce frontier life vividly illustrated by the real people'.

Above: Buffalo Bill, photographed in London in 1887, quintessential hero of the American West.

1846
Born in Iowa and emigrated to Kansas eight years later

1864
Enlisted in the Seventh Kansas Cavalry and fought in several campaigns

1868
Buffalo hunter for the railroad and appointed Chief of Scouts to the Fifth Cavalry

1883
Formed his 'Wild West Exhibition'

1887
The 'Wild West' paid its first visit to London

1917
Died at Denver, Colorado, on 10 January

Artifacts courtesy of Gene Autry Western Heritage Museum, Los Angeles, California

William Frederick Cody, alias 'Buffalo Bill', was perhaps one of the most important characters ever to appear in the Old West, not necessarily for what he achieved (which was to his credit), but because he more than anyone else publicized the Old West and its myriad characters to world-wide audiences in a manner unsurpassed before or since.

All this, of course, was very much in the future when he was born on 26 February 1846, at Leclaire, Scott County, Iowa. By 1854 the family had moved to Missouri, and was one of the first to cross the line when the Kansas–Nebraska Act was signed in May 1854 and the territory was opened up for settlement. His father, a staunch abolitionist frequently aired his views against slavery and was stabbed for his trouble; he survived only to die from a severe chill in 1857. Mary Cody, with a family to support, obtained employment for eleven-year-old William with Russell, Majors & Waddell, then the largest freighting firm on the frontier. He was employed as a messenger riding between their office in Leavenworth to Fort Leavenworth, some three miles away. In later years, Cody was to claim that he rode for the company's Pony Express, which began to run on 3 April 1860. The truth is that he was never a Pony rider – that claim came years later when he wrote his autobiography and he wished to embellish an already impressive career!

In the late 1850s, the young Cody met James Butler Hickok, at that time called 'Bill' by most people, but some years were to pass before the word 'Wild' was added. Hickok befriended the young man during a wagon trip to Denver in 1860, and they became firm friends.

Right: Buffalo Bill and 'friends' photographed at Staten Island in 1886. To his right are Pawnee scouts and to his left Sioux chiefs. Both tribes were hereditary enemies in the old days on the Plains, but Cody persuaded them to 'bury the hatchet'.

Below: One of Buffalo Bill's saddles. During the life of his Wild West he had several ornate saddles for use in the ring. This one is ornately hand-tooled with the addition of silverwork that enhanced its appearance and well suited its owner.

Above: James Butler ('Wild Bill') Hickok, who first met the Cody family at Leavenworth, Kansas, in the mid-1850s, was a role model for Cody. As a favor to Cody he joined his theatrical Combination in 1873; but he disliked acting and left to return West.

Right: A brown leather cigar case with the inked inscription 'From Chief Bull to Buffalo Bill'. Like most of his generation, Cody was 'partial to the weed' and liked a fine 'seegar'.

Below: Buffalo Bill sits and admires his saddle (the same one illustrated left). This photograph was made in Paris where the Wild West appeared at the Exposition Universelle in 1889.

Above: Edward Judsen, alias 'Ned Buntline', who first publicized 'Buffalo Bill'. He was a notorious womanizer and drunk. His own life would have made an ideal subject for his prolific output of dime novel yarns. He wrote his first Cody play in four hours!

During the Civil War Cody served with the 7th Kansas Cavalry Regiment. Later, following his marriage to Louisa Maude Frederici in 1866, he left her at Leavenworth and headed West. He again met up with Hickok, now generally called 'Wild Bill', who was at that time a scout for the army. Cody secured employment with the Union Pacific Railway Company (Eastern Division) as a grader, but later when he proved his ability as a buffalo hunter he was employed to supply meat for the track workers. Soon he was generally known as 'Buffalo Bill' rather than Bill Cody.

By 1869 Cody had achieved a reputation both as a buffalo hunter and scout, and at General Sheridan's request he was appointed chief of scouts to the Fifth Cavalry. During a skirmish with Indians in Nebraska during 1872, he displayed great courage and was later awarded the Congressional Medal of Honor. Years later this was taken back by Congress because he had been a civilian at the time and not a serving soldier. However, in recent years the medal has been restored.

Cody's meeting with Ned Buntline in 1869 and the subsequent publicity he received when Ned 'wrote him up' for the *New York Weekly* and other papers as 'Buffalo Bill, King of the Border Men' (a story based more upon the adventures of Hickok than Cody) established him as a 'frontier hero' and, following some persuasion from Buntline, Cody and his friend John B. Omohundro (Texas Jack) resigned from scouting and took up acting.

From 1872 until the early 1880s, Buffalo Bill's Combination, a theatrical troupe, toured the eastern states with melodramas based upon Western life. Buntline initiated Cody's success, and when the pair parted from him in 1873 they persuaded Hickok to join them; he only lasted eight months, disillusioned by the 'sham' of acting. Texas Jack later set up on his own, and Cody was joined for a time by Captain Jack Crawford. Eventually, he was on his own and thriving. In 1883 his Wild West was organized and for thirty years it toured the United States and parts of Europe.

Buffalo Bill died on 10 January 1917, mourned by millions, who regarded him as their hero. Despite controversy over his penchant for stretching the truth when it suited him, and an ego that irked some of his contemporaries, Cody's fame is assured.

Above: John Crawford, alias 'Captain Jack, the Poet Scout' who joined Cody's Combination before branching out on his own. In later life he lectured on the Old West and Wild Bill Hickok in particular. He paid several visits to Hickok's family at Troy Grove.

WILD WEST SHOWS

The Wild West Show has been a featured attraction for more than a century. For sheer spectacle it easily outclassed its older rival the circus, which relied to a large extent upon animal acts. On 17 May 1883, the Cody–Carver combination gave its first public performance at Omaha, Nebraska, and was an instant success. People who had lived most of their lives on the frontier and were familiar with its characters nevertheless were thrilled by the spectacle of cowboys, Indians, buffalo and other facets of Western life.

The Wild West Show is now an established part of Western legend. Although Buffalo Bill is generally credited with its origin, the facts suggest that shows of this type were promoted many years before his own venture in 1883. As early as 1843 the Great Barnum organized something of the sort, employing an expert rider and lasso artist, together with fifteen starved and weary buffalo calves, to put on a 'Grand Buffalo Hunt' at Hoboken, New Jersey. Dancing Indians and other attractions brought in the crowds, but when the buffalo were released and escaped into the crowd there was panic. In 1860 Barnum tried again, this time with the celebrated James Capen ('Grizzly') Adams and his California Menagerie. But there were few successes. A later and surprising entrant into the area of such events was Joseph G. McCoy, who took a break from organizing cattle transportation to promote the new venture with a variety of wild animals and riders with some success. He later organized a 'Grand Excursion to the Far West! A Wild and Exciting Chase after the Buffalo, on his Native Plain'. This event ('bring your own firearms') attracted a large number of sportsmen. And then in 1872, Colonel Sydney Barnett produced his Grand Buffalo Hunt at Niagara Falls, with Wild Bill Hickok as master of ceremonies, which proved a financial failure.

Buffalo Bill's decision to embark upon a similar venture in 1883 was prompted by the success of an

Below: A remarkable photograph of some of Buffalo Bill's Indians made at Chicago in 1893. Cody recalled that the Sioux, Cheyenne and Arapaho were 'more hardy than the others'; he tended to recruit new ones for each trip.

Above: Buffalo Bill and Sitting Bull photographed together in Montreal, Quebec, 1885.

1843
Barnum's Grand Buffalo Hunt

1883
Cody–Carver Wild West

1887
Buffalo Bill's first European tour

1892
Buffalo Bill's second European tour; his last is over by 1905

1916
Buffalo Bill's last season

BUFFALO BILL'S
WILD WEST
PAWNEE BILL'S
FAR EAST

Above: A poster, circa 1910, advertising the combined Buffalo Bill and Pawnee Bill show, with cowgirls as a feature.

'Old Glory Blow-Out' in 1882 which had attracted cowboys and others anxious for fun and a feast. The original partnership was between Cody and William Frank ('Doc') Carver, a dentist turned marksman with a world-wide reputation. The venture failed and the pair split up. Cody was then joined by Nate Salsbury who proved to be an astute businessman. Thanks to him Cody's 'Wild West Exhibition' (he never used the word 'show') became so popular that in 1887, to coincide with the 'Exhibition of the Arts, Industries, Manufactures, Products and Resources of the United States' (generally called the 'American Exhibition') being held in London, the Wild West

was invited to come to England. The fact that 1887 was also Queen Victoria's Jubilee proved a great benefit, for the queen insisted upon visiting the Wild West on several occasions, which set the seal upon its status. And when Her Majesty rose in her box to bow as the United States flag was paraded past together with the Union flag, the Americans went wild; at long last any resentment felt by England against the former colonists was laid to rest.

With Cody came a large number of Indians, cowboys, and assorted buffalo, elk and other 'frontier' animals. Among the crack shots accompanying the troupe were Lillian Smith and Annie Oakley. Lillian was presented to the queen and demonstrated the Winchester rifle. She later left the company, some believe because of a personality dispute with Annie Oakley. It is debatable who was the better shot, but it was Annie who was to be immortalized and celebrated in both song and story.

The sheer spectacle of the Wild West enthralled audiences wherever it appeared. Cody's role increasingly became one of 'Master of Ceremonies' but it is doubtful that that worried him, for his presence in the ring always received great applause. By 1913, however, with many rivals, business problems and advancing age catching up with him, together with continual problems over his marriage which had never been a success, Cody was tired and disillusioned. But such was the appeal of Buffalo Bill's Wild West, that long after both it and its creator had faded into history, its memory as perhaps the most spectacular event of its kind ever to be produced lingers on.

Above: Major John ('Arizona John') Burke, Cody's erstwhile theatrical manager-cum-actor turned press agent. Arizona John served Cody well for more than forty years, and even after Buffalo Bill's death, continued to keep his name before the public.

Above: Phoebe Anne Moses, better known world-wide as Annie Oakley, who was dubbed by Sitting Bull as 'Little Sure Shot', and proved to be one of the finest women 'shootists' of her generation. Annie Oakley knew all the tricks of the trade.

Left: A re-enactment of the 'Battle of Summit Springs', and the rescue of white women captives. There is no wasted space in the arena!

Below: A copy of the 1893 Programme. By this time a number of new acts had been added to the show, which necessitated a change of name.

Right: This panoramic view of the Wild West was made at Omaha, Nebraska, in 1907, by Cheyenne photographer Joseph Stimson. His glass plate negatives (eight by ten inches) are among the best ever made of Cody's enterprise. The view also makes us appreciate how compact was the spectacle.

INDEX

Page numbers marked in *italic* indicate illustrations or mention in captions.

CREDITS/ACKNOWLEDGMENTS

The publisher wishes to thank the many organizations and individuals who have supplied photographs for this book, credited here by page number and position. For reasons of space, certain references have been abbreviated as follows: **AHCUOW**, American Heritage Center, University of Wyoming; **AHSL**, Arizona Historical Society Library; **BBHC**, Buffalo Bill Historical Center, Cody, Wyoming; **CHS**, Colorado Historical Society; **CJCLDS**, Church Archives, The Church of Jesus Christ of Latter-day Saints; **CSCSL**, California Section, California State Library; **DPLWHD** Denver Public Library, Western History Department; **Haley Memorial Library**, The Nita Stewart Haley Memorial Library, Midland, Texas; **ISHS**, Idaho State Historical Society; **KSHS**, Kansas State Historical Society; **MHS**, Missouri Historical Society; **MontHS**, Montana Historical Society; **NA**, National Archives; **NHS** Nevada Historical Society; **NSHS**, Nebraska State Historical Society; **PNWA**, Peter Newark's Western Americana; **Robert G. McCubbin**, Collection of Robert G. McCubbin, El Paso, Texas; **SHSW**, State Historical Society of Wisconsin; **UALSCD**, University of Arizona Library Special Collections Department; **UPR**, Union Pacific Railroad; **WFB**, Wells Fargo Bank; **WHCUOL**, Western History Collection, University of Oklahoma Library; **WSM**, Wyoming State Museum. Other sources of photographs are cited in full.

Key to positions: a, above; b, below; l, left; r, right; m, middle; pan(s), panel(s), and combinations thereof.

Endpaper NSHS; **i** SI; **ii** (a) California State Railroad Museum Library; **ii/iii** KSHS· **iv/v** WFB; **v** (artifacts) BBHC; **vi/vii** U.S. Department of Agriculture; **vii** (artifacts) BBHC; **8** (a) CHS, all others SI, (artifacts) Salamander Books; **10/11** photographs SI, (artifacts) Salamander Books; **12/13** BBHC. Gertrude Vanderbilt Whitney Trust Fund Purchase; **14** (a) In the Collection of the Corcoran Gallery of Art, Washington, D.C.; **15** National Museum of American Art, Washington, D.C./Art Resource, NY; **16/17** Amon Carter Museum, Fort Worth; **18/19, 18** (a) U.S. Geological Survey; all others PNWA; **20** (a) BBHC, (b) Salamander Books; **21** (r) BBHC. Gift of The Coe Foundation, (b) SHSW, (a) KSHS, (a) CHS; **22** (a) SHSW; **23** (b) Salamander Books, (pan, a) CHS, (pan, b) MHS; **24/25** Gift of Maxim Karolik for the M. and M. Karolik Collection of American Paintings, 1815–1865. Courtesy, Museum of Fine Arts, Boston; **26** (a) NA, (b) Courtesy United States Naval Academy Museum; **27** (l) WHCUOL, all others The Alamo, Daughters of the Republic of Texas; **28** DPLWHD, (m) ISHS; **29** (a) CJCLDS, (b) DPLWHD, (pan) NSHS; **30/31, 31** (m) KSHS; all others MHS; **32**, (a, b) NSHS; **33** (a) C.F. Taylor Collection, (m, ar) MinnHS, (b, r) ISHS; **34/35** all CJCLDS; **36** (a) Salamander Books, (a) Department of Defense, (r) Salamander Books; **37** (pan, a) The Alamo, Daughters of the Republic of Texas, (m) PNWA, (pan, b) Joseph G. Rosa; **38/39, 38** (a) U.S. Department of Agriculture, all others CSCSL; **40** (artifact) WFB, (b) MontHS, (r) CHS; **41** (pan) Library of Congress, all others CSCSL; **42** (a) CSCSL, (b) MontHS; **43** (a) DPLWHD, (b) AHCUOW, (pans) MontHS; **44** all WFB; **45** (a) AHSL, all others WFB; **46** (a) St Joseph Museum; **47** (a) Oakland Museum, (pan, a) St Joseph Museum, (pan, b) BBHC, Garlow Loan, all others WFB; **48** CHS; **49** (a) ISHS, (b) CSCSL, (pans) WFB; **50** (pan) AHSL; **51** (b) BBHC, all others WFB; **52** (a) Salamander Books; **52/53** (pan, b) Robert G. McCubbin, all others Haley Memorial Library; **54/55** Robert G. McCubbin; **56** (a) KSHS; **57** (pan, a), (b) California State Railroad Museum Library, (a) KSHS; **58/59** all NHS; **60** (a) National Portrait Gallery, Smithsonian Institution, (b) Library of Congress; **61** (pan, a) SI, (pan, m) New York Historical Society; **62** (a) General Sweeny's Museum, Republic, Missouri; **63** (a) KSHS, (b) KSHS, (pan, a) General Sweeny's Museum, Republic, Missouri, (pan, m, pan, b) KSHS; **64** (a, b) NA; **65** (a, b) NA, (pan, b) Valentine Museum; **66** (pan, a) NA, (pan, m) Salamander Books, (a) Library of Congress, (m, b) NA; **67** (pans) Salamander Books; **68** (a) PNWA, (artifact) The Museum of the Confederacy, Richmond, Virginia; **69** (a) Lloyd Ostendorf Collection, (artifact) Civil War Library and Museum, Philadelphia, Pennsylvania (pan, a) U.S. Army; **70** (a, b) PNWA, (artifact) The Museum of the Confederacy, Richmond, Virginia. Photography by Katherine Wetzel; **71** (pan, a) PNWA, (pans m, b) General Sweeny's Museum,

Republic, Missouri; (a) SI; **72/73** all General Sweeny's Museum, Republic, Missouri, except (pan, a) BBHC; **74** (a) Haley Memorial Library; **75** (pan, a) Joseph G. Rosa, (pan, b) KSHS, others Haley Memorial Library; **76/77** all KSHS except (pan) NA; **78** (a) C.F. Taylor Collection; **79** (a) U.S. Department of Agriculture; all others Solomon D. Butcher Collection, NSHS; **80** (a) UPR, (b) SI, Division of Transportation; **81** (b) Oakland Museum, (a) Southern Pacific Railroad Co., (b, r) California State Railroad Museum, (pans) PNWA; **82/83** California State Railroad Museum; **84** (pan, a) PNWA, (a) CSCSL, (m) KSHS, (b) Salamander Books; **85** (a) Burlington Northern, (b and pan, b) UPR Museum Collection; **86** (a, and b) CHS; **87** (r, and pan, b) KSHS, (pan, a) CHS; **88/89** BBHC; **90/91** all CHS except 91 (b, r), Salamander Books; **92** (pan) and (m) CHS, (r) MontHS; **93** CHS except (pan) KSHS; **94/95** BBHC. Gift of Charles Ulrick and Josephine Bay Foundation Inc.; **96/97** all KSHS except 97 (a) Joseph G. Rosa; **98/99** all KSHS except 99 (pan, a) Jack DeMattos; **100** (a) WFB, (b) MontHS; **101** (a and b) AHSL, (pan, a) Joseph G. Rosa/Wadsworth Atheneum, Hartford, Conn., others PNWA; **102/103** NA; **104/ 105** all KSHS except 105 (a) Robert G. McCubbin, and (pan, m) West of the Pecos Museum, Pecos, Texas; **106** (a) AHSL, (m) AHCUOW; **107** (a) Robert G. McCubbin, (m) AHCUOW, (b) CHS, (pans) KSHS; **108** (a) Joseph G. Rosa/St Joseph Museum, (b) Jesse James Farm Museum; **109** (r) BBHC, (pans) Joseph G. Rosa/MinnHS, all others Jesse James Farm Museum; **110/111** all BBHC except (pan, m) Robert G. McCubbin, and (pan, b) WHCUOL; **112/113** Courtesy Amon Carter Museum, Fort Worth; **114/115** all Joseph G. Rosa except 114 (b) South Dakota Historical Society; **116** (a) BBHC, (b) WHSUOL; **117** (a, l) Fred R. Egloff, (a, r) Joseph G. Rosa; (pan, a) MontHS, (pan, m) Boot Hill Museum, (pan, b) KSHS; **118** (a) NA; **119** (b) PNWA, (a) MontHS, (pan, a) SI, (pan, b) KSHS; **120** (a) NA, (b) SI; **121** all MinnHS except panels, all SI; **122/123** all SI except 122 (a and b) MinnHS; **124/ 125** BBHC. Gift of William E. Weiss; **126** (a) Joseph G. Rosa, (b) SI; **127** (a) NA, (m) SI, (b, r) C.F. Taylor Collection, (pan, a) Joseph G. Rosa, (pan, b) PNWA; **128/ 129** BBHC. Gertrude Vanderbilt Whitney Trust Fund Purchase; **130** (a) SI, (b) NA; **131** all Peter Palmquist except (pan, b) PNWA, (artifact) © The National Museum of Ethnography, Stockholm, photograph Bo Gabrielsson; **132/133** all SI except (pan, b) PNWA; **134/135** all SI; **136** (a) Library of Congress, (b) SI; **137** all SI except (pan, a) PNWA, (artifact) U.S. Army Military History Institute, (pan, b) CHS, (artifacts Salamander Books); **138** (pans) all UALSCD, (m) SI, (b) NA, (artifacts) © The National Museum of Ethnography, Stockholm, photograph Bo Gabrielsson; **139** (a and pan, a) SI, (pan, b) DPLWHD, (artifact) Hampton University Museum, Hampton, Virginia; **140** (a) Robert G. McCubbin (m and b) AHSL; **141** (a) MontHS, (pan, a) Haley Memorial Library, (pan, m) UALSCD, (pan, b) AHSL; **142/143** all Robert G. McCubbin, except (pans, m and b) WHCUOL; **144** (a) BBHC, (b) Courtesy Museum of New Mexico, photograph J.R. Riddle; **145** (a) DPLWHD, all others Robert G. McCubbin; **146** (pans)UALSCD, (a and b)·Haley Memorial Library; **147.** (b) Lincoln County Heritage Trust, (r) BBHC, (pan) Robert G. McCubbin; **148** (a) BBHC, (a) AHSL; **149** (b) DPLWHD, (pans) AHSL; **150** (a) Salamander Books, (b) PNWA; **151** (a, b) PNWA, (a, r and pan, a) WHCUOL, (pans, m, b) Robert G. McCubbin; **152** (a) NA, (b) and 153 (a, r) PNWA; **153** (a) Department of the Interior, (b) WHCUOL; **154/155** PNWA; **156/157** all AHCUOW except 157 (m) and (pans, m and b) WSM, (pan, a) DPLWHD; **158** (a) WSM, (b) AHCUOW; **159** (pans) AHCUOW; **160** (pans) WSM, (a, b)AHCUOW; **161** WSM; **162** (a) SI, (b) MontHS, (artifact SI); **163** (a) DPLWHD, (artifact) SI; others NSHS, except (pan, a) SI, (pans, m and b) courtesy James S. Hutchins; **164** (a) WSM, (b) WHCUOL; **165** (b) AHCUOW, (pans) DPLWHD; **166/167** all SI except 167 (a) and map, BBHC, (b) NSHS; **168** (a) Joseph G. Rosa; **169** all BBHC except (pan, a) Joseph G. Rosa, (pan, b) Haley Memorial Library; **170** (a) SI, poster and (a, r) BBHC; **171** all Joseph G. Rosa; **172/173** Joseph G. Rosa/WSM; endpaper KSHS. All artifacts published with the kind permission of the Buffalo Bill Historical Center, Cody, Wyoming, and the Gene Autry Western Heritage Museum, Los Angeles, California, have been acknowledged on the relevant pages. While every effort has been made to acknowledge photographs reproduced in this book, the editor would be pleased to hear if any have slipped the net.